# Out of Conflict
## From War to Peace in Africa

*edited by*

Gunnar M. Sørbø & Peter Vale

Nordiska Afrikainstitutet, Uppsala 1997

This book is published in cooperation with the Chr. Michelsen Institute, Bergen, Norway

**Indexing terms**

Armed conflicts
Peace-keeping
Mediation
Organization of African Unity (OAU)
Africa

*The opinions expressed in this volume are those of the authors and do not necessarily reflect the views of Nordiska Afrikainstitutet*

Cover painting: Mohamed A. Abusabib

ISBN 91-7106-413-3

Printed in Sweden by Motala Grafiska, Motala 1997

# Contents

# Preface

Since the 1970s, Africa has been the site of many of the world's most deadly conflicts. Most of them have been internal conflicts but with profound effects on neighbours, sub-regions and the continent as a whole. Thus, South Africa's destabilization of its neighbours, particularly in the 1980s, was a direct extension of its own civil war. Seven wars—in Angola, Ethiopia, Mozambique, Rwanda, Somalia, Sudan and Uganda—have taken between 500,000 and 1,000,000 lives each, either on the battlefield or through war-induced famine and disease. Two other conflicts, in Burundi and Liberia, took over 100,000 lives each. As this book is being prepared for publication, a new human tragedy has been unfolding in Zaire, showing that the turmoil in the Great Lakes region of Central Africa can no longer be seen as a series of small wars in tiny countries; it is a conflagration affecting tens of millions of people over a huge area.

While more internal conflicts have occurred in Africa in the post-Cold War era than in any other major world region, the continent is becoming increasingly marginalized in US and European foreign policy. Declining resources for engagement, including development aid, coupled with a fatigue borne of the apparent intractability or complexity of conflicts in Africa, has led to a situation in which it is difficult for policy makers to engage in preventing or ending armed conflicts. In the United States particularly, the "Mogadishu syndrome", which refers to the general lack of political will for engagement in Africa following the deaths of US soldiers deployed in the UN-peace-keeping operation in Somalia in 1992, seriously limits the ability to make credible policy commitments in this area. At the same time, peace enforcement and humanitarian intervention have drawn resources and attention away from assisting countries in Africa that have a chance to develop in benign directions. Although armed conflicts have been brought to an end in Namibia, South Africa, Mozambique, Angola and Ethiopia, the perception of conflict in Africa—and the record of the international response to them—is grim. "Afro-pessimism", a term that reflects the widespread disenchantment, obscures the reality of the mixed record of conflict management achievement in Africa.

To promote better understanding of the nature of armed conflicts in Africa, the Chr. Michelsen Institute organized a Workshop of leading authorities in Bergen, Norway, on September 7–8, 1995. The purpose of the meeting was to identify lessons learned from recent conflict management experiences and to develop recommendations for a more consistent, coherent, and effective international response. The Workshop was attended by 12 core participants—a majority of whom were Africans with considerable experience in African peacemaking and peacekeeping—and 35 observers representing Nordic governments, non-governmental organizations involved in conflict resolution, humanitarian relief organizations, and academic institutions.

During the Workshop, we were struck by the depth of African leaders' commitment to developing a regional capacity to prevent, contain, and resolve armed conflicts, relying principally on their own peace-making capabilities but supported and reinforced by the international community. The involvement of Africans has been of critical importance in efforts to end armed conflicts on the continent in recent years; and African political and civic leaders have played pre-eminent peace-making roles in initiatives in countries like Angola, Lesotho, Rwanda, Liberia and Zaire. Although there is a general awareness of these factors outside Africa, a key message of the Bergen Workshop is that concerned Africans would like to see more urgent attention devoted to developing an effective internal capacity to respond to conflicts on the continent. In 1993, the Organization of African Unity created a conflict prevention mechanism in its Secretariat. Subregional organizations have also become more actively engaged in mediation and, in Liberia, peace-keeping. Furthermore, locally based non-governmental organizations are playing an increasing role in humanitarian relief, human rights monitoring, and conflict resolution at the community level.

The Workshop was inspired by a shared vision of active partnership, co-operation, and coordination between Africans and the outside world in responding vigorously, and pre-emptively, to armed conflicts. We believe this conception of a more integrated, co-operative response to conflicts in Africa—with a sensible division of labor and balanced and complementary responsibilities between Africans and the international community—can significantly improve the response to conflicts, thus both saving lives and minimizing extraction.

The editors wish to express their deep appreciation to Svein Gjerdåker and Øystein Rygg Haanæs for editorial assistance. The Chr. Michelsen Institute gratefully acknowledges the financial support of the Norwegian Ministry of Foreign Affairs.

May 1997
Bergen and Cape Town

*Gunnar M. Sørbø*                                    *Peter Vale*

# PART I

*Thinking about peace...*

# The International Community and Armed Conflict in Africa—Post Cold War Dilemmas

*Richard Joseph*

The anticipation of enhanced possibilities for international peace, security and cooperation at the end of the Cold War has given way to confusion and disillusionment as a result of the intensifying conflicts in parts of Africa, Asia and Europe. The belief that ideological rivalry would be succeeded by an international system that would adhere more strictly to shared norms and protocols has yielded to an awareness of the lack of a strong consensus concerning the criteria that should govern international involvement. A pattern is emerging in which conflicts will continue for several months and even years, as in Bosnia, before the world community arrives at an agreed arrangement for collective action. In Africa it appears that the more intense and destructive the conflict, as the cases of Burundi, Liberia, Rwanda, and Sudan exemplify, the greater the paralysis of the international community in acting decisively to bring an end to the violence.

Salim Ahmed Salim, the Secretary-General of the Organization of African Unity, has stated that the major problem confronting Africa is that of armed conflicts, a position echoed by the International Peace Academy.[1] Africa is the world's poorest continent and these conflicts deepen her impoverishment and sow chaos and instability that spill across state boundaries. Although the termination of these conflicts usually take the form of a negotiated agreement, what usually happens is that they end because one or more factions have reached the point of utter exhaustion, their external resources to finance the fighting have dried up, and their leaders seize the chance to leave the battlefield with some dignity and a package of material inducements. In their wake, they leave behind destroyed communities which have often long forgotten the reasons for the fighting.

William Zartman contends that most interstate conflicts in Africa do not change anything. They usually reach a point of stalemate at which a third party steps in and helps the combatants disengage and extricate themselves from a

---

[1] International Peace Academy, "The OAU Mechanism for Conflict Prevention, Management and Resolution". Report of a Conference co-sponsored by the IPA and OAU, Cairo, 7–11/5 1994, p. 11.

no-win situation.[2] This evaluation applies as well to many intra-state conflicts. One aspect of post-cold war dynamics is that although none of the warring parties in these internal conflicts is usually able to defeat the others, the international leverage to get them to desist has also weakened. As Witney Schneiderman points out, "where the superpowers often exacerbated conflict in Africa, they also were well-positioned to influence the termination of conflict".[3] The balance has today shifted towards leaders of warring groups who "will not hesitate to return to war; far from it—it is their business".[4] Even when, at great expense and after many painstaking efforts, the faction leaders are brought to the negotiating table, they often treat such exercises as tactical moves to ease the diplomatic pressure on them and obtain a breathing spell to re-group and re-arm, a scenario that has been repeatedly enacted in Angola, Liberia, and Somalia. The United States Institute of Peace (USIP) has consequently called attention to the stockpile of "orphaned agreements" brought about by these actions and attitudes.[5]

There are many factors responsible for the increasing sense of confusion and bewilderment associated with armed conflicts in Africa: the uncertain priorities of the major actors in global geopolitics; the increasing activity of continental and sub-regional organizations (unmatched by any demonstrated effectiveness); and the political turmoil within many African nations including those, such as Nigeria and Zaire, which have assumed expanded responsibilities for helping resolve conflicts in their sub-regions. Finally, with the erosion and collapse of African states, the warring groups that emerge from the wreckage are today highly opportunistic in nature. One author, with some exasperation, describes the Somali militias as really having "no issues...no ideological differences...nothing to negotiate".[6]

AFRICAN SELF-DETERMINATION

It seems axiomatic that the first responsibility for mitigating conflicts in Africa should lie with Africans themselves and their collective organizations.[7] The first recommendation of the USIP based on its 1994 symposium is that "Africans

---

[2] William I. Zartman, "Conflict and Conflict Management in Africa", paper prepared for the Sub-Committee on Governance and Democracy, The Global Coalition for Africa, 1992.

[3] "Conflict Resolution in Mozambique", in David R. Smock (ed.), *Making War and Peace: Foreign Intervention in Africa*. Washington DC: United States Institute of Peace, 1931, p. 235.

[4] Seifulaziz Milas, "What to do with the Warlords?", *Humanitarian Monitor*, no. 2, February 1996.

[5] "The US Contribution to Conflict Prevention, Management and Resolution in Africa", Report of a USIP Symposium of 28 September 1994.

[6] Maren, Michael, 1996, "Somalia: Whose Failure?", *Current History*, 95, 202. In the same issue of this journal, see the related article by William Reno, "The Business of War in Liberia", pp. 211–215.

[7] See the call by the Institute for African Alternatives (IFAA) for "an African strategy in the realm of conflict resolution" that would develop "Africa-specific mediation and negotiation techniques", *West Africa*, 24–30 October 1984, p. 1823.

should determine under what conditions it is helpful to have the international community engage in conflict resolution efforts".[8] The USIP suggested a strategy of "layered responses" to resolve conflicts, beginning with local organizations, then proceeding to sub-regional, regional, and finally international organizations "as a crisis escalates".[9] The IPA, however, endorsed the more conventional position: "the OAU should be the continent's "first port of call" in dealing with internal conflicts".[10] There are apparently no commonly agreed guidelines, what the IPA calls a "Peace Operations Doctrine", that would indicate which organizations, at what level, and in what combinations, should embark on peace initiatives in Africa.[11] This was therefore one of the key issues discussed by the participants in the 1995 Bergen Workshop and the reason it recommended a concerted effort to review the "architecture" of institutional capabilities in conflict prevention and resolution with the aim of reducing the prevailing "incoherence".[12]

In his keynote address to the IPA's Vienna Seminar on Peace-keeping and Conflict Resolution, Salim stated that a prime role of regional organizations such as the OAU is to "devise regional solutions to regional problems".[13] Such organizations should, he went on, "take primary ownership of their own problems". Yet, as reflected in his own discussion of the considerable difficulties the OAU has faced when seeking to play the lead role in resolving major armed conflicts in Africa, there is a large gap between assertions about African "ownership" and "leadership" and the blunt realities of African organizational weaknesses and external dependence. These failings were made glaringly evident in the months immediately preceding the Rwandan catastrophe of April 1994 when the OAU and the UN were unable to coordinate their efforts to obtain the fullest implementation of agreements reached between the Rwandan government and the insurgents. In this case, the principal actors were all African—leaders of the OAU and the UN and senior officials of the Tanzanian government—and they still could not get their institutions to collaborate effectively.

Salim has contended that the declining enthusiasm of the outside world for getting involved in African issues, and the escalating demands on the UN for peace-keeping missions, should lead to a greater devolution of responsibility for conflict resolution onto regional organizations such as the OAU. He also believes that such devolution should include the conduct of peace-keeping

---

[8] USIP, "Conflict Prevention, Management and Resolution", p. 1.

[9] Ibid., p. 3.

[10] IPA, "The OAU Mechanism", p. 40.

[11] Ibid., p. 33.

[12] *The International Response to Conflict in Africa: Conclusions and Recommendations, The Bergen Workshop 1995*. Bergen: Chr. Michelsen Institute, 1995.

[13] *The Role of Regional Organizations in Conflict Management*, IPA 25th Annual Vienna Seminar, 2–4 March 1995, p. 113.

operations.[14] In this regard, he is in step with his UN counterpart, Boutros Boutros-Ghali, who has emphasized the need to pursue better cooperation with regional organizations in accordance with Chapter VIII of the UN Charter.[15] While Boutros-Ghali includes all aspects of conflict management in this scenario—preventive action, peacemaking and peace-keeping—the IPA has taken a somewhat different position and suggests that the appropriate division of labour between the UN and the OAU "at this stage" should be for the OAU to focus its efforts on conflict prevention and peacemaking while leaving peace-keeping and peace-enforcement to the UN.[16]

In July 1993, the OAU Assembly of Heads of State and Government, meeting in Cairo, adopted a declaration establishing a Mechanism for Conflict Prevention, Management and Resolution. Some member states continued to express reservations concerning the OAU's involvement in peace-keeping operations. Nevertheless, this was a highly significant development in the history of the OAU, whose statutory Commission on Mediation, Conciliation and Arbitration had never become operational, and which was for long hampered in its capacity to resolve intra-state conflicts.[17] The stage is therefore formally set for progress to be made in overcoming the ambiguities and even contradictions regarding the relative responsibilities of the UN, the OAU and the various sub-regional organizations in peacemaking in the continent. While African governments and other international actors will continue to play a major, and often determining, role in seeking to end armed conflicts in Africa, it is these three sets of organizations that will continue to claim primary responsibilities in this area. Unfortunately, despite this promising step, the evidence still suggests that the gap between aspirations and achievements will not be speedily bridged.

THE OAU AND THE UN

Despite the polite diplomatic language used in most documents, the OAU and the UN are still struggling to find a mutually acceptable way to coordinate their responses to African conflicts. In 1996, the meetings of leaders of countries bordering the Great Lakes of east and central Africa, spearheaded by former US President Jimmy Carter, and the peace talks arranged by International Alert between the government and insurgent forces in Sierra Leone, are indicative of the role that non-African actors continue to play in fostering communication among the opposing sides in African armed conflicts while intergovernmental

---

[14] Ibid., pp. 7 and 14.

[15] *An Agenda for Peace*, 1992.

[16] "The OAU Mechanism", p. 30.

[17] It should not be overlooked, however, that the OAU had developed a commendable record in using the good offices of particular African leaders to help resolve interstate conflicts and should take some of the credit for the relatively small number of such disputes in Africa that erupted into actual fighting.

organizations are immobilized by the complexities of both the conflicts and their own internal operations.

While the OAU and UN agree on the objectives of "improved consultation, exchange of information, coordination of joint action", they are still groping for the modalities to achieve them.[18] The conflictual interaction of these two organizations during the period preceding and during the Rwandan catastrophe of 1994 makes painful reading today, especially in light of the scale of that tragedy. Salim refers to the UN's "laissez-faire" attitude in Rwanda at a time when the OAU was urging the rapid dispatch of a peace-keeping force to replace the OAU's fifty observers and to obtain implementation of the 1993 Arusha Agreement. "Timely intervention", Salim went on, "and the support of regional efforts were areas where the UN should not cut costs".[19] The IPA, which jointly organized with the OAU the symposium in Addis Ababa in May 1994 on its new Mechanism, had even planned to discuss the Rwandan initiative as a "success story". It had hope to use the Rwandan experience as a case-study of how an African state, Tanzania, and the OAU acted promptly and energetically to promote a peaceful resolution of the fighting that began in 1990. Instead, when the plotters struck on April 6, 1994 and the genocidal attacks began, the OAU and the Africa group in the United Nations were unable to get urgent action from the UN and the world powers. The UN's initial response was to reduce its already small contingent and then take another three months to replace it with a force just twice as large (5,500).

A comprehensive multi-volume review of the Rwandan catastrophe has now been completed and its findings should provoke the action needed to achieve the level of institutional coordination recommended by the 1995 Bergen Workshop.[20] The energies that are devoted to such exercises, however, must now be matched by appropriate action. Alongside the stockpile of unimplemented peace agreements in Africa is another growing stockpile of recommendations about what should be done to improve coordination among concerned external actors. The USIP has suggested that African nations should provide troops for UN peace-keeping operations while the UN handles command, communications and coordination. European powers with a strong African interest were assigned in this configuration the task of assisting with logistics and material supplies. This division of responsibilities is not likely to evoke a positive response in Africa as it appears to downgrade significantly the potential role of African institutions.[21] Also added to the stockpile is a detailed communiqué to the OAU Secretary General from the British and Nigerian UN ambassadors in 1995 in which they reviewed the "ways and means of improving practical cooperation and coordination" between the UN and regional

---

[18] Salim, "The Role of Regional Organizations", p. 12.

[19] "The OAU and Conflict Resolution in Africa", IPA Roundtable Series, 30 September 1993.

[20] *The International Response to Conflict and Genocide: Lessons from the Rwanda Experience*, Copenhagen: Joint Evaluation of Emergency Assistance to Rwanda, March 1996.

[21] USIP, op. cit., p. 7.

organizations. Their communiqué included a number of practical suggestions: technical assistance, staff exchanges, liaison offices, joint missions, training of forces, and pre-positioning of equipment.[22]

A similar suggestion by John Roper, in his contribution to the IPA's Vienna Seminar, stressed a form of partnering between regional organizations in Europe and their counterparts in other areas such as the OAU in Africa, which would involve the sharing of training, equipment, transport and other facilities.[23] Finally, in a paper for the Global Coalition for Africa entitled, "Africa and the United Nations Agenda for Peace: A Proposal", Herman Cohen advanced several concrete proposals for UN/OAU Cooperation based on the shared premises of the UN's "Agenda for Peace" and the OAU's "Mechanism".[24] There is clearly a widespread recognition of the lack of institutional coordination and the need for an agreed division of responsibilities among international, continental and sub-regional organizations. It is yet to be demonstrated, however, that the political commitment exists to move from the crafting of recommendations to the actual designing of a programme of action that can enjoy wide and sustained support.

SUB-REGIONAL ORGANIZATIONS

There have been high expectations of the role that sub-regional organizations could play in the resolution of armed conflicts in Africa. Africa is a vast continent and the cultural and linguistic variations within its sub-regions are often considerable. It seems reasonable, therefore, that this devolution of responsibilities would bring specific advantages. The sub-regional organizations that have recently become involved in peacemaking—ECOWAS in West Africa, IGADD in East Africa and SADC in southern Africa—were not initially designed for this purpose.[25] The record of the best-known initiatives, however, ECOWAS in Liberia and IGADD in Sudan, suggest that the capabilities these bodies bring to peacemaking is currently overwhelmed by the logistic, political and financial challenges they encounter.

William Zartman identifies the multinational peace-keeping effort in Chad in 1981 led by Nigeria, which failed to achieve any of its objectives, as the first

---

[22] Letter to OAU Secretary-General from Ibrahim A. Gambari and David Hannay, 11 April 1995 on conflict prevention and peace-keeping in Africa.

[23] Roper, John, *The Contribution of Regional Organizations*. IPA Vienna Seminar, 1994.

[24] For a revised version of this paper, see Herman J. Cohen, 1995, "African Capabilities for Managing Conflict: The Role of the United States", in David R. Smock and Chester A. Crocker (eds.), *African Conflict Resolution: The US Role in Peacemaking*. Washington DC: Institute of Peace Press, pp. 77–94.

[25] ECOWAS is the Economic Community of West African States; IGADD is the Inter-Governmental Authority on Drought and Desertification; and SADC is the Southern African Development Community.

such initiative in Africa.[26] The Liberian exercise, which at its height involved as many as 15,000 troops from several nations, is certainly the most complex and sustained exercise of this nature that has ever been attempted by African nations.[27] Several years have now elapsed since the first detachment of ECOMOG (ECOWAS Monitoring Group) troops fought its way ashore in Liberia in August 1990. Virtually every aspect of conflict resolution involving sub-regional authorities has since been attempted in Liberia: mediation, peace-keeping and peace-enforcement. The OAU has not played a major role in deference to the extensive involvement of the sub-regional authorities. Nevertheless, a special envoy of the OAU Secretary-General, Rev. Canaan Banana, took part in the negotiations that culminated in the Cotonou Accord of July 1993, which set up the first transitional government that included representatives of warring factions and civilian political groups. This government, however, turned out to be just as unsuccessful as its predecessor.[28]

What the Liberian experience demonstrates is that there is a great gap between the theories and arguments regarding "the comparative advantage of sub-regional organizations" and the reality on the ground.[29] Salim outlines some of the tensions that exist between the knowledge and concerns that neighbouring states bring to peace efforts and the problems that derive from their tendency to become implicated in the conflict. One way of trying to overcome this tension, he suggests, is by "combining the principle of neighbourhood with the principle of distant impartiality".[30] In Liberia, there have been several attempts to achieve this particular mix. Senegalese troops were added to the original forces provided by Liberia's neighbours, but they were withdrawn in 1993 after a confrontation in which several soldiers were killed. Tanzanian and Ugandan detachments were added to the West African forces in 1993–94 but they also experienced much loss of life and were eventually withdrawn.

In the report of its 1994 Cairo conference, the IPA highlighted the following observation whose double negative followed by a conditional clause is indicative of the difficulty commentators find in assessing these exercises: "ECOMOG proved that it is not impossible for African states to mount peace-keeping operations if the political will is there".[31] What ECOMOG does not prove, however, is that it is possible for African states at the present time to mount successful peace-keeping operations. Perhaps it is our expectations about these operations that are unrealistic. What are the examples of successful Asian or Latin American peace-keeping operations in their respective continents? India's dis-

---

[26] "Conflict and Management", p. 8.

[27] This author is conducting a comprehensive study of this conflict and the various peacemaking activities under a grant from the US Institute of Peace for 1995–1997.

[28] Following the Abuja Accord of August 1995, in which the UN, OAU and ECOWAS pooled their efforts, another ill-faced set of interim institutions was established.

[29] USIP, op. cit., p. 7.

[30] "The Role of Regional Organizations", p. 3.

[31] "The OAU Mechanism", p. 18.

patch of troops to help end the armed conflict in Sri Lanka was just as disastrous as Nigeria's interventions in Chad and Liberia. Even the European Union was unable to take effective charge of peacemaking in Bosnia. For the foreseeable future, it appears that the position of the IPA is the most persuasive: peacekeeping in Africa should be conducted under the auspices of the United Nations with African forces serving alongside soldiers from non-African nations as they have done quite effectively in many operations world-wide.

The IGADD experience has been of shorter duration than that of ECOMOG and has not included a peace-keeping dimension. However, the fact that two of the members of IGADD have broken relations with the government of Sudan (Eritrea and Uganda), and that IGADD meetings have generated successive proposals with little subsequent progress toward a settlement, suggest that it is highly doubtful that this body will contribute significantly to the resolution of the Sudan civil war. SADC has had a hand in moving the faltering Angolan war toward a resolution. It also provided the context for a concerted effort to end a military challenge to the democratically-elected government in Lesotho in 1994 and in keeping the peace process and elections from being derailed in Mozambique. These initiatives were obviously enhanced by the towering prestige of Nelson Mandela and the ANC-led South African government.

Southern Africa bids fair to be a zone of peace, democracy and development in Africa. The complex web of relations among the political leaders and organizations in this region during the long struggle against the apartheid system now serves as a resource in containing the outbreak of armed conflicts. The deeply-polarized struggle along racial lines in southern Africa has left behind political structures and relationships that facilitate peacemaking. Elsewhere in the continent, however, where the struggle to end colonial rule and racial domination was much shorter in duration, African nations are obliged to create institutions without the benefit of such tangible and intangible resources. Outside of southern Africa, therefore, sub-regional organizations cannot draw on a strong sense of commitment and shared understanding among their member countries. If anything, these organizations tend to complicate rather than facilitate attempts to resolve intra-state conflicts. It is therefore advisable that such organizations revert to their more general, and especially economic, objectives. When confronted with the outbreak of conflicts within their member states, they should concentrate on "doing no harm", encourage third-party mediation, and avoid mounting operations for which they currently lack the collective will and the necessary material and other resources.


THE PAX AFRICANA

It is necessary to make the seemingly trite observation that the problem in Africa is not conflict per se but the inability to manage and peaceably resolve inevitable social and other conflicts. Moreover, there is the added complication of the deliberate provoking of violent conflicts for political and other ends, especially as many authoritarian regimes reluctantly restored competitive multi-party politics. William Zartman began an overview article by discussing the conflicts that are inherent in the process of creating new African states and in the search for domestic and continental order.[32] The crises in which Sudan, Somalia, Rwanda and Liberia are mired are not *sui generis*: they can be associated with more generic struggles that have long been underway in Africa to determine "the structures and practices of government in the future and its beneficiaries".[33] In short, these intractable conflicts can be traced to the fundamental tasks of nation-building, state-building and governance that *all* African countries have had to pursue, whether their sovereign existence dates from the period 1955–1975, or a century earlier as in the case of Liberia.

Zartman identifies three fundamental sources of conflict in contemporary Africa: internal consolidations, boundary disputes and structural rivalries.[34] I would suggest the following terminology to make the differences clearer: struggles to consolidate political power, boundary disputes and interstate hegemonic rivalries. In general, Zartman underplays the role of external forces in fomenting conflict in Africa for their own hegemonic reasons. Nevertheless, his formulation calls attention to an important point: all three sources of actual and potential conflict in Africa were contained in the past by certain forces and factors: Cold War geopolitics; the African policies of particular European and Middle Eastern states; the commitment to preserve African boundaries and observe principles of non-interference in the internal affairs of the OAU and other continental bodies; the "apolitical" postures of multilateral and bilateral providers of aid and loans which provided extensive financial resources regardless of the nature of the regimes in power; and the consolidation of authoritarian rule throughout the continent.

Despite the armed conflicts that erupted in one African country or another during the post-colonial period, a *Pax Africana* based on the preceding factors emerged to replace European partition of the continent. Only minor boundary adjustments were permitted by the Pax Africana which was itself anchored to the preservation of colonial borders. No scission of any African nation occurred until Eritrea gained its independence from Ethiopia after three decades of war. With regard to internal power configurations, and despite occasional flurries of competitive elections in a few countries, ruling regimes in most countries could only be changed via military coups (or the occasional replacement of rulers following their natural deaths).

As the 1980s drew to a close, this entire edifice came under challenge. The demise of the USSR and the collapse of Eastern bloc communist governments removed an important source of support for authoritarian regimes in Africa. These changes simultaneously took away the principal arguments that western

---

[32] "Conflict and Conflict Management", p. 2.

[33] Ibid., p. 3.

[34] Ibid., p. 2.

nations had relied on to justify their support of these regimes. The removal of Africa from the arena of global geo-politics did not, however, mean that the continent was now free of external intervention. In fact, cold war geopolitics tended to divert attention from the extensive involvement and intervention in Africa of middle-level states, especially France, Israel, Libya and South Africa. While Libya has recently been constrained by international sanctions, and South Africa has undergone a dramatic change in its external policies with the end of apartheid, France and Israel have continued to pursue their national interests in Africa in ways that essentially sustain the political status quo.[35]

As for the international donor community, it was finally induced to confront the fundamental contradiction between its "developmental" policies and the non-developmental nature of most of the states to which financial resources had been regularly transferred. Finally, agitation for more open, participatory and accountable governments in most African countries increased, and political groups emerged to fill the political spaces opened up by these structural and policy shifts. As the major western nations began to provide significant support for the burgeoning forces demanding political liberalization and democracy after 1989, the *Pax Africana* implicitly came under challenge. Before long, however, as these political transitions were accompanied by an increase in the number of complex emergencies, western nations gradually tempered their support for them. As a consequence, the main ingredients of the *Pax Africana* have been gradually restored.[36]

In retrospect, it can be seen that this post-colonial system served to maintain interstate peace in Africa as well as uphold the regimes established within African states. In a now classic formulation, Carl Rosberg and Robert Jackson have argued that African states were sustained by these external frameworks although they had steadily lost domestic legitimacy and efficacy.[37] After 1989, with the upsurge of long-suppressed social and political struggles, the governing structures which formerly relied on repression were weakened or dismantled before alternate systems of accommodation and conciliation could be established. The African continent therefore entered the final decade of the twentieth century with the quest for political renewal via democratic transitions encountering strong countervailing forces and factors. Most significant among

---

[35] Other Middle East countries, such as Iran and Saudi Arabia, are active in particular countries, especially where political mobilization on Islamic issues are prominent, such as Sudan and Northern Nigeria.

[36] One of the recommendations of the working group on democratization and human rights of the White House Conference on Africa, June 1994, which this author co-chaired, was for assistance to be provided for the emergence of a community of African democratic states. Such an initiative was seen as helping sustain the momentum for political reform. It would also have provided a counterpoint to the active assistance Africa's authoritarian leaders provide each other as was most recently demonstrated in the 1996 elections in Benin in which the former military ruler, Mathieu Kerekou, returned to power.

[37] Jackson, Robert H. and Carl G. Rosberg, 1986, "Why Africa's Weak States Persist? The Empirical and the Judicial in Statehood", in Atul Kohli (ed.), *The State and Development in the Third World*. Princeton: Princeton University Press.

them were the decline in economic resources, the upsurge of conflict along ethnic, communal and religious lines, and the persistence of regimes seeking to re-establish authoritarian controls as soon as external pressures for democratization slackened. In this conjuncture, it is unlikely that a wholly revamped *Pax Africana* based on respect for democratic governance, the rule of law and human rights would be established.

CONCLUSION: PROMOTING PEACE AMONG STATES AND NON-STATES

Of all the problems that beset African countries today, perhaps none is more daunting than the erosion of the state itself. There has been a steady increase in the number of countries in which the national territory effectively under state control has contracted. The more extreme cases such as Somalia and Liberia, in which the state has effectively disappeared, could increase as there are several lurking candidates. Most at risk are those countries in which not just the composition and policies of the government are challenged but the legitimacy of the state itself is highly contested as a result of the deep estrangement of large sections of the population. In this regard, the political turmoil in Nigeria since the annulment of the presidential elections of 12 June 1993 has grave implications both for Nigerians themselves and the peoples of several neighbouring countries in west and equatorial Africa.

The erosion or complete collapse of African states, and the failure of competing groups to defeat their rivals, are transforming areas of the continent into zones of combat between marauding bands. Achille Mbembe has used the term "nihilism" to characterize certain defining features of the resulting conflicts.[38] These include the absence of any significant idea or programme much less ideology associated with these conflicts; their extreme social destructiveness in which the norms, cultural institutions and basic authority structures of communities are torn apart; their seemingly irrational qualities as fighters rip apart the very structures in which they will have to live; the predatory economic activities that strip away the minimal resources on which the population subsist including those provided by relief organizations; and the unrestrained pursuit of power by faction leaders that include using child soldiers, terrorizing civilian refugees, and razing churches and health clinics.

There is a tendency to refer to these characteristics of armed conflict in post-Cold War Africa as indications of a spreading "anarchy".[39] In fact, as the case of Liberia demonstrates, even the chaotic fighting that periodically erupts can be traced to deliberate instigation by faction leaders. These leaders lack the means to organize disciplined armies and the capability to defeat their rivals and re-establish central state-power, as was accomplished in Uganda by Yoweri

---

[38] "Complex Transformations in late 20th Century Africa", *Africa Demos*, 3, March 1995.

[39] Notably in Robert Kaplan's tendentious but influential article, "The Coming Anarchy", *Atlantic Monthly*, February 1994.

Museveni and the National Resistance Movement and in Eritrea by Isaias Afewerki and the Eritrean Peoples Liberation Front. Moreover, the ending of great power rivalries in Africa after 1989 has meant that the smaller state actors still actively involved in the continent are able to support particular governments or insurgencies but lack the capacity to bring these conflicts to a definitive conclusion.

According to Mbembe, parts of Africa have returned to the nineteenth century with a mixture of states and organized groups seeking to augment their control of territory and peoples through raiding and other military and predatory activities.[40] Another author has compared them to "the conscripts of Europe's and Asia's medieval hordes who considered the spoils of combat to be their perquisites".[41] What implications, it must be asked, does such a scenario hold for the pursuit of peace on the continent. Some authors have suggested that the answer lies in the external imposition of a new form of colonialism or international trusteeship on the continent.[42] Others, such as the noted African scholar, Ali Mazrui, have proposed a reconfiguration of African states that would make particular states responsible for assuring order among the smaller countries in their periphery. None of these grand schemes, however, are likely to be implemented. Africa is obliged to seek progress incrementally. The most promising path remains the encouragement and support for open and accountable democratic governments. Where, as in Somalia and Sudan, there is little immediate prospect of restoring a unified government based on democratic principles, the international community should act decisively to protect civilian populations from the devastation and use vigorous diplomacy to reduce the scale and intensity of the fighting until the possibility of a more definitive resolution of the brute struggle occurs.

Since 1989, armed conflicts in Mozambique, Namibia and South Africa have been brought to a peaceful resolution by sustained diplomacy and the achievement of political inclusion and power sharing via democratic elections. Sierra Leone, following the elections and peace talks in 1996, may soon be added to this list. Countries in which these options have been blocked, as in Liberia, Rwanda, Somalia and Sudan, have found themselves catapulted into prolonged warfare. It is also important to recognize that transitions from war to peace by the establishment of an open and accountable government following democratic elections can proceed in the reverse direction. A democratically elected

---

[40] Mbembe explores the parallels between the pursuit of power and the resulting conflicts in pre-colonial Africa and contemporary Africa in a forthcoming study to be published by the University of California Press.

[41] Milas, "The Warlords", p. 12.

[42] Pfaff, William, 1996, "Trusteeship is the Solution for Much of Africa", *International Herald Tribune*, 25–26 May. James Jonah, a special representative of the UN Secretary-General, has suggested that the most practical solution to the Liberian situation would be for the UN to take control of the territory, echoing recommendations made at the height of the Somalia crisis. See Stedman, Stephen John, 1996, "Conflict and Conciliation in Sub-Saharan Africa", in Michael E. Brown (ed.), *The International Dimensions of Internal Conflict*. Cambridge MA: The MIT Press, p. 255.

government in Zambia since 1991 has systematically undermined the very basis of the pluralist democracy which had enabled it to come to power. As a consequence, on the eve of the second set of multiparty elections in 1996, the country is confronting the prospect of a sharp descent into greater authoritarianism and political violence.

The temptation to retreat from Africa, as a result of these frustrating developments, will obviously increase within the international community. Yet, violent conflicts and societal collapse within Africa will not remain limited in their impact to the continent: they will show up on the doors of more stable nations in the form of increased refugee flows and a range of illicit activities. In addition to such recommendations of the Bergen Workshop as the promotion of greater coordination among organizations pursuing the peaceful resolution of conflicts and sustained support for democratic transitions, greater attention should be devoted to combating external forces that contribute to the erosion of African states through arms and drug trafficking, the fostering of corruption and money laundering, and the smuggling of precious stones and other commodities.

Efforts to contain these externally-promoted operations are essential if the fragile process of state rebuilding along democratic lines is to have any chance of succeeding. There is also a need to take the long view of African renewal and the restoration of the material and political conditions for civic life within war-torn areas of the continent. On the eve of the twenty-first century, the balance between the forces of construction and those of destruction in Africa is tipping in favour of the latter. Reversing this alarming trend is one of the major challenges facing Africans and the international community. While the end of the Cold War has removed some of the causes of armed conflict, it has also created opportunities for a new class of actors, "small men lusting after power and loot", who, for tactical reasons, are prepared to enter into peace agreements that they have "no intention to honour" while their people are subjected to unspeakable horrors.[43] Said Samatar goes so far as to speak of his nation, Somalia, as consisting today of two nations, one of victims and one of criminals. While the former faces the constant threat of starvation, the latter grows "fat off loot taken from the hungry and powerless".[44] An estimated 6.5 million Africans have died from civil wars between 1960 and 1990.[45] In short, Africa has suffered the equivalent of the Holocaust in the numbers of lives lost between the end of colonial rule and the end of the Cold War solely as a result of internal conflicts. In view of the continuation of some of these conflicts after 1990, and the initiation of new ones, the international community must redouble its efforts to assist Africans in finding appropriate institutional and other remedies.

---

[43] Michael Maren, "Somalia: Whose Failure?", pp. 202–203.

[44] Samatar, Said S., 1995, "Somalia's Prospects for a Lasting Peace", *Humanitarian Monitor*, February, p. 14.

[45] Stedman, "Conflict and Conciliation", p. 238.

# Thinking about Peace and Peace-Making in Africa

*Tom Vraalsen*

## INTRODUCTION

African countries have since the 1960s been beset by an extraordinarily heavy burden of warfare. Close to two dozen civil wars have been fought. Nearly one third of all overt military interventions in the world between 1960 and 1985 were aimed at African countries. Most of them came from within Africa. At present, more than ten African countries are suffering from violent conflicts and civil disorder. Propaganda campaigns, border skirmishes, terrorism and other forms of low intensity conflict have been the order of the day.

Africa's refugee population constitutes one half of the global total. 72 communal groups in Africa have been identified as being at risk of involvement in future conflicts and being subjected to victimization. Such findings, which in the aggregate account for slightly less than half the population of the region, suggest that the incidence of future conflict may equal, or even surpass, previous levels of conflict.

Against such a backdrop, peace and peace-making in Africa emerge as issues of the greatest importance; issues which are not only the concern of governments. These are not matters of intra-state or inter-state affairs in an abstract sense. The fact is that the well being—and even life and death—of millions of individuals is involved.

The point of departure for any successful attempt to resolve conflicts and make peace in Africa must be a genuine recognition of, and respect for, the identity of the peoples of the continent, their traditions and their proud cultural heritage. To this should be added an intimate knowledge of the historical facts as well as an understanding of the prevailing social and economic conditions on the continent as fashioned by centuries of colonial domination and oppression.

Africa's economic and political problems defy easy solutions. They cannot be approached in purely military or political terms. That would in most cases be too simplistic and could more often than not compound the problems and thus further aggravate the situation. National security will depend on whether states can create an environment in which problem solving can succeed. I believe that the way to such an environment lies in social and economic justice, respect for the fundamental rights of the individual citizen, the rule of law and the independence of the judiciary, popular participation at all levels of the decision-making process and freedom to act under social and legal responsibility. Such an environment is rare in Africa today. Contributing to fulfilling these criteria is in my view true peace-making. Safeguarding them and securing their continuous implementation is true peace-keeping.

I will in the following give a snapshot of Africa's past history and present situation, and offer some thoughts on what should be done in order to create a security environment conducive to peace-making and peace-keeping. I will subsequently discuss the use of regional and international mechanisms for conflict prevention and resolution in Africa.

Of course, not all the present 52 members of the OAU came out of the same mould. There were major differences both between and within the various subregions: differences in the level of economic, social, infrastructural and political development as well as in the material and human resource base. However, I believe that for the purpose of this article, generalization is in order.

## BACKDROP

What is the impression of Africa in the Western World? People in distress, people fleeing from civil war, hunger and disease. Mismanaged and neglected economies, corruption, autocratic one-party systems, military dictatorships and abuse of power. A continent caught in an unbreakable downward spiral, a continent about to be decoupled from the global development process, a continent which is already marginalized in a political and economic sense. This is the picture of Africa generally portrayed by Western media and often accompanied by statements from so-called experts that Africa is a lost case; the continent cannot be saved. And the question is asked: why should the rest of the world really care? They postulate that in a post-Cold War situation Africa is no longer of importance, be it in a political, strategic or economic sense. The answers these people give to their own questions tend to be: Let Africa drift in her own sea of misery and hopelessness. It is of no concern to us!

Such attitudes and statements not only demonstrate a very disheartening disregard for fellow human beings. They also reveal a high degree of ignorance, or lack of understanding, of the magnitude of the problems and the extent to which they transcend regional boundaries. The heart of the matter is that Africa's problems are our problems. We will all suffer if the situation is not brought under control. Pressures from a galloping population growth coupled with ruthless exploitation of the continent's natural resources will ultimately cause ecological catastrophes. The poor and unjust socio-economic conditions are breeding grounds for political and social destabilization with ensuing disorder and violent conflicts. The situation can best be compared with a time-bomb of tremendously destructive power. If it detonates, the shock-waves will be felt deep within our own societies. The international community has—for its own protection, if for nothing else—every reason to feel concerned about Africa and the developments on that continent; it has every reason to be supportive of the African countries, to help them reverse the present trend, to stabilize the situation and create a basis for social, economic and political justice. That would be a significant contribution to securing peace and good neighbourly relations in Africa.

Africa is poor, but even so, so infinitely rich; it has been oppressed, but is not subdued; it is a continent with its own clearly established identity, bearer of proud traditions and a unique cultural heritage; it possesses a strong resource base in material and human terms. Like any other continent, Africa's history is a tale of dynasties in growth and decay, of prosperous trading centres and extinct cities, of good times and bad times.

The peoples of Africa demand satisfaction and respect having been subjected to the slave trade, colonialism, racial discrimination and oppression. The peoples of Africa seek support in regaining what is their birthright: freedom, respect, economic and social justice. To grant them that right through active and generous support is true peace-making.

THE SOCIO-ECONOMIC ENVIRONMENT

Since the 1970s the economies of most African countries have been in deep trouble. This is in part due to clear and unforgivable mismanagement by their political leaders. But equally important have been adverse external developments. In recent years there has been a growing realisation that new approaches will have to be found if Africa is to recover from her present economic and political crisis. African representatives have themselves come to the forefront of this debate, with new and bold initiatives. At the same time, there is an increasing frustration over several aspects of the present modalities for North–South cooperation. Many countries in the South have felt that the state of unequal dependency has pushed them further into a position with even less influence over conditions determining their development patterns.

**The debt burden**

External debt is the Achilles heel of African countries as they attempt recovery and transformation. Since 1984 the African countries have persistently urged the international community to address in a comprehensive manner the critical economic situation confronting them as a result of the mounting debt service burden. In 1994 Sub-Sahara Africa's debt represented 254 per cent of the regions export income and 83 per cent of its GNP. The corresponding figures for 1980 were 90 per cent and 30 per cent. Africa's debt burden is unsustainable, even after various debt relief initiatives, including cancellations.

African leaders have repeatedly reaffirmed that their external debts constitute contractual obligations which they intend to honour to the best of their ability. They have argued for agreement on a viable debt strategy that would take fully into account their economic and social development needs; a strategy based on cooperation, continuous dialogue and shared responsibility.

This call has largely been ignored. The international financial institutions and the creditor nations have not demonstrated the necessary will to take the oppressive debt burden off the shoulders of the African peoples. It seems that Africa's bi- and multilateral debt is not sufficiently large in global financial terms to warrant the necessary attention from the major creditor countries and the international financial institutions. Unlike for some Latin-American countries, African defaults and non-servicing of their debt cause only a ripple in the world of international finance. Nor do African countries any longer have, like some Middle Eastern and Eastern European countries, strategic leverage which might be used to obtain significant debt reductions.

The problem of indebtedness is historically linked with that of underdevelopment; its long term solution lies primarily in Africa's own ability to generate real development. Since 1986 more than 100 structural adjustment programmes have been signed between the IMF/IBRD and dozens of African governments. Measures have been taken by African countries to implement the commitments they have made individually or collectively. They have instituted far-reaching reforms at great social and political sacrifice and costs to their own peoples.

These reforms and their efforts have, however, yet to yield the desired results. Part of the reason lies in the backwardness and very poor state of African economies. Equally important is the fact that African efforts to implement reforms and adjust their policies have been undermined by exasperating and excruciating debt service payments, worsening terms of trade, an international economic and political environment characterized by benign neglect and the failure of the international community to live up to its commitments to provide Africa with substantially increased resources.

Generous debt-relief, not least from the international financial institutions, and increased support from the same institutions, as well as from bilateral donors, would be significant contributions to improving socio-economic conditions in Africa. If this could be accompanied by an improvement in the terms of trade for Africa, we could really be on our way towards creating the right environment for peace and stability.

## Trade and finance

Over the last 20 years most African countries have suffered a decline in per capita income. This is set to continue despite higher growth projections for the remainder of the decade. The already wide gap between them and the developed countries of the North will continue to widen. Foreign direct investment (FDI) in Africa is down to a trickle, official development aid (ODA) is being reduced in real terms and the latest Uruguay Round is expected to hit African countries hard with lower export earnings and higher import prices. Some erosion of trade preferences is also evident, particularly for African exports of cocoa and coffee to Europe. The purchasing power of Africa's exports has over a long period of time been substantially reduced. Even when GATT negotiations have been successfully concluded, many developing countries have felt marginalized from the process. To them the multilateral negotiating process is a very unequal process. In recent years many developing countries have radically liberalized their trade and foreign investment regimes and have been pressed by industrial governments to make concessions on services and intellectual property rights. In return they have received only limited and grudging improvements in access to markets in sensitive sectors. They face trade barriers estimated to cost them more than twice the value of all aid.

African countries' weak production structures limit their ability to fully benefit from future improvements in market access. They need help to improve their competitiveness in the new international trade environment. Given the links between international trade patterns and poverty in Africa, African countries should be given compensation for their short term losses. Removal of preferences under the Uruguay Round should be deferred, while special aid is provided to help finance preparatory phases of commodity diversification projects, particularly in the non-traditional sector. The international community and specially the World Trade Organization (WTO) have a vital role to play in helping African countries through a difficult transition. However, it is equally important that African countries themselves look beyond the short term and take measures to transform their production and trade structures. Competitive advantage cannot be shielded permanently by trade preferences. There is a need for strong measures to raise economic competitiveness. African countries have to improve their services infrastructure and investment climate and to take advantage of technological developments.

Such measures would encourage more foreign investors to explore opportunities in Africa. The fact is that Africa today offers very profitable investment opportunities. An inter-regional study of FDI profitability for foreign affiliates of American companies show that net income as a proportion of owners' equity was considerably higher in Africa than in other developing country regions. African countries must further liberalize FDI legislation and should be given foreign assistance in developing local capacity for investment promotion. Individual donors and international organizations should come forward and respond to calls for support.

ODA to Africa has been falling in real terms through the 1990s despite promises made by the donor community to do its utmost to increase such aid. Overall Western ODA relative to the size of donors' economies is at present at its lowest point. With much of what is made available going to emergency relief, long-term development needs are being doubly starved. Donors are now responding to the almost continuous calls for strengthened international support with increasing selectivity in which countries get aid.

The list of conditions the recipient countries have to satisfy steadily become longer and tougher. Many African countries argue that their economic and political circumstances make it impossible for them to meet all of a growing profusion of conditionalities.

ODA is generally considered as providing a marginal input into a country's development process. A healthy growing trade and increased volumes of FDI and other financial transfers are of much greater importance in securing sustainable growth and improved social conditions. This is certainly true in most cases. However, a number of African countries simply cannot sustain themselves through their own efforts. They are critically dependant upon predictable and continuous external financing whilst they re-organise and restructure their societies. To decouple such countries from the general development process by denying them necessary economic and political support could be a recipe for future instability, disorder and conflict.

The developed countries have a moral obligation to extend political, economic and financial support to African countries in the fields of trade, FDI, ODA and finance. The donor community's present performance in all these areas is at best lacklustre. Budgetary constraints are no excuse. A more generous policy is a small price to pay for future peace and stability.

### Popular participation

Foreign governments and international lending institutions hold certain expectations for the socio-economic policies of African countries as expressed by the conditionalities they place on aid and assistance. In so doing it is of vital importance that the donor community place Africa's brief history of modern state-building in a historical perspective.

I regret to say that this is often not done. Expectations held, demands made and conditionalities imposed are too often unrealistic and simply not achievable—at least not in the short or medium term. The expectations and demands stem from applying Western standards of state responsiveness to countries with little ethno-linguistic unity and few economic resources, states that from independence suffer from a deficit of legitimacy—in brief: states that are not nations. The standards of responsiveness set for African countries were in fact only recently attained by the Western industrialized states themselves.

State-building in the Western World was a lethal process. European states reached their high levels of domestic consensus on issues such as social and political organization only after lengthy instability and upheaval. State-building in Western Europe was intimately linked to wars against external enemies and coercion of domestic groups. Responsive politics and distributional economics rose from drawn-out bargaining during which states learned to make accommodations with their citizens in order to survive in a world of warring countries.

The state formation process in Norway, for example, began in the 9th century. Universal suffrage was not introduced until 1913. In the United States, the most important issues of national identity and political legitimacy were forged over a century. It took fifty years to consolidate a competitive party system; the separation of the state from gross political patronage took over one hundred years.

Coercion and violence should of course not be condoned for the states of Africa simply because the Western countries used such methods. The point I wish to make is that expectations and demands placed on African states should be realistic. Conditions in Africa are far less favourable to the development of strong states and democratic policies than those that existed when Western countries undertook state making and nation building. The challenge today is for the countries of Africa to build strong states without recourse to violence— to turn the immense power of nation states away from war and toward the creation of justice, personal security and democracy.

The word "democracy" expresses the concept of a political system which allows for popular participation and contestation for power. A system which contains checks and balances as well as freedom to organize opposition. To be resistant to different kinds of political machinations and subversion from destructive forces—be it external or internal—it should be solidly rooted in the traditional values of the country concerned. This is what we all should be working towards. Let us focus on the substance of the matter and not the appearance. The essential thing is that Africa develops systems which allow for true popular participation and powersharing.

Our system of democracy and the way we have organized our societies is not necessarily suitable for African countries. The Westminster system of parliamentarism may be right for the United Kingdom, but not necessarily so for Tanzania, Rwanda or Burundi, to mention just a few. Systems for the exercise of popular power must be developed from within. Only then will they attain the necessary strength and legitimacy. Systems super-imposed from outside will ultimately collapse and disintegrate.

A recognition of these facts by the international community—and in particular the Western donor countries—would help promote peace and social harmony in Africa; that is, provided this recognition is translated into practical policies. We must decisively move away from the arrogant assumption that only the Western countries know how to govern and that our system of democratic government is superior to everything else. It takes conscious efforts of leadership to establish and develop a state or to put it back together again after a violent upheaval. Such leadership can only be indigenous.

### Framework for economic cooperation

Since the Lagos Plan of Action was adopted by the Organisation of African Unity (OAU) in 1980 a number of initiatives have been taken to set the continent on a new development track. However, these initiatives have not yielded the anticipated results and alternative courses of action have been sought. As a contribution to this debate, I have suggested that the structural adjustment programmes which have been imposed on developing countries by the international financial institutions at a time when the former are in a particularly weak bargaining position, should be replaced with a different kind of relationship in the form of a development contract or compact.

The main basis for a development contract—which would be of a political and not legal nature—would be the mutual interest of the contracting parties in promoting development in the poorer country. Such an arrangement would be binding on both parties. It would involve obligations to remain valid over a considerable period of time, say a decade. The contract would deal with political and social issues: debt, trade, finance, direct investment and aid flows. It could encompass a number of these elements or be limited to only a few. Such an arrangement would give assurance of predictability in political and economic terms as long as both sides abide by the contractual obligations. This should in sum secure a better basis for political, social and economic stability in the developing country.

A development contract would imply a relationship between equal partners as opposed to one between powerful donors and weak recipients. The contracts would have to be entered into voluntarily, resulting from a genuine process of negotiations. I still believe it would be worthwhile to pursue and further develop this idea in our search for avenues towards improved socio-economic conditions in Africa.

Of course, the primary responsibility for developing their societies rests with the African governments and peoples. It is for them to develop the right policies. It is for them to take the necessary measures. However, in their present economic and social situation they simply cannot be expected to pull themselves up by their own bootstraps. They are in desperate need of support and they deserve such support.

In this chapter I have highlighted some political and socio-economic factors which are basic to the establishment of stable societies in Africa. These factors are an indispensable part of the equation in any discussion about African peace and peace-making. They are particularly relevant in discussing conflict prevention. Until these issues are addressed in a generous, altruistic and constructive manner through a cooperative and mutually supportive effort by African leaders and the political leadership in the industrialized countries, Africa will continue to suffer and be exposed to internal strife and inter-state conflicts. It will not experience peace.

MECHANISMS FOR CONFLICT RESOLUTION

## The new setting

Another indispensable part of the equation in discussing African peace and security is the establishment of effective procedures and mechanisms for conflict prevention and resolution. This part of the equation is—in a global sense—topical and has moved high up on the political agenda not only for governments and international organizations, but for academia, NGOs and for concerned individuals. The end of the Cold War and the East–West ideological struggle, the collapse of the Soviet Union, the emergence of a unipolar world with some additional smaller centres of excellence and power, have with great speed created a new and very different international setting. Not, however, the setting many had hoped for; a setting where peace and social harmony (the New World Order) would prevail; where the world's natural and human resources would be used not for enhancing the war fighting capacities of individual countries, but rather for the betterment of the socio-economic conditions for the underprivileged, the poor and the vulnerable in our "Global Village". Instead, the world has experienced political turmoil and violence. Old conflicts have resurfaced with terrible destructive force. Numerous new conflicts—not least in Africa—have caused immense human suffering and material destruction.

Conflict resolution, peace-keeping and peace-making are at a cross roads. The fact that conflicts—violent or not—today occur within rather than between states has dramatically changed the role of peace-makers and peace-keepers. There are no simple and clear cut answers to present day problems; there is no quick fix and there are no ready made prescriptions. The challenge presently confronting the international community is to devise procedures, systems and mechanisms which can respond to these new challenges and provide a road map which shows the avenues to conflict prevention and resolution.

There is a strong sense of urgency in these matters. In a situation with pressing demands for action to prevent conflicts and provide peace and security, it is important to bear in mind that urgency does not mean undue haste. We are dealing with matters of great political sensitivity. In dealing with these problems patience and perseverance are essential requirements. We must pursue these matters relentlessly. We simply cannot afford the luxury of giving up the struggle for improved mechanisms, which can effectively deal with the world's present very complex problems.

## Information and analysis

Whatever mechanism or procedure is chosen to deal with a conflict, one aspect stands out as absolutely fundamental: there has to be sufficient comprehension of the conflict in question. Too often the international community has responded to conflicts in Africa (or elsewhere) without fully understanding the complexity of the forces generating these conflicts. Somalia and Rwanda are but two examples. Very few outside Somalia had a proper understanding of the intractable ethnic and social networks prevailing in that country. On Rwanda, most of the world was taken aback, standing totally perplexed by the hatred and the violence that suddenly erupted.

It is not that some people did not know. The problem is that they were not asked for their advice; that there were not—and still are not—procedures and systems in place through which such people can be mobilized, their knowledge and experience listened to and processed, and their advice sought.

It should be a basic requirement for any organization involved in conflict prevention and resolution, peace-making and peace-keeping to have a well developed system of information gathering. These organizations should possess the professional expertise needed for top quality analytical work, so as on short notice to provide the decision makers with the best possible advice on how to proceed. At present, they are not adequately equipped or staffed. To improve on this situation on a global as well as regional basis, should be a matter of the highest priority. It would be one way of reducing the risk of "the Councils for Peace" (in the UN/OAU) taking wrong and unimplementable decisions (suffice it to mention Somalia and Rwanda). Faced with quick, well considered and highly publicized international expert advice, it might be somewhat more difficult for the major powers to allow domestic considerations to dictate their positions when it comes to decision-making. We might also achieve a better balance between what the international community asks the organizations to do and the resources put at their disposal.

### The principle of layered response

It is increasingly apparent that the United Nations cannot address every potential and actual conflict troubling the world. Regional and sub-regional organizations sometimes have a comparative advantage in taking a lead role in the prevention and settlement of conflicts and to assist the United Nations in containing them.

A pro-active and constructive interplay between the global, regional and sub-regional organizations in conflict prevention and peace-making allows for what is called a layered response. The theory of layered response plays on a complete set of instruments, horizontal and vertical. From global to regional to sub- and sub-sub-regional. From one individual to two or more individuals at all levels. From inter-governmental organizations to non-governmental organizations. Each problem, each crisis is distinctly different, and it cannot a priori be said what part in the structure of layered response should be the first port of call. There is no toolkit which provides for ready made solutions.

A layered response can involve several actors. It is vital to bear in mind that conflict resolution and peace-making is not a competitive sport. It revolves around the ability to cooperate and sacrifice one's own ego and interest at the altar of peace. This ought not be too difficult as there is enough work for every-one who aspires to be a peace-maker. However, in the real world the situation is unfortunately somewhat different. Therefore, where several actors are involved, it is essential that someone takes charge of the situation and sees to it that objectives and division of labour be clearly established at the early stages of an operation.

It is equally important that the mandate is comprehensive; that is to say, it should contain provision for implementation and follow-up in the post-conflict period. This is very relevant to the resolution of conflicts in Africa where, as I have already described, conflicts are often caused by depressing socio-economic conditions and deepened by ethnic rivalries. If the underlying sources of con-flict are not addressed on a sustainable basis in a post-conflict situation, new conflicts are bound to erupt. Sufficient resources must be available to help con-solidate agreements once they are reached. Too many settlements and agree-ments have collapsed due to inadequate follow-up.

## The Organization of African Unity (OAU)

The Organization of African Unity (OAU) with its inclusive membership, the shared history of colonial oppression and exploitation, the egalitarianism that prevails in the organization and the principle of African solidarity, should in many ways be the ideal body to resolve Africa's conflicts. It should be an important link in the chain of layered response. However, its track record so far has not been impressive. OAU has been caught in its perennial dilemma of wanting to promote peace in cases of civil war while at the same time con-demning all secessionist movements and always supporting the government in power. OAU has almost without exception been a defender of status quo, both in terms of boundaries, how the various countries are structured and of political leadership. These positions, although understandable, have severely limited the peace-making effectiveness of the organization since its founding. This seems now to be changing, even though slowly.

Another constraining factor has been OAU's limited resources, both finan-cial and resources of expertise in such complex fields as peace-making and peace-keeping, and organizing and monitoring elections. Under the prevailing economic conditions on the continent, it seems unlikely that such resources will be available in the foreseeable future. A multilateral approach is required through which OAU's own efforts would be supported by external forces pro-viding political leverage, moral authority, credibility, legitimacy, and financial and physical resources.

The common thread that runs through various suggestions on improving the effectiveness of OAU's role in conflict resolution and prevention, is the call for a stronger OAU. The impression is sometimes given that strengthening the OAU is primarily a constitutional matter. What is often overlooked is that OAU as currently constituted was the only structure African states could agree on.

Talks about constitutional amendments have always come to naught. They rather serve to distract attention from the real and substantial problems.

The reality of African regional politics dictates that any search for measures to enhance the competence of OAU in peace-making and peace-keeping should build on the existing structures of the organization and the African network of sub-regional bodies. The principle of versatility should be applied. Versatility in this context includes the notions of dynamism, flexibility and inventiveness. The search for solutions should focus not only on the OAU. It should focus on African states and their leaders, on their perspectives on regional and domestic conflicts and on what processes would be culturally and politically acceptable. Such an approach would give a good basis for turning the theory of layered response into real life action. The experience gained through the ECOWAS operation in Liberia might offer valuable insights into the pros and cons of sub-regional operations.

Any significant movement forward for the OAU in search for regional peace depends upon the political will of the members of the organization. In this respect recent decisions to establish an OAU Mechanism on Conflict Prevention, Management and Resolution, to agree upon certain rules and procedures for peace related activities and to strengthen the relevant section of the Secretariat give grounds for cautious optimism. There is yet a long way to go, but a beginning has been made.

## The OAU and the UN

Improving Africa's capacity for conflict prevention and resolution should be viewed as a cooperative endeavour between the United Nations, the OAU and sub-regional organizations with a view to optimizing the use of available resources. Progress in this respect will facilitate and encourage increasing practical application of the theory of layered response.

African forces suffer from shortfalls in specialized and heavy equipment and will often face logistical and financial problems. To overcome some of these problems the Secretary-General of the United Nations has promoted the concept of bilateral "partnerships" among nations with complimentary strengths. According to this idea, one country would make the necessary troops available while another would provide the equipment and the logistics required to meet anticipated shortfalls. These "partnerships" would include training in the use and maintenance of the equipment on a bilateral basis. It could also include pre-positioning equipment in Africa for use by African contingents. It is in my view an interesting and promising concept which should be pursued with vigour.

Other measures to prepare African contingents for peace-keeping operations could be the holding of regional workshops and seminars on carefully chosen topics, development and distribution of manuals and guidelines, and command post exercises and related simulations for staff officers, logisticians, communications officers and commanders. The establishment of an all African training centre for peace-keeping should be encouraged and externally supported materially and financially. It is also to be hoped that some countries pick up and carry forward the invitation from the Secretary-General of the United Nations for contributions to a Trust Fund that would be dedicated to enhancing preparedness for conflict prevention and peace-keeping in Africa. Such support is desperately needed.

Even though the United Nations and the OAU now consult regularly on key African questions with a view to coordinating initiatives and actions on a broad spectrum of political issues, including the prevention and resolution of conflicts in Africa, there is a clear need for a further strengthening of the mechanisms for coordination, consultation and cooperation in the respective headquarters as well as in the field.

Exchange of liaison officers, staff exchange programmes, development of separate but interconnected early warning databases and joint reviews should offer a good basis for structured and continuing exchange of information on emerging crises at a sufficiently early stage. However, successful peace-making will depend upon the capacity for sustained support and assistance. The OAU must be helped in mobilizing the necessary financial and logistical support if it is to be able to be an important player in the act of preventive diplomacy, peace-making and peace-building.

The United Nations will continue to play a central role with regard to peace-making and peace-keeping in Africa. A strengthened OAU would, however, in a significant manner contribute to widening the scope and adding flexibility to the international community's joint efforts to establish and maintain peace and security in Africa. It would give added weight to the principle of layered response.

In fairness, it is not only the OAU, but every link in the chain of layered response which needs strengthening. Many academic studies and expert reports on the efficiency of various international organizations (the UN family and the OAU) have raised the question whether there is a need for major structural reforms or if some modifications and adjustments of the existing machinery will do the job. My own answer to such questions is as follows: Be ambitious and set high goals. Mobilize the will of governments to act and not only talk. But be realistic. Do not produce and argue in favour of beautiful blueprints which in the real world of power politics can only be mirages. To produce such mirages and actively promote them in high profile political campaigns can even be counterproductive as it might weaken public confidence in and support for the existing peace-making institutions. After all, we do have a fairly finely masked network of organizations covering virtually all bases be they global, regional or sub-regional, be they state or private, be they large or small. I believe we can best use the resources available through modernizing and strengthening this system.

And let me repeat: If peace-keeping is to succeed and the larger goal of lasting conflict prevention and conflict resolution is to be achieved, it must be accompanied by essential ingredients such as economic and social development, the promotion and protection of human rights, good governance and national institution building.

CONCLUDING REMARKS

Contemporary Africa is, as a continent, in some respects living through its second revolution. The first revolution brought the end of colonialism and the emergence of a large number of independent states. Even though transition from colonial status to independence in most cases was done in an orderly manner, the newly born independent countries were—virtually without exception—launched without the necessary means and tools needed for developing into strong and viable entities. Their self-appointed leaders—who might have performed well in the pre-independence struggle for liberation—lacked legitimacy in the new setting, they had no experience in or knowledge of how to manage the affairs of an independent state. Qualified middle and lower level officials were at best in very short supply. The economies of these countries had been developed and structured for the primary purpose of supplying their colonial masters and the rest of the industrialized world with raw materials and cheap labour; they had no industrial base, hardly any processing industry, and only a rudimentary infrastructure. Under such conditions it would be a formidable task to break the shackles of colonialism and realize the full political and economic potential. In sum: the new born countries had achieved their formal independence, but not true political and economic freedom.

In the post-independence period, most African countries have experienced social disorder and political violence. Autocratic rulers unfit for governing have come and gone, many of the countries have suffered negative growth and further impoverishment of a rapidly growing population. This negative and utterly destructive development trend has to be not only broken, it has to be reversed. Only then will genuine peace come to Africa.

This is what the second revolution is about and I believe it is under way. However, it is still a long and difficult way to go for most African countries. Developments are unfortunately very uneven. Among countries whose economies are growing there seems to be a significant and sustained upward trend. But for those which continue to be in crisis, there will be less foreign help and support available. The question to be addressed—not least in the context of peace and peace-making—is how can the countries on the road to socio-economic growth sustain that development trend. How can the economies of the collapsed states recover?

First and foremost: The African leaders must take full control of the development and the destiny of the continent with the outside providing support and assistance rather than trying to supplant Africa's own initiatives and priorities. Mechanisms must be developed and refined for realizing the potentials of Africa's human and material resource base and for dealing decisively with its challenges and problems. These measures include the development by Africans of the courage, the self-confidence, integrity and self-esteem needed to build on their own values and to implement their own blueprints. African leaders must commit themselves to their pronouncements and fully accept and encourage popular participation at all levels of the countries' political, economic and social life. The days of deceit, megalomania, corruption and ignorance should belong to the past. Responsible government for and with the people must be the order of the day.

Africa has for too long tried to copy systems of government and development—often imposed upon them from outside powers—which have been foreign to their way of life. As happens in medical transplants, the foreign element will often be rejected with the gravest consequences for the patient. Africa needs no transplants. The continent is so rich in social values and traditions, in compassion and concern and in creativeness. These values represent a solid foundation for the building of strong and healthy societies. The key to success, to peace and harmony lies in bringing these values to the forefront, cultivating them and letting them blossom.

Whilst it is only the Africans themselves that can bring the second African revolution to a successful conclusion, they are in their current state of affairs dependent upon foreign support, particularly in two areas: debt-relief and preferential trading arrangements. Without generous assistance in these two areas the Africans' own efforts—however strong, unselfish and persistent—are likely to come to naught.

The developed countries and the international financial institutions have shown that debt forgiveness and other relevant arrangements can be organized and implemented if it is seen as politically expedient and the political will exists. The industrialized countries must be sensitized to the fact that Africa matters. The extreme population growth in the poorest African countries, the destabilizing migratory movements and the ecological damage done with global consequences are just some of the facts which should open the eyes of the Western world. What is needed now is to demonstrate political will in support of Africa's own efforts. This is in my view the most important contribution the industrialized world can make to promoting peace in Africa.

In a potential conflict situation or in a situation where conflict has erupted, the principle of layered response should be applied with ingenuity and resourcefulness. It is essential from the outset not to lose sight of the purpose of the exercise: to seek and promote a lasting solution to the problem in question. It is irrelevant who does the job. Fights for turf and prestige amongst aspiring peace-makers will in most instances undermine the peace effort. Peace-making is a cooperative, and not a competitive enterprise.

In situations where two or more actors are involved in the peace-making effort, total and continuous coordination is of the utmost importance. There have to be open lines of communication between those involved, sharing of information, joint planning, preparedness to offer mutual support and if necessary call upon and give way to other actors who might be better positioned to deal with the matter.

The OAU and the sub-regional organizations in Africa are important parts of the structure of layered response to African problems. The OAU has since its inception in 1963 been important to its members as a highly visible political manifestation of the continent's independence. During these years it has not been able to fulfil its Charter obligation to be a forum for conflict prevention and resolution. Two essential ingredients have been missing: political will and resources, ingredients which should have been provided by the member states. Recent decisions taken by the members of the OAU seem to indicate that the majority—although not without objections and resistance from some members —are now inclined to give the organization a greater role in African conflict prevention and resolution. This change in attitude should be encouraged. The African governments should be told in no uncertain terms that they are expected to deliver on their promises. If they do, foreign support should be rapid and generous. One important foreign contribution would be to compensate for Africa's own lack of material and financial resources. The United Nation's Secretary-General's suggestion of "partnership" arrangements and the establishment of a trust fund should be pursued.

The OAU and the sub-regional organizations would often be the natural first port of call for continental problems. Other situations might lend themselves to a cooperative and joint effort by African as well as external forces. When it comes to peace-keeping, extra-regional material and financial support will be needed as the African countries with some exceptions lack the equipment, the communication facilities, the logistics and the finance.

Again as African governments indicate a political willingness to take upon themselves greater responsibility for conflict prevention and conflict resolution on the continent, they deserve to be supported. This apparent willingness is another aspect of the ongoing "second revolution" in the sense that Africa and Africans wish to take greater responsibility in dealing with the problems of the continent. This is a very promising development. It gives hope for a better future for the peoples of Africa.

REFERENCES

Adedeji, Adebayo (ed.), 1996, *South Africa or Africa—Within or Apart?* Ijebu Ode: African Centre for Development and Strategic Studies.
Haas, Ernst B., R.L. Butterford and J.S. Nye, 1972, *Conflict Management by International Organizations*. Morristown: General Learning Press.
Job, Brian (ed.), 1992, *The Insecurity Dilemma: National Security of Third World States*. Boulder: Lynne Rienner Publishers.
Ofstad, Arve, Arne Tostensen and Tom Vraalsen, 1991, *Towards a Development Contract*. Bergen: Chr. Michelsen Institute.
Ohlson, Thomas, Stephen John Stedman and Robert Davies, 1994, *The New is Not Yet Born. Conflict Resolution in Southern Africa*. Washington DC: The Brookings Institution.
OAU, 1985, *Africa's Priority Programme for Economic Recovery 1986–1990*.
OAU, 1987, *African Common Position on Africa's External Debt Crises*.
OAU, 1989, *African Alternative Framework to Structural Adjustment Programme for Socio-Economic Recovery and Transformation*.
OAU/Africa Leadership Forum/ECA, 1991, *The Kampala Document: "Towards a Conference on Security, Stability, Development and Cooperation in Africa"*.
Smock, David R. (ed.), 1993, *Making War and Waging Peace. Foreign Intervention in Africa*. Washington DC: US Institute of Peace Press.
Stenseth, Nils Chr., Kjetil Paulsen and Rolf Karlsen (eds.), 1995, *Afrika—natur, samfunn, bistand*. Oslo: AdNotam Gyldendal.
Tilly, Charles (ed.), 1975, *The Formation of National States in Western Europe*. Princetown University Press.
UN, 1987, *UN Programme of Action for African Economic Recovery and Development 1986–1990*.
UN, 1991, *UN New Agenda for the Development of Africa in the 1990s*.
UN Secretary-General, 1995, *Improving Preparedness for Conflict Prevention and Peace-keeping in Africa*.
UNDP, 1995, *Human Development Report 1995*.
Zartman, William I. (ed.), 1995, *Collapsed States. The Disintegration and Restoration of Legitimate Authority*. Boulder: Lynne Rienner Publishers.

# Peace-Making in Southern Africa
# —Time for Questions

*Peter Vale*

It appears perverse—even mischievous—to generate questions on the multi-layered processes which appear to be moving Southern Africa towards the goal of peace. After all, the sub-continent has been blighted by violence for most of this quickly closing century; simple logic suggests that every (indeed, any) impulse in the opposite direction should be encouraged. But, as the ending of the Cold War has painfully taught, movement and making are not the same things. This is why simple logic also suggests that there is no end of history. It also explains why the search for a "new world order" in Southern Africa is bedevilled by a range of negative late-20th century signs: porous borders, recalcitrant tribalisms, broken promises, failing states.

This is not the place to provide a genealogy of the "new world order", but its enunciation by George Bush at the time of the Gulf War has set it up as another lodestar—a truth-dream, to coin a phrase—of international relations practice. Its relevance for this essay is two-fold: firstly, complicity in the goals—primarily US hegemony of the international system—implied in the phrase will profoundly influence the kinds of pressures exerted on regions and strong players in them. Secondly and possibly as a result of the first, the phrase has become much loved by South African foreign policy-makers; it has been used by the Foreign Minister and his Deputy and President Mandela's speech-writers have cued him to use the phrase. This should not be taken to mean that South Africa is a compliant state for US global interests. The Mandela government has made significant policy stands—on Cuba, on Iran, on Libya, in peace issues these have been less significant, although, undoubtedly, South Africa's cautious approach to the Clinton Administration's idea of a US-sponsored African peace-keeping force was a set-back for the idea.[1]

Interpretations of the "new world order" are however crucial to the possible answers to this question: Why will the road to lasting peace prove elusive in Southern Africa? The search for an answer provides the central theme of this essay, and is central to the concerns of this book.

---

[1] Clinton, 1996, "To intensify US role in Africa", *Guardian Weekly*, October.

The idea that Africa is a continent in permanent decline is endemic in opinion-making circles throughout the world.[2] For many across the world, Southern Africa represents a beacon of hope in this otherwise troubled picture. This is why the idea of building a strong Southern Africa which will act as an anchor for a continent in despair has become a priority in the thinking of the many who unquestioningly accept the idea of a "new world order". The anchor's anchor—as it were—is of course South Africa[3] with its successful transition, strong economy and pivotal location.[4] In this vision, South Africa is the region's hope; and the region is Africa's.[5]

These understandings account for the indecent haste in which South Africa was ushered towards accepting a role in international peace-keeping efforts. Suggestions that a post-apartheid South Africa would be drawn into direct participation in peace-keeping operations—and so join her northern neighbour, Zimbabwe—occurred almost immediately after the inauguration of Nelson Mandela as South Africa's President. In a very public display of pressure (it almost happened on national television) Al Gore, the US vice-president, raised the issue of South African support for international intervention in the Rwandan crisis which was then breaking.

These urgings played into the hands of South Africa's military which, at the time, remained uncertain of the long-term role that they were to play in the new South Africa. The influential military think-tank, the Institute for Defence Policy, had been anxiously pursuing a programme which was seeking to entrench the South African Defence Force beyond the apartheid years.[6] And other opinion-formers, like the South African Institute for International Affairs, were quickly crossing the divide between their traditional interest in diplomacy towards a focus on security issues.[7] Through these developments, the location of military security thinking—both in the transitional process and in the affairs of peace in the region—was secured under the hegemonic social constructs of post-Cold War thinking.

This was a lost opportunity in the search for a lasting regional peace. At the moment when intellectual energy should have been geared to rethinking long-term ideas about peace (and its making) in the region, the powerful South

---

[2] There are many accounts of this; for one drawn from outside the Anglo-Saxon tradition see Schaepman, Kees, 1996, "Geen nieuws is nooit goed nieuws in Afrika", in *Vrij Nederland*, 40(5) pp. 34–37.

[3] See for instance Chase, Robert S., Emily B. Hill and Paul Kennedy, 1996, "Pivotal States and US Strategy", *Foreign Affairs*, 75, pp. 33–51.

[4] Ibid.

[5] "The Economist sees SA as a potential uplifter of neighbours", in *Sunday Independent* (Johannesburg), 13 August, 1995.

[6] For an example see Celliers, Jakkie and Markus Reichardt (eds.), 1995, *About Turn. The transformation of the South Africa Military and Intelligence*. Johannesburg: IDP.

[7] See Celliers, Jakkie and Greg Mills (eds.), 1995, *Peace-keeping in Africa Vol. 2*. Johannesburg: IDP and SAIIA.

African discourse fell back on the cherished values associated with the power and might of the state.

Success for this particular interpretation of the future came quickly; by October 1994, six months after South Africa's new government was in power, the Foreign Minister, Alfred Nzo, suggested that South Africa's role in peace-keeping was "inevitable".[8] South Africa's seemingly successful efforts at averting a domestic conflict had sanctioned its path towards fulfilling its role in the new order by helping to build peace through fulfilling a set of regional and continental obligations.

The drift of these events was almost inevitable. As nature abhors a vacuum, international relations adapt to change by stressing continuities. In an age of intense change, the discourse of international relations readily embraced the ideas of a new world order build on neo-liberal and neo-realist theory. A new hegemony replaced the long-revered ideas of the Cold War with its simple binary logic and policy orientation. The resulting policy implications have been profound. As the rhetoric of globalisation has squeezed domestic budgets, the international burdens of western governments have—seamlessly, it seems—been passed to anchors—like South Africa—in the poorer corners of the globe.

It should be no surprise that this development has favoured the status quo both in South and, it follows, Southern Africa. A leading South African banker put it this way:

> After the long isolation of the sanction years, South Africa can now as a full democracy, rejoin the community of nations with pride. This is a more challenge but must also be seen as an opportunity for South Africa's business community to play its full part, alongside the Government of National Unity, in conceiving new policies for this new age. These policies will have to synchronise our realities with those of the world in which trade and global competitiveness are as important as the political dimensions of diplomacy.[9]

This perspective illustrates the tenor of much orthodox writing and thinking on the region's future, the discourse quickly moving between the celebration associated with endings—the cold war and apartheid—and the triumphs associated with new beginnings: an "order" of "realities" in which peace and prosperity hinge on the unquestioned assumption that continuity is preferable to change.

Between these moments—celebration and triumph—there is however seldom pause to rethink assumptions, to probe long-held truisms, or to debunk some obvious myths. As a result considerations of peace- and of war-making in the region are caught within the limiting explanatory range offered by a hegemonic discourse—in security questions, neo-realism; in economics, neo-liberalism. Because both are bounded by limited imagination, they both place

---

[8] *The Argus* (Cape Town), 27 October, 1994.

[9] Dr Conrad Strauss, 1995, preface to Mills, Greg, Alan Begg and Anthonie van Nieuwkerk (eds.), *South Africa in the Global Economy*, p.v. Johannesburg: The South African Institute of International Affairs with the Assistance of The Standard Bank Foundation.

blinkers on the potential for exploring peace and the process of its making in the region.

In the hope of prising open new perspectives, this contribution shows why the answers to the questions of peace in the region which are currently on offer are only partial ones. To do so, it poses a series of questions which lie—in most cases not very far—beyond the current explanatory frameworks. Its form is critique, and like all critique, it looks beyond simply explaining the world; with Marx, it believes the point is to change it.[10]

## RACE, DEMOCRACY AND THE NEW SOUTHERN AFRICA

The region's transformation from war to peace has been near miraculous. A short decade ago—when apartheid scuttled the Commonwealth Eminent Person's Mission to South Africa—it appeared that the region was in the throes of disintegration; today, things are very different. But this historical leavening says more about recent world affairs than it does about Southern Africa itself. In any other moment, Southern Africa's turnabout would have been judged remarkable. In today's world it appears commonplace, ranking no higher than the transformation of Latin America, or the relatively painless end to the divide in Europe.

There is nonetheless a unique dimension to what has happened in the region, and it must be set down. The ending of apartheid has closed a desperately unhappy chapter in the history of mankind. Multiracial Zimbabwe, independent Namibia and the "new" South Africa all attest to an elasticity in racial questions in a part of the world in which—for a cruel century—race was the single most determining factor.[11]

Race and its twin, ethnicity, remain potent forces in international politics; the conflict in the Balkans was a reminder of their bloody power. And in Africa, as Rwanda has tragically shown (and Burundi surely will), politics cannot be freed from considerations of colour, caste or creed. But these reservations, important though they are, do not detract from the fact that in helping to turn the proverbial corner on race, Southern Africa has delivered to the world an immeasurable gift, a lasting achievement.

The lasting outcome of the region's struggle for democracy—and its link to regional peace—is regretfully less certain. As the following paragraphs attest, however, there is evidence that movement towards a democratic culture is steady, if not spectacular.

The long conflict over Namibia was ended in 1989. This had involved the United Nations in a legal and political struggle with South Africa over the

---

[10] See Devetak, Richard, 1996, "Critical Theory", in Burchill, Scott et al., *Theories of International Relations*, p. 146. London: Macmillan.

[11] From Booth, Ken and Peter Vale, 1995, "Security in Southern Africa: after apartheid, beyond realism", in *International Affairs*, 72, pp. 285–304.

future of this former German colony. In the 1970s, South Africa had tried to bring it directly under its control; in response, SWAPO, a political movement chiefly formed by Ovambo activists, had escalated its guerrilla war against South Africa's occupation. But the acceptance by South Africa and Angola of a peace plan which was underwritten by the United States and the Soviet Union led both to the country's independence and the installation of a democratic government under the leadership of SWAPO president, Sam Nujoma.

As the 1980s closed, Frelimo ended one-party rule in Mozambique and relax state control of the economy. In 1992, Frelimo and the rebel group, Renamo, signed an accord which formally ended their conflict. Free elections followed in October 1994; Frelimo President, Joaquim Chissano won the presidency and his party won control of the parliament.

Elsewhere in the region things have also been encouraging: in November 1991, Kenneth Kaunda was defeated at the polls by Frederick Chiluba's Movement For Multiparty Democracy in the first multi-party elections to be held in Zambia for twenty years. And in June 1993, a combination of rising internal dissent and the decision by Western donors to conditionally suspend aid forced a referendum over the future of the one-party state in neighbouring Malawi. Almost a year later, the country's citizens overwhelmingly voted to end one of Africa's longest-running dictatorships. Finally, there was South Africa's own transition which culminated in the inauguration of Nelson Mandela as the State President of the country on 10 May 1994 and positioned South Africa's African National Congress as the majority party in the country's parliament.

FRAMING THE LIMITS TO PEACE

The ending of apartheid and the search for democracy have spawned discussion on the creation of a range of new security institutions to underwrite peace in Southern Africa. Almost without exception, these ideas have turned on the notion that the region's states system enjoys a new legitimacy.[12] The road to lasting peace, it has been held to follow, is to build upon the potential offered by this new condition. And using the continuities associated with the rituals of post-Cold War international relations, some success has been registered.

When Lesotho experienced a constitutional crisis in August 1994, swift consultation by three Presidents—South Africa's Nelson Mandela, Botswana's Quett Masire and Zimbabwe's Robert Mugabe—agreed a course of action which helped to return an elected government to power.[13] This success encouraged further engagement with a regional peace process along the same lines. So, in February 1996 when faced with a deteriorating political situation in

---

[12] Like the recently established SADC Organ for Politics, Defence, Security.

[13] *Cape Times* (Cape Town), 15 September, 1994.

Swaziland, regional leaders discussed the possibility of launching a "Lesotho-type initiative" for dealing with the political conflict in that country.[14]

In approaching regional peace-making in this way, Southern Africa's leaders have reinforced the idea that states provide the building blocks around which the idea of "community" can be fostered.

However, quite elementary questioning reveals a deep paradox in this approach. Traditionally, the region's states have discouraged a sense of community in Southern Africa. Instead, they have relied on the idea of conflict, and on preparing for it, as the central motif of the regional modus operandi. This was even so in SADCC where, it will be recalled, there was little (rather, no) inclination to share sovereignty.

The idea of achieving a regional peace, therefore, has traditionally been associated with the building of nationalism and the defence of national sovereignty. It comes therefore as no surprise that the answer to the region's peace "problem" was to use strong measures to secure a regional state system.[15] The record shows that Southern African states have not build robust and tolerant polities: indeed, the opposite is true.

Given this, it was unlikely that simply ending apartheid and holding elections could bring peace to the region. This is why significant corners of the region are still at war. In Angola, despite a formal cessation of hostilities and an internationally-certified election, fighting continues between the MPLA government and its UNITA opponents.[16] almost daily the prospects for an end to strife appear to be receding.[17] While in South Africa's province of Kwazulu-Natal, notwithstanding the end of apartheid and promising talk of peace, bloody conflict continues between the African National Congress and the ethnically-centred Inkatha group.

These instances suggest that decades of strife have bequeathed legacies of deep mistrust and crippling misunderstanding. As economic circumstances deteriorate and small arms are readily at hand, prolonged—indeed, renewed—conflict appears inevitable in these and other parts of the sub-continent.[18]

How to end these conflicts is an immediate challenge to the regional peace-making process. But finding durable answers to them is difficult, if not impossible, within the peace possibilities offered by the neo-realist framework favoured in the "new world order" discourse.

---

[14] On Swaziland's recent crisis, see *Weekly Mail & Guardian* (Johannesburg), 2 February, 1996 and Dlamini, Kuseni, 1995, "Swaziland. The Winds of Change", in *Indicator SA*, 21, pp. 18–22.

[15] Booth, Ken and Peter Vale, 1995, "Security in Southern Africa: after apartheid, beyond realism", in *International Affairs* (London), 72, pp. 285–304.

[16] See "Angola on the brink" in *New African* (London), September, 1996, pp. 18–19.

[17] See "UN officials worry as UNITA edges away from peace", *Inter Press Service* via MISANET, 9 October, 1996.

[18] There are countless examples of this kind of non–state conflict; for tension in Zambia, for instance, see "Unita barter may supply arms to Lozi seccessionists", *SouthScan* (London), 10 March 1995, p. 79.

Not that the security concerns at the root of this perspective have remained static; inevitably the new dynamic has established a range of new concerns. Indeed, the security discourse in the region has sought to re-invent itself with the changing times.[19] So, for instance, traditional thinking has shifted towards what has been called the "new security agenda". Items like migration, cross-border arms flows and drug smuggling, banditry, and cattle rustling are now included within the region's "new" security basket. But managing these conflicts—let alone building peace from them—is proving difficult—no, impossible—for the military and political elites in Southern Africa. Why?

Eight clusters of conflict have been isolated in Southern Africa:[20] those associated with war termination and reconciliation as in Mozambique and Angola; those associated with political participation as in Lesotho and Swaziland; those over the distribution of resources which have been acutely affected by efforts to restructure economies; those over identity, whether local, national or regional; those which spillover borders like refugees, arms smuggling or drugs; inter-dependency conflicts associated with the spread of disease or water shortages; asymmetry conflicts—particularly South Africa's domination of the region; and those over land claims like the one between Botswana and Namibia over an islet[21] in the Chobe River.[22]

Of these, only the latter directly involves the strategic perspectives associated with the inter-state conflict which was the region's over-riding concern in the 1980s. (In this particular case incidentally, a joint commission between the two states has been able to avert direct conflict and there are plans to take the case to the International Court of Justice in The Hague.)[23] The point is that conventional thinking on peace-making in the region remains primarily geared to the idea that the major source of conflict will be between states. And yet, as the listing shows, state-to-state conflict plays only a minor role in its prioritisation.

Understanding this raises questions around the peace goals of a country like Botswana. Although considered by many to be the quintessential model of democratic governance, it is in the processes of building its military forces. The army is said to be increasing from about 7,500 to more than 10,000 soldiers.[24]

---

[19] See Rupauh, Martin, 1996, "Security Options in Southern Africa", *SAPEM* (Harare), May, pp. 20–22.

[20] See Ohlson, Thomas and Stephen John Steadman (with Robert Davies), 1994, *The New is Not Yet Born. Conflict Resolution in Southern Africa*. Washington: The Brookings Institution.

[21] The uninhabited Kasikili island, known as Sedudu in Botswana, lies in the Chobe River on Namibia's north-eastern border with Botswana. In April 1996 Botswana deployed troops on the island during an operation to eradicate a bovine disease. Namibia's foreign minister protested arguing that the responsibility for this task lay with Namibia's Defence Force. *SABC Channel Africa Radio* (Johannesburg), in English 1500 gmt. 23 April, 1996.

[22] "Sources of Domestic Insecurity in Southern African States" (A Conference Report by John Bardill). *Backgrounder 12*. Bellville: Centre for Southern African Studies, 1994, pp. 41–44.

[23] See "Kisikili will not lead to conflict", *The Namibian* (Windhoek), 16 September, 1996.

[24] The *Weekly Mail & Guardian* (Johannesburg), 4 April, 1996.

and it has recently purchased second-hand fighter planes from Canada.[25] Can these developments buy security for Botswana and assure its neighbours? Despite elaborate arguments to the contrary,[26] the answer it seems is no. Indeed there have been suggestions, supported by remarks by the head of the Botswana armed forces,[27] that Botswana's military build-up was aimed at preventing South Africa's instability from spilling into Botswana. Or is Botswana's build-up aimed at the possibility of domestic political ructions as a result of its own skewed economic growth?[28]

These questions reinforce the idea that within the existing conceptual frameworks, the prospects for the region may be narrowed, rather than extended, by the belief that states (and the institutions they foster) can bring peace to the region. If this thread of the new world order perspective is bare, what of the idea that South Africa can anchor a regional peace?

For worse rather than better, South Africa occupies a central position in the affairs of the region and a pivotal position in international relations. Despite South Africa's understanding that "regional order should be developed by the people of the region—not imposed by a regional power, the pressure upon South Africa to offer leadership in the region may be too overwhelming to ignore.[29]

As it does so, South Africa will favour particular outcomes in regional conflicts.[30] In cases where South Africa believes it can act decisively (and presumably with efficacy) to defuse a situation, it has done so within the confines of achieving policy outcomes rather than creating new processes. The 1996 conflict in Swaziland seems to be such a case. Although the direction of South Africa's pressure remains, at the time of writing, wholly uncertain, South African reports have suggested that President Mandela is ideally placed because he "enjoys a special relationship with the Swazi royal house through the marriage of his daughter...to...a senior Swazi prince".[31]

This trend, if continued, will strip peace-making of its own necessary democratic culture. This has already been reflected in important ways by the

---

[25] *The Botswana Gazette*, 2 October, 1996.

[26] Heitman, Helmoed-Romer, 1996, "Botswana finds itself in a rough neighbourhood", *Business Day* (Johannesburg), 8 May.

[27] SABC SAfm Radio (Johannesburg), in English 1500 gmt 23 April 1996.

[28] In 1994 Botswana's per capita gross national product of 2,800 US dollars per annum was higher than that of middle-income nations like Russia and Costa Rica. In Africa, only Gabon, Mauritius and South Africa achieved higher scores. Its foreign reserves grew by 10.5 per cent during 1994/ 1995 to about four billion dollars, sufficient to finance 23 months of imports—a situation many other developing countries would envy. However, about 60 per cent of its 1.4 million people are poor; many are also jobless. Unemployment affects 25 per cent of the active population, according to official estimates, but the real figure is probably between 45 to 50 per cent.

[29] Department of Foreign Affairs, South Africa, Occasional Papers No 1/96, p. 6.

[30] See "SA backs Botswana against Namibia, presses for arms build-up in region", *MRB Southern Africa*, 5(7) (July, 1996), pp. 1–3.

[31] SAPA Press Report by George Starita, 15 March, 1996.

recently-created Organ for Politics, Defence and Security which was cobbled together at the SADC meeting in January 1996[32] and confirmed at a SADC meeting in June.[33] This aims at promoting "lasting peace in the region" and will link with other peace-keeping efforts on Africa.[34] Intended to operate at heads of state and ministerial levels, the institution's co-ordination would not be permanent but would rotate amongst the member states. It has been claimed that the new arrangement reflects the changed political situation in the region, particularly because the Front-line States' mission was no longer relevant to the times: while excepting this, the underlying mechanism remains, it seems, the non-transparent "clubby" process which was used by the Front-line States.

As seriously, the evolving structure of peace-making in the region rests on a mix of formal and informal arrangements. The lasting test of these will not be whether they can intervene effectively in a series of legitimacy crisis in the region, but whether—when it becomes necessary; as it certainly will—they will over-ride the interests of one of the three countries—South Africa, Zimbabwe and Botswana—which increasingly dominate the process of regional peace-making.

The limits offered by the present peace discourse seem to distort efforts to balance the practice of regional relations and encourage, instead, South Africa's positioning as "the first among regional equals".[35] Can there be lasting peace in a situation which so obviously favours the strong?

Then there is the question of military power. The international debate over South Africa's pivotal role in securing the region's peace simply encourages the country's military to act as its custodian. This may produce unintended consequences. In the 1970s and 1980s when the debate in international military circles was precursor to the hard-line security policies of the second Cold War, anti-communism became the standard diet of South Africa's defence establishment.[36] This appears to have been replaced by an equally compelling diet of peace and its keeping.[37]

Approaches to building peace in the region therefore seem caught in the trap of understanding the "others'" aspirations, interests and intentions in

---

[32] Radio Botswana (Gaborone), in English 1110 gmt, 19 January, 1996.

[33] SAPA New Agency (Johannesburg), in English 1624 gmt 29 June, 1996.

[34] See Celliers, Jakkie, 1996, "Co-operation the key to African peace effort", in *Business Day* (Johannesburg), 27 June.

[35] See Vale, Peter, 1996, *Southern Africa: Exploring a peace dividend*. Briefing Series. London: Catholic Institute for International Relations, 20 pp.

[36] A discussion of the themes which have underpinned international studies in South Africa are to be found in Dyer, Hugh C. and Leon Mangasarian (eds.), 1989, *The Study of International Relations: The State of the Art*. London: Macmillan in association with Millennium, pp. 201–220.

[37] This idea is borrowed from Sandra Whitworth's important paper "Gender, Race and the Politics of Peace-keeping". Paper presented at the International Studies Association Annual Meetings, San Diego, USA, April 16–20, 1996.

order to control the "other's" behaviour, or to outwit and outmanoeuvre the "other" conceived as adversary.[38]

## FRAMING AN ALTERNATIVE PEACE DISCOURSE?

Within this immediate canvas, there is no space to detail the increasing drift of non-state forces which now mark the course of inter-state relations in Southern Africa. Concerns over water, migration, drug and arms smuggling: these issues, rather than the traditional security concerns, are at the base of new regional relations. How will they be met?

The hope of the region's leaders appears to be that inter-regional co-operation—including the establishment of a free trade area—at the SADC level will provide answers to these new challenges.[39]

Their faith seems firmly placed in the idea that trade, investment and self-reliance might deliver an adequate peace to enable international relations to flourish. But prospects that this can happen without state intervention look quite grim. On almost every social indicator the region is in deep trouble: six—Angola, Lesotho, Malawi, Mozambique, Tanzania, and Zambia—of its eleven countries are classified in the low human development index; the other five—Botswana, Namibia, South Africa, Swaziland and Zimbabwe—are in the medium human development band.[40] This means the states of the region are outside the core of countries which may prosper and deliver security in the next century.

Appreciating this points to the structural paradox which underpins the search for peace in Southern Africa. Although formally divided into twelve states, a single economy is built in the region; this is centred in the strongest country, South Africa. But the sheer size and power of South Africa is itself a cause for regional insecurity because, while it is rhetorically committed South Africa is a hesitant partner in the building of a vibrant self-assertive region which is not subservient to the dominant international system. And, by twist of history and circumstance, the predilections of the emerging international system towards South Africa are not amicable to the needs of the region.

To change this, new ways of looking again at the region's history must be explored.[41] For the sake of illustration consider this alternative narrative. In the 1880s, the coincidence of British capital, American technology and African muscle turned a geographical backwater in southern African into a candidate for modernisation. Prior to this, a set of quasi-states—mainly Boer Republics

---

[38] Linklater, Andrew, 1996, "The achievements of critical theory", in Steve Smith, Ken Booth and Marysia Zalewski (eds.), *International theory: positivism & beyond*. Cambridge University Press, p. 292.

[39] See "SADC in moves to establish free trade", *Business Day* (Johannesburg), 26 August, 1996.

[40] *Human Development Report 1995*. UNDP. Oxford University Press, 1995, p. 226.

[41] The paragraphs which follow are from Vale, Peter, 1996, "Regional Security in Southern Africa", *Alternatives*, 21(3), pp. 363–391.

and scattered colonial fragments—operated within a crude political system notwithstanding the efforts of both the Dutch and the British to develop a state diplomatic system within the region which would favour their interests.

The turning point came with the establishment of the region's first Westphalian-type state, the Union of South Africa in 1910. It took nearly fifty years for the next orthodox state in the region—Tanganyika in 1962—to emerge. By the time it did, South Africa and its interests dominated the region in every possible way. Other states when they emerged were modelled in, and on, the modernisation core represented by South Africa.

The idea of state structures followed from rather than predated the thrust towards both regional economic development and regional integration. And states in the region, as South Africa has always shown, were required to enforce and legitimise the power of markets.[42] South Africa set the conditions for membership of the region's inter-state system; put differently, and drawing from historical sociology, the other states in the region were defined not so much by an interaction of internal forces but by their external setting towards the apartheid state.

All the region's maps were drawn upon and, indeed, around South African interests. The most obvious example was the recruitment of mine labour from the region—a process which commenced not long after the discovery of gold in what is now called Gauteng. But other examples followed—the region's extensive and relatively efficient railway system, the powerful electricity grid, veterinary research and the creation of a customs union, to cite four of possibly a dozen.

The moment of state creation in 1910 enshrined a series of power relations in the region in which, to deliberately belabour the point, South Africa is the first among regional unequals. This conclusion is inescapable: South Africa's hold distorts, not balances, the region in its own direction. Given this, can lasting peace follow except that South Africa must (in the Vattel's words) "lay down the law to others"?[43]

UNDERSTANDING THE UNSTATED PROBLEM OF REGIONAL PEACE AND ITS KEEPING

As the growing migration of Southern Africa's people suggests, the regional dilemmas are wider than those offered by states. Approaches to understanding the regional condition however have set parameters which privilege states above people. New ways of looking at inter-state relations in the region,

---

[42] This follows Robert Latham's assertion that "capitalist markets are perhaps the ultimate modern form in that they smash all sorts of relations before them". Latham, Robert, "Modernity and Security: An Argument Sketch". Paper presented at the 1996 Annual Meeting of the International Studies Association, San Diego, California, April, 1996, p. 5.

[43] Evans, Graham and Jeffrey Newnham, 1992, *The Dictionary of World Politics*. London: Harvester Wheatsheaf, p. 26.

although difficult to embed, can however change understandings both of peace and its making.

In this, outsiders can help, but will they look beyond the narrow frameworks? Evidence suggests not. As we have seen, the perspective that South Africa should anchor the region has its roots in the country's own successful transition. This has promoted the idea that a regional peace-keeping capacity is desirable.[44] Outsiders have embraced this idea and encouraged the proposal that South Africa has a role to play in sustaining a peace-keeping capacity in the region and beyond. As a result, "two Scandinavian funded projects were launched with the aim of creating a Southern African capacity for meaningful participation in future multinational peace operations, especially those which may be mounted in the sub-region or elsewhere in Africa".[45]

As South Africa's military budget has been threatened, the idea of the country's participation in peace-keeping has been pushed to the fore. With the international debate on peace-keeping as a lever and institutional support from the North, South Africa's military are reasserting a role for themselves both in the national life of the country and in the region.[46]

South Africa's military have been at pains to stress that the declared goal in peace-keeping is a professional one.[47] By casting it this way however they ignore (conveniently, perhaps) the limits of their own understandings. Throughout the 1970s and 1980s, they singularly failed, as did others of course, to anticipate the collapse of Soviet Communism and mis-read the nature of the changes within their primary domestic/international adversary, the exiled African National Congress. In the celebration of the moment and in the triumph of re-discovery few lasting questions in this direction have been posed. Of these, perhaps the most telling might be Baudrillard's "If their culture was so mistaken about others, might it also be mistaken about itself?"[48]

By drawing extensively on western (read: NATO) perspectives on peace, South African peace-warriors (to coin another phrase) have drawn extensively from external doctrines[49] which, by emphasising technical aspects, for instance, of the "mission", cast the peace process in narrow "non-ideological" terms. Is this possible?

To approach the issue through technical language avoids asking a number of important political and moral questions which are as much at the foundation of peace and its keeping. So this one, how peaceful are peace-keepers?, is asked

---

[44] Some of the debates around this are to be found in Spanger, Hans-Joachim and Peter Vale (eds.), 1995, *Bridges to the Future: Prospects for Peace and Security in Southern Africa*. New York: Westview.

[45] Malan, Mark, 1996, "Foundations for Regional Security: Preparing to Keen the Peace in Southern Africa", *African Security Review*, 5, p. 4.

[46] See " SA officers gear up for regional peace-keeping role", *SouthScan* (London), 21 June 1996.

[47] Some of these arguments are to be found in Celliers, Jakkie and Greg Mills (eds.), 1995, *Peacekeeping in Africa (Vol. 2)*, Johannesburg: IDP and SAIIA, pp. 187–198.

[48] Turner, Bryan (ed.), 1996, *The Blackwell Companion to Social Theory*. London: Blackwell, p. 411.

[49] See Celliers, Jakkie, "Peace Support Operations", in Celliers and Mills, op. cit., pp. 57–88.

too seldom for comfort.[50] Ironically however, by turning the debate on peace-keeping in a technical direction, new South Africa warriors have by-passed a question to which, in its recent past, the South African state had an all-too-ready Clausewitzian answer: is peace only politics by a different term?[51] The weight of this interpretation is particularly important when set against the persistent reports that South Africa has sold weapons to Burundi.[52]

The idea that South Africa should act as a major peace-keeper is mercifully not an uncontested one in the country.[53] Reports have suggested that the Cabinet of South Africa's (transitional) Government of National Unity was divided on the issue.[54] Both the National Party and the Inkatha Freedom Party—political parties with a traditionally hard-line record—opposed the sending of South African Blue Helmets to Angola. South Africa's ruling African National Congress took a distinctly ambivalent line; it was reported that South Africa's defence minister and his deputy favoured this option.[55] Other indications have pointed to a possible South African role in peace mediation in Burundi.[56]

In too few of these cases however is there a determination to set these peace goals up against the largely untold—and quite simply, unrecorded—story of South Africa's destabilisation of Southern Africa.[57] While South Africans have been quite sensitive about this, few outside the continent have made the connection. In the search for a new world order, neo-realist perspectives are nourished by the relative comfort of continuity rather than the challenge of change. As a result, the full horror of South African experience in making regional wars is being lost to public consciousness both in South Africa and the region.[58]

The debate on making regional peace is conducted only within the confines of limited understandings—around the idea of legitimate states and anchored upon South Africa. The region's peace, it follows, can only be a peace which supports the peace interests of its hegemony. And, to draw a tighter analytical circle around the same idea, the region's peace can only be the peace determined by the power discourses within South Africa. This accounts for the (re)-

[50] Whitworth, op. cit., p.2.

[51] I am grateful to Klaus van Walraven of Clingendael for pointing this out to me.

[52] See "Criticism mounts as SA agress of sale of arms to Rwanda", *SouthScan* (London), 4 October 1996.

[53] See Laufer, Stephen, 1996, "Focus on SA's role as ethnic conflict boils up in Burundi", *Business Day* (Johannesburg), 15 July.

[54] "Battle of the blue helmet troops", *The Weekly Mail and Guardian* (Johannesburg), 2 December 1995.

[55] *Weekly Mail* (Johannesburg), 2 December 1994.

[56] "Mbeki strives for compromise political solution in Burundi", *SouthScan* (London), 9 August 1996.

[57] For an exception see Hanlon, Joseph, 1986, *Beggar your Neighbours*. London: Catholic Institute for International Relations.

[58] For a discussion of the amnesia in orthodox international relations See Rosenau, James N. (ed.), 1993, *Global Dialogues: Dialogues in International Relations*. Boulder: Westview Press, p. 9.

emergence of the astonishingly narrow debate on what constitutes South Africa's national interests in Southern Africa.[59]

However welcome and celebrated South Africa's transition might be, it is not the end of history in the region. It has opened only another phase of struggle; much of this will turn on the nature and behaviour of the state we now call South Africa. The triumphalism over South Africa's undoubted success in ending formal apartheid has made it very difficult to appreciate that embedded within the same state "is a strategic culture which has not changed. As the state reaches into its collective memory it...(is discovering)...that routine responses to challenges are more likely that even the acknowledgement of the necessity to think long and hard about creative responses".[60]

The re-assertion of the neo-realist thinking of the "new" South Africa is to be found in the deepening paranoia around migration to the country.[61] A reflective debate on migration to South Africa belongs not on these but on other pages: the issue remains however the litmus test of prospects for peace. Will the country share the gains of its triumph over racism? Or will, as now, sovereignty remain the only real force which binds South Africans?

CONCLUSION

As suggested at the outset, it appears disingenuous to question the idea of peace in a region which—for a century and more—has only known war and conflict; quite clearly, "jaw, jaw" is infinitely preferable to "war, war". It is however too simple to equate this with peace. In the search for quick answers to the unfolding challenges of the region, the idea of peace—its making, its keeping— has been de-linked from the many layers of complexity which underpin relations—international, inter-community, inter-personal—throughout Southern Africa.

Throughout the sub-continent, a range of identities are asserting themselves; [62] many of these, it seems, are premised on the nation state's inability to deliver peace. This confirms that identity (and its national equivalent, sovereignty) is not pre-ordained: like all products of social intercourse, these change with time.

The discourse around peace in Southern Africa has not, it seems, been liberated by political change; instead, it appears to have been frozen by the limits of time and space set by an analytical framework which stresses states above people.

---

[59] See for instance the leader "National interest", *Business Day*, (Johannesburg), 24 April 1996.

[60] Vale, Peter, 1995, "Some Conceptual Concerns for Policy Makers", in Mark Shaw and Jakkie Celliers (eds.), *South Africa and Peace-keeping in Africa*. Halfway House. Institute for Defence Policy, p. 17.

[61] Hussein Solomon. On this see "Defending Borders. Strategic Responses to Illegal Immigrants", *Indicator SA*, 13 (Winter 1996), pp. 9–13.

[62] Some of these are discussed in Vale, Peter and Khabele Motlasa, 1995, "Beyond the Nation State: Rebuilding Southern Africa from below", *Harvard International Review*, XVII (4), pp. 34–37; 83-84.

Peace is not simply the absence of war in the aftermath of the great victory over race and the dawn of democracy. To succeed, ideas around lasting peace must explore the possibilities of "new forms of community in which individuals and groups can achieve higher levels of freedom".[63] This includes groups previously excluded: women in particular whom as the many examples from the region's community life indicate, have much to offer.

Given its history and the accomplishments of its struggles, Southern Africa should be ideally geared for these new explorations of peace. The only remaining question, although theoretically cast, is pregnant with policy options. Will its peoples be allowed to try?

---

[63] Linklater, op. cit., p. 279.

# PART II

*Doing it...*

# Conflict Resolution and Peace-Keeping —The Organization of African Unity and the United Nations

*Margaret Aderinsola Vogt*

## ANALYSIS OF THE POST COLD WAR DIMENSION OF CONFLICTS IN AFRICA

The cessation of the competition for influence by the superpowers in Africa which followed the end of the Cold War in the early 1990s marked the beginning of a new phase in the African security landscape. Conflicts erupted in many parts of Africa from the beginning of the 1990s, and unlike the period before the end of the Cold War when most of the post-colonial conflicts in Africa were interstate disputes largely related to the definition of colonial boundaries, many of these conflicts were internal. There were some instances of civil war before the beginning of the nineties, some of which attracted international attention or intervention. These included the civil war in the Congo, the Nigerian civil war, the civil war in Chad, the wars in Ethiopia for the independence of Eritrea, the territorial dispute over the Ogaden, and the civil war within the Ethiopian state itself following the overthrow of the Emperor Haile Selassie, and the anti-colonial wars of liberation, mostly in Southern Africa. Africa was a major front-line of competition, not only between the United States and the Soviet Union who sought to expand their spheres of influence, but also between the erstwhile colonial powers, particularly France, Britain, Belgium, Germany and Portugal, which wanted to retain their influence and protect their economic interests in Africa. The major powers invested heavily in the development of the economic and social sectors of those countries in Africa that were considered important for the promotion of their own interests, and in the security of those African regimes that were considered important allies in the maintenance of their influence and of a politically stable environment conducive to the promotion of their influence. For this reason, many African regimes were encouraged to maintain various forms of defence alliances and military assistance programmes which provided the facility for military intervention in the event of external aggression and were often used in the event of internal wars or domestic political problems as legal platforms to justify the deployment of intervention forces into some African countries.[1]

The OAU stipulation which charges in Chapter III of the Charter that states were to avoid interference in the affairs of other states was respected more by the Africans to prevent the effective mediation of some of these internal crises by the regional organization. For example, it was effectively exploited during the Nigerian civil war to deny legitimacy to the rebel cause and to discourage a larger number of African states from recognizing "Biafra". Because the war was seen as an internal affair of Nigeria, any effort made to open a pan-African discussion of the problem was seen as interference in Nigeria's internal affairs. On the other hand, the invasion of Angola's territory by South African forces in support of UNITA (The National Union for the Total Independence of Angola) was used as an effective argument by the MPLA (People's Movement for the Liberation of Angola) government to justify the invitation to Cuba to support the defence of Angola and to station troops in that country. Many African countries, notably Nigeria, fully endorsed the MPLA government after the intervention by South Africa, shifting positions from their previous refusal to recognize any single faction and insisting that they form a government of national unity upon the withdrawal of Portugal from Angola.

The post colonial African political landscape was characterized by the evolution of military governments or one party regimes, many of which had been in power since independence. These regimes, in many cases, received international recognition and legitimacy because the post-colonial epoch in African history was thought to be a learning stage for African countries to develop their own systems.[2] The internal states of social and political development were considered to be secondary to political stability and economic development, the latter being largely measured by the extent to which the countries allowed effective foreign partnership and by the size of the foreign trade sectors. Erstwhile latent problems of national integration and ethnicity were worsened by the methods used for economic development. Uneven distribution of resources and facilities, and the dominance of political control by an elite or specific ethnic group, often further undermined the ability of different peoples to co-exist peaceably. Existing ethnic differences which were delicately man-aged in pre-colonial Africa to prevent conflicts, have often been further worsened by

---

[1] The 1970s witnessed several such interventions, either directly by the Rapid Deployment Unit of the French armed forces, especially the foreign units, or often in alliance with a group of franco Zaire, and in 1978 and 1979 to remove a head of state in the Central African Republic, Jean Baptist Bokassa, and replaced him with another, David Daco. Cuban troops, financed and facilitated by the Soviet Union, intervened in Angola to repel an invasion of South African forces, who were in support of the FNLA. For an analysis of foreign intervention in Africa, see M. A. Vogt "Nigeria and the World Powers" in *Nigerian Defence Policy: Issues and Problems*, edited by A.E. Ekoko and M.A. Vogt, (Malthouse Press Ltd., Lagos, 1990), p. 68.

[2] This was when scholars thought that the military, because of their structure and professional orientation, might provide a progressive frame for national integration. Scholars such as Huntington, Inis Claude and Ruth First described the revolutionary role of the military in the development of the political systems in Africa.

the post-colonial patterns of economic development and political control. Such problems lie at the root of those conflicts that have witnessed major ethnic wars, such as Liberia, Somalia, Rwanda and Burundi.

The pattern of external involvement in African conflicts equally changed following the end of the Cold War. The major powers became reticent to get involved in African crises, and they became champions of democratization. This reluctance was particularly strong when there was demand for the use of external African military personnel in African conflict situations. The reluctance to deploy forces to Africa was particularly reinforced following the Somali operations when American forces were attacked and their bodies denigrated by Somali militia. One of the most recent indicators of such a change in the management of regional security issues, especially by France, which in the past conducted military interventions to replace undesirable governments by regimes they considered more favourable, was the French reaction and military intervention in 1995 in the Comoro Islands following a coup d'etat facilitated by a group of French mercenaries led by Bob Denard. The French intervened to revere the coup but did not reinstate the deposed government. Instead, they established a transitional government with the mandate to manage the affairs of the island country and organize elections for a democratically elected government.[3] The action by the French military was preceded by a similar threat of intervention in Lesotho by the members of the Southern African Development Community (SADC). By threatening to intervene militarily SADC successfully prevented a coup in that country.[4] This action was taken with the approval of the member states of the sub-region and the tacit approval of the OAU. Similarly, the OAU gave an approving nod to the French action in the Comoros.

The new generation of conflicts in Africa, apart from being intra-state in character, has been generated by the following major factors:

1. Struggle for the reform and transformation of political systems and for changing the political process from an overly exclusive system to a more inclusive system, from a more authoritarian to a democratic system. In all instances, this has been through demands for regime change. In some cases the former regimes have been changed, in others, some interim accommodation and arrangement were worked out in a gradual process of change. Many conflicts were successfully prevented from degenerating into war through the active involvement of the international and regional organizations, especially the UN and the OAU, and other groups of actors, in the democratic process that consisted of election monitoring and observation of the political processes in countries such as Namibia, South Africa, Congo, Gabon, Zaire, Côte D'Ivoire and Togo. Before the 1990s, it would have been inconceivable for a member state to allow an external body to supervise and monitor elections in their territory, not even the OAU. By 1994, the OAU had

---

[3] French Intervention in the Comoros: See *The Mail and Guardian*, 8 Dec., 1995.

[4] South African intervention in Lesotho.

monitored about 39 elections and referenda in 25 member states. It must, however, be noted that in many of these countries the political conflicts have not yet been successfully resolved, only frozen.

2. Ethnic and religious competition, and the struggle to redefine the formula for power sharing mechanisms; with the state unable to depend on external support for economic and military assistance, the people began to challenge the way in which they were governed, and the denial of access to them to sources of economic and political power. This was the case, for example, in Somalia, Liberia, Ethiopia, Rwanda, and Burundi. In most of these instances, while the conflict assumed an ethnic character, the underlying causes were usually economic and political, reflecting competition over the allocation and access to dwindling resources, and in some cases over land space. The near total control by the state over the management and distribution of resources and other development facilities account for the fact that the control of political power is often perceived as an end game and as the only means of access to power and the restoration of economic balance.

3. Disputes over traditional land boundaries, questions of internal land boundaries between communities, grazing and farming rights, resource sharing and equitable distribution of political and economic power within the state system have assumed important dimensions in terms of the impact they have had on the generation of violent conflicts. The problem of nomadic Africans such as the Tuareg in their search for grazing lands in such West African states as Mali, Niger and Senegal, Mauritania, the Fulani area in Nigeria, where inter-communal fighting has been fairly persistent in the last ten years, and northern Ghana are evidences of contests over internal land space and access. Many African countries have different manifestations of such hegemonic wars of attrition. In the more powerful states, where the central governments exercise a tight control over the internal and external dissemination of information, such conflicts often do not make the news.

Many of these conflicts have elements of more than one of the factors listed above at play at any given time. The most significant factor that characterizes the continent in the period following the cold war is the weakening of the political, social and economic systems in many African states. However, in spite of this negative image, some hopeful developments have occurred in such countries as Benin, Ghana, Namibia, Malawi, Zambia, South Africa, Sierra Leone and Uganda and others that have successfully engineered interim political arrangements that they hope will help create the consensus-based democratic systems around which sustainable peace can hopefully be developed.

THE MANAGEMENT OF CONFLICTS IN AFRICA

At its creation in 1964, the OAU developed tools which were meant for the effective mediation of inter-state conflicts. The OAU Charter provided for a Commission on Mediation, Reconciliation and Arbitration. This legal mechanism was created to encourage member states to submit their disputes for regional arbitration. Most of these were expected to be disagreements on the definition of colonial boundaries. This Commission is a legal entity and adopts a juridical approach, relying on the member states to voluntarily submit their cases to the body for adjudication. The Commission's facility was hardly ever used; this was why the OAU evolved a more traditional African concept of intervention by respected elders and fellow heads of state. The use of ad hoc Committees of two or three heads of state to mediate and facilitate the negotiation of issues that were in contention between states expanded the scope of the regional organization to interstate disputes. The envoys and heads of state sought to prevent disputes from escalating by inviting the parties to allow third party mediation. This was the case, for example, in the territorial disputes between Algeria and Morocco in 1971, between Somalia and Ethiopia and Somalia and Kenya, Nigeria and the Cameroon over the Bakassi Peninsula, and Ghana and Togo over the Volta region. The adoption of the mechanism of an ad hoc committee of heads of state has allowed the OAU an entry point to prevent the escalation of several of the conflicts, even when it was not possible to resolve them fully.

The post-Cold War conflict landscape in Africa resulted in the initiation of a new generation of multilateral and international interventions, in many cases with multi-dimensional characteristics in response to the change in the character of the conflicts confronting Africa. In many of the post-Cold War conflicts, the nature of the state and of leadership itself was in question and came under challenge by groups within civil society. The type of international action that was needed, therefore, was an intervention between the state and leadership on the one hand and its people on the other, as well as among contending groups of people within the state. In most cases, the international community needed to reconstruct fractured societies and develop civil society, especially in countries where the central government had collapsed, for example in Somalia and Liberia. Because the inter-state conflicts not often are confined to a specific geographic area but often engulf the entire society, the use of traditional inter-positionary peace-keeping forces for the management of such conflicts becomes impossible In most cases, intervention is required even when there is no peace to keep. The United Nations, the OAU, other multilateral organizations such as the Commonwealth and some sub-regional organizations (IGAD, the Economic Community of West African States ECOWAS, SADC and the countries of the Great Lakes) have initiated various levels of intervention. These range from political and election monitoring missions, military and civil police observer groups, peace enforcement operations in both Somalia and Liberia, and humanitarian support missions in Liberia, Somalia and Rwanda. In Southern Africa, SADC appears to be evolving a set of political principles and codes which should guide their interaction and collaboration with each other. As mentioned earlier, they successfully reversed a coup d'etat against an elected government in Lesotho, insisting on adherence to democratic principles by its members. Also, Zambia has been criticized by its Southern African neighbours for its treatment of political opposition.

The new pattern of international intervention, unlike traditional, inter-positional peace keeping, calls for elements of several types of missions, including peace-building, or for mandates to be changed and expanded mid-stream as the conflict situation assumes new complexities. The other distinction in the post-Cold War intervention in Africa is that all such deployments have occurred within independent states to re-establish central authority and maintain law and order, the only exception being the missions to Mozambique and Angola where there were long civil wars deriving from unresolved colonial rivalries. This trend markedly contrasts with the classical concept of peace-keeping in which international facilitation was invited by a government or parties in dispute to assist with the implementation of previously concluded agreements including cease-fires. In classical peace-keeping, the parties asking for international support shared responsibility for its implementation and success. In the post-Cold War era, however, multilateral intervention often has to be imposed to prevent a further decline of security. The most recent examples are the crises in Liberia, Somalia, Rwanda and Burundi.

International response to the new, post-Cold War generation of conflicts in Africa has had varying degrees of success. In Somalia, the initial objective of the United Nation's intervention led by the United States in 1992, the support of humanitarian relief action, was expanded after the death of the American Rangers and the group of Pakistani soldiers on 5 June 1993. UNITAF, under the command of the United States, launched a military attack and a search for Mohammed Aïdid, the leader of the Somali National Army, who was held responsible for provoking these attacks. Not only did the efforts to arrest Aïdid fail, they also caused serious damage to the confidence of the Somali people in the sincerity of the multilateral force that was deployed to assist them, including the successor United Nations force, UNOSOM I and II. The international effort was no longer perceived as a neutral force by some of the Somali factions on the one hand, while many of the force-contributing states lost interest in peace-keeping in Somalia and decided to withdraw as a result of constant attacks on their personnel by various Somali factions. UNISOM II, the UN force that took over the operations in UNITAF in Somalia in 1994, operated under a changed mandate. For the first time in United Nations history, a mandate was written clearly authorizing enforcement action in support of restoration of order to Somalia. However, since the enforcement measure was not conducted as a full Chapter VII operation, the military support for a Chapter VII operation was never made available. Instead, the United Nations gave a Chapter VII mandate to a force that was configured to perform peace-keeping roles. UNOSOM II's function was to remain largely that of peace-keeping and support for humanitarian action that was the earlier stated objective, expanding to peace building efforts such as the search for political reconciliation, the demobilization of fighting forces and the restoration of certain institutions such as the police and the judiciary. However, with the withdrawal of UNITAF, the UNOSOM II operations had even fewer personnel to work with. At its peak, the force had only about 25,000 men and women, and was deployed very thinly throughout Somalia except in the Northeast and Northwest. As of August and September 1994, when the drawdown of UNOSOM II started, the bulk of the force of less than 20,000 men was pulled back to Mogadishu and gradually withdrawn. The process ended in March 1995 with neither peace nor order restored to Somalia. The country has reverted to a state of instability. While some parts of Somalia are gradually becoming stable, because the people are evolving their own means of co-existence following the withdrawal of the international community, Somalia is far removed from a situation where national and political reconstruction can be conducted in a concerted manner.

In order to grasp the main lessons of the Somali operations, it is important to clearly understand what the UN did in Somalia and the implications. Some have concluded, based on the UN actions in Somalia and the complexities of protecting "safe havens" in the former Yugoslavia, that enforcement action conducted by the United Nations resulted in tremendous complications and damaged the concept of impartiality. Thus it should not be applied again as a tool of conflict management, especially by the United Nations. This conclusion was partially responsible for the reluctance to allow effective and timely international action to prevent the massacre of 500,000 people in Rwanda in 1994.

Some analysts have recently pointed out that judging the effectiveness of enforcement action based on the Somali experience would remain inconclusive because the mission to Somalia, even though so labelled, was not a Chapter VII operation. Nor was it provided with the resources to operate a mandate for enforcement. The disposition of the forces was also not designed to support enforcement action. The Security Council did not provide the UN with the wherewithal to effectively discharge an enforcement mandate. One should add that with the structure of the United Nations, especially the lack of a centralized command system to direct what would have become a large scale military operation, and given the political nature of the UN system of reportage, could UNOSOM II have effectively carried out an enforcement mandate even if it had the resources required? Enforcement action requires the deployment of a force that would be overwhelming enough, both in numbers and in capability, to force the warring factions to accept the terms laid down in the January 1993 Addis Ababa agreement. In a civil war situation where practically the entire society is armed, a much larger UN force would have been required and it would have been necessary to disperse them all over Somalia. Following the death of the American Rangers and Pakistani soldiers, the enforced disarmament of the warring factions was abandoned. While the revised UNOSOM II's mandate called for voluntary disarmament in exchange for demobilization and reintegration, no resources were made available for demobilization until October 1994, when a token sum of $2m was provided for, two months prior to the beginning of the drawdown process. The expenditure of this was made conditional on proof of effective disarmament, which could not take place in a hostile security environment.

While the international community was reluctant to employ enforcement action in Somalia, some West African states did use enforcement action in Liberia. This was justified by the need to prevent attacks by Liberian warring factions on the ECOMOG Forces which were deployed by the West African sub-regional organization, ECOWAS, in August 1990. The West African states embarked on peace-keeping in Liberia after more than 150,000 people had been either killed or displaced in the civil war which started in 1989. By July 1990, a large number of civilians, many of them nationals of member states of ECOWAS and Liberian refugees, were trapped in Liberia. The warring factions, including the government forces, openly violated international norms and attacked and killed unarmed civilians who had ran to churches, United Nations offices and foreign embassies for protection. International response to the critical situation in Liberia was non-committal, as the event occurred at the height of the war in the Persian Gulf and received little international coverage. The member states of ECOWAS, frustrated by the deterioration of the Liberian crisis, mounted a multilateral force that landed in Monrovia in August 1990. ECOMOG was immediately engaged in a battle to stop its landing by the Charles Taylor-led NPFL. The decision was taken that the multilateral force should fight its way into Monrovia, create a beach-head and evacuate the large number of civilians who were stranded at the port and in Monrovia to refugee camps in various African countries. Following this, enforcement action was pursued to create a secure zone, first around Monrovia, and then Greater Monrovia, by securing strategic assets, such as the water reservoir, electricity generation capacity, and the local and the international airports. Enforcement action was again taken in 1992, after the NPFL launched Operation Octopus to try to capture Monrovia, which played host to over 70% of the population of the entire country. ECOMOG's operations were intended to push back the attacking forces and to weaken their operating base.

The ECOMOG has remained in Liberia since 1990. The mounting of the force was only retroactively and reluctantly endorsed by some of the member states of ECOWAS. The adoption of enforcement action raised questions about the credibility of the force for carrying out a peace-keeping mandate while remaining an impartial arbiter. The concept of a multinational monitoring force in the African sub-region was an innovative one in that it represented the first time that a sub-regional force had been mounted for peace-keeping in an internal war situation and in support of humanitarian action. Secondly, Liberia represented the first time that a collaborative effort was entered into at three levels of international action, the sub-regional (ECOWAS), the regional (OAU) and the United Nations. Similar arrangements have been subsequently tried in Bosnia and Haiti. The use of peace-keeping forces to facilitate the discharge of humanitarian assistance and to back the activities of international non-governmental efforts was subsequently tried in Somalia, Rwanda and Bosnia by the United Nations. African police forces had been used to maintain law and order in Tanganyika during the army mutiny in 1961; and in Chad in 1982, an OAU peace-keeping force was deployed to support the Government of National Unity (GUNT) in a power-sharing arrangement, and to facilitate the withdrawal of Libyan forces. When that same force was requested to support the government of Chad in an enforcement capacity to repel the invading forces of the former defence minister, the OAU argued that it was not part of the force's mandate to do so. The OAU force to Chad was withdrawn in the middle of rebel incursion, leaving Hissein Habre to overrun the country.

In Liberia, an exclusively African mounted and financed force was injected into a state where the central authority had collapsed and there was no national authority in control. Learning from the lessons of Chad, the ECOWAS force was quickly reinforced to enable it to carry out its mandate, which was the protection of the refugees. According to the first ECOMOG Chief of Staff, the choices before them were highly unattainable:

1. Withdraw and abandon the thousands of refugees that were waiting at the port for evacuation. Given the precedence set by the warring factions, the chances were high that many would have been killed.

2. A UN-negotiated withdrawal would have necessitated an aggressive defence of the exit of the force for they would have had to fight their way out.

3. A UN-negotiated or aggressive withdrawal would have forced them to abandon most of their equipment in Liberia, which in the hands of the warring factions, would have raised the threshold of the war.

The ECOWAS states concluded that an assertive defence of the mandate was the only viable option.[5]

Six years after ECOMOG's intervention in Liberia, while the civil war has been largely contained, the situation in the country still remains delicate, especially following the mid 1996 war which, for the first time since the beginning of the Liberian civil war, destroyed a large part of Monrovia. The disarmament of the warring factions has yet to be implemented. Problems with the disarmament phase led to the collapse of previous agreements in Liberia. However, Liberia still provides an interesting example of the kind of partnerships that can be established in the management of international security and of conflict situations. These include:

---

[5] Iweze, C.C., 1993, "The ECOMOG Operations" in M.A. Vogt and A.E. Ekoko (eds.), *Nigeria in International Peace Keeping, 1960–1992*. Lagos: Malthouse Press Ltd.

1. The military efforts of the sub-regional organization, ECOWAS, which took the lead in mounting the peace-keeping force and later the peace-enforcement force, shows that sometimes the politically difficult decision to intervene in a charged conflict situation where there is no pre-agreed cease-fire may be more easily taken at the sub-regional level. Enforcement action is expensive, in terms of both men and material, and few countries are willing to sacrifice both where they do not have vital national interests. Sub-regional states with a great deal to lose through such conflicts are more likely to agree to act.

2. The ECOWAS action was complemented by the political representative of the Secretary-General of the OAU, former Zimbabwean President Canaan Banana, who followed the political aspects of the Liberian crisis almost from the beginning.

3. A political representative of the UN Secretary-General, who headed the United Nations Observer Mission To Liberia from 1994. Before UNOMIL was established, the UN complemented the ECOWAS intervention in Liberia with the deployment of a United Nations Observer Mission and the expanded ECOMOG consisting of troops from two East African countries, Tanzania and Uganda. These troops were to be deployed to the NPFL-held territory as part of the conditions for disarmament stated in the Cotonou and Akossombo Accords. These agreements could not be implemented because the disarmament process was disrupted by renewed fighting.

The Liberian crisis, even though militarily more stable than before in that the destruction of life and property has greatly reduced, is yet to be totally resolved. The last peace accord in Abuja, Nigeria in May 1995, while addressing many of the issues previously under contention created a new set of problems as some of the groups that were assumed to be inconsequential suddenly developed aggressive teeth. For the first time, the oldest and the most militarily and politically influential of the factions, the NPFL led by Charles Taylor, not only participated in the negotiating process, but was among the first to report in Monrovia for the swearing-in of the new Liberian Transitional National Government with a Council of State that was to administer the country for one year.[6] Elections were then supposed to be held with the military and administrative support of ECOMOG and the UN and the financial backing of the international community. The disarmament, demobilization and reintegration of the fighting forces, which was to begin in December 1995 as a prelude to the elections, did not hold on schedule as a result of renewed fighting led this time by the ULIMO—Johnson and the LPC—who feel left out by the Abuja agreement.

---

[6] Liberia's New Council of State Assumes Power, in *This Day*, Vol. 150, Friday and Saturday, 1&2, 1995 (Leaders & Company Ltd. Nigeria), p. 1.

The United Nations in Rwanda assumed the lead role in the management of the brewing crisis in that country in 1990. The Arusha agreement of August 1993, hosted under the sponsorship of the OAU and the neighbours of Rwanda, called for the establishment of a neutral force. The United Nations Assistance Mission for Rwanda was established in October 1993, with the mandate of assisting with the provision of a secure environment for the installation of a democratically elected government, the demobilization of fighting forces and the verification and monitoring of a demilitarized zone. The security situation in Rwanda deteriorated at the time of the deaths of the Presidents of Rwanda and Burundi. Some of the international contingents, especially the Belgian forces, were targeted for attack by some of the Rwandese factions. This prompted the decision of the Belgian government to recall its forces, even at a time when the political situation was getting more tense. The security problem of Rwanda finally reached a peak when in April 1994 about 500,000 Rwandese, mostly Tutsi, were massacred even with the presence of the small UN force that still remained in Rwanda. Even though the massacre was being predicted, the UN Secretary-General was not able to extract the consent of the Security Council to intervene with a more robust force because the member states who had the capability were not prepared to deploy their forces into Rwanda. The situation was further complicated by the military gains made by the Rwandese Patriotic Front against the Hutu-dominated Government Forces, resulting in the outflow of hundreds of thousands of Hutu refugees fearing retribution to neighbouring countries.

The situation in Rwanda, following closely the death of the American Rangers and the Pakistani soldiers in Somalia, suffered from the consequences of the Somali experience and the reaction to the deliberate targeting of international peace-keepers. This raised comment about "Afro-pessimism" and "peace fatigue". The major powers were unwilling to embark on another major military offensive in Rwanda and risk losing their men. African member states of the UN were called upon to contribute forces and this was coordinated by the OAU. However, even after the African forces were earmarked, they could not be deployed for almost five months because the United Nations had problems mobilizing the necessary funding, logistics and transportation. The African contingent did not have the basic requirements of communications equipment, personal weapons and even food rations. The delay greatly exacerbated the crisis. While the Rwanda situation has gradually been stabilized, the general contention is that the international community must be better prepared to act to prevent the 1994 experience in Rwanda.[7]

---

[7] The statement by the Secretary-General of the OAU, "Resolving Conflicts in Africa: Proposals for Action" sums up the OAU's sense of helplessness. Amb. Salim states: "Many times, we have looked around for the OAU to intervene constructively in a conflict situation only to find that it is not there, and when present, to realize that it is not adequately equipped to be decisively helpful." (Extracts from a speech delivered before the 56th Ordinary Session of the Council of Ministers in Dakar, Senegal on 22–27 June 1992 ). [OAU Press and Information Series (1) 1992]

A similar situation in Burundi has generated discussions on what the inter-national community should do to avert a crisis. The Secretary-General of the UN has called for the advanced preparation of a multilateral force that could be rapidly deployed, operating under Chapter VII to enforce security and to pro-tect the threatened civilian population. The Secretary-General's proposal states that the enforcement force will consist of troops of those member states that have the capability to rapidly deploy their forces and carry through an offen-sive military action. This force will be deployed to Burundi if the situation dete-riorates further and is assessed as threatening to the civilian population. It is proposed that the enforcement action be employed until conditions stabilize enough for the force to be withdrawn, at which stage the intervention force will then be replaced by a UN peace-keeping force.

The countries of the Great Lakes have assumed the lead role, not only in the political mediation of the Burundi crisis but also in the implementation of punitive action against the military-led government that assumed power in a coup d'etat. Under the leadership of the former Tanzanian President Julius Nyerere, who mediated the Arusha talks on Burundi, the sub-regional states had called for an international enforcement action into Burundi to stop the killings in that country. While the former government of Burundi strongly opposed international intervention, they initially endorsed the concept of an African military intervention. However, powerful interest groups within Burundi were opposed to any form of external military intervention.[8] The UN Security Council at an earlier stage concluded that an intensification of political negotiations should be pursued.[9] With the deterioration of the security situa-tion within Burundi, and following the Tutsi-led military coup, the sub-regional states have imposed punitive sanctions, including an embargo on the transport of all but essential humanitarian services to Burundi. They are being supported in this by the major powers.

However, the problematic missions in Somalia, Liberia, Rwanda and Burundi have diverted attention and acclaim from the successes achieved by the international community. In Namibia, collaboration was forged among various levels of actors, the Commonwealth, the Contact Group, the OAU and the United Nations to effect a successful transfer of power, through a demo-cratic process, to a new set of actors in a country that had been at war for sev-eral decades. Another international coalition of facilitators encouraged the internally controlled negotiations that resulted in the epoch-making elections in South Africa in 1994. The United Nations led a team of facilitators, including the church and the major powers, in supporting the negotiations leading to the Rome Accord, the subsequent disarmament and demobilization of the warring factions, and the internationally supervised elections in Mozambique in

[8] OAU Foreign Minister's meeting at Addis Ababa, OAU/Burundi, (Reuter) 27/2 1996, Bulletin #1.

[9] Security Council Report of the Secretary-General on the Situation in Burundi: S/1996/116, 15 February 1996; see also the concept of preventive deployment to Burundi in the Secretary-General's Letter to the Council of 29 December 1995 (S/1995/1068).

November 1994. In the Congo, OAU electoral monitors played a significant role in the successful transition to a democratically elected government. International multilateral facilitation of political negotiations, often involving and even led by non-state actors, and international election monitoring and supervision of internally conducted elections are major successes of international collaboration which, because they were successful, are too quickly forgotten. The lessons learnt from these successes also need to be extracted.

LESSONS LEARNED FROM SOMALIA AND LIBERIA

It is certainly not very fair to compare two operations such as the ones deployed to Liberia and to Somalia. The only similarity in the two situations lay in the fact that the missions were deployed to countries where the state system and governance had collapsed and there no longer existed a central coordinating political organ, at the national level and in many instances even at the regional and district levels, around which consensus could be constructed and on which a national platform could be constructed. However, one is tempted all the same to draw a non-analytic comparative list that can highlight the impact of differences in approach.

1. The ECOMOG intervention in Liberia was organized and executed by a group of member states of ECOWAS, countries that had geographic and political contiguity with the zone of conflict, states which believed that they had a responsibility to arrest the carnage and the massacre of thousands of innocent people, many of whom were nationals of their countries. They also believed, rightly or wrongly, that their own security could be affected by events in Liberia.[10] This same logic informed the action of the countries of the Great Lakes in Burundi. In Somalia, the intervening multilateral force was largely drawn from countries that had no geographical or political connection with the zone of conflict. The intervention was largely driven by the need to provide humanitarian support in response to the tragedy, and perhaps also driven, in the case of the United States, by the domestic political calculations of the Bush administration.[11] The troop contributing states shared no ethnic or geographic affinity with the country in conflict, and had no fundamental national interests to protect. The difference in response was, therefore, that while the member states of ECOMOG were willing and have continued to make the sacrifices of lives, material resources and political capital in Liberia, they had and still have interests to protect. The United Nations could not extract the consent of its major financial backers to con-

---

[10] *Africa Confidential*, Vol. 32, No. 10, May 1991 and Gen I. Babangida, "The Imperative Features of Nigerian Foreign Policy" referred to in *The Liberian Crisis and ECOMOG*, M.A. Vogt (ed.) (Gabumo, Lagos, 1992), p. 336.

[11] Clarke, Walter and Jeffrey Herbst, "Somalia and the Future of Humanitarian Intervention" in *Foreign Affairs*, March/April 1996.

tinue with the support of the Somali operation, which became one of the most expensive in the history of the organization. However, the political interests of the member states of ECOWAS complicated the search for a solution to the problem as these interests had to be factored in. Their national rivalries affected the conduct of the operation. To some extent, the member states became part of the problem of the Liberian crisis.

2. The ECOWAS member states, at the very beginning, sought to create a political Liberian coalition made up of several political and religious groups —the Inter Faith Group, social groupings including women organizations, human rights organizations and others—around which a national political coalition was constructed. This balanced the power and influence of the ethnically based warring factions. By mobilizing this constituency at the very beginning, and by encouraging the emplacement of an Interim Government and the involvement of this government at all stages of its operation (even though IGNU limited its activities to Monrovia), ECOMOG was able to rely on a Liberian political authority for support. This also maintained a national front for Liberia at the international level. IGNU could always claim to speak for the Liberian people and did use this to good effect to undermine the ability of the warring factions to harness and sustain international support. In Somalia, it was not possible for such a coalition to be formed. The Addis Ababa Agreements of 1993, through which such a coalition was to be formed, could not be implemented, especially following the killings that occurred in 1994.

3. Liberia was perceived as an attempt to provide an African solution to an African problem. Some of the member states objected to the domination of ECOMOG by Nigeria and Ghana and frowned at the centralization of decision-making concerning the use of the force in the capitals of the two major force contributing states. However, few of them could openly oppose Nigeria on the issue, and in the usual African manner, a consensus of support for ECOMOG was always eventually extracted, both at the ECOWAS subregional level and at the OAU regional level. The OAU Secretary-General gave full support to the concept of ECOMOG at an early stage of the intervention. In Somalia, the sub-regional states were individually involved. They did not have a collective platform for intervention in the form of a viable sub-regional organization similar to ECOWAS. The Ethiopian head of state was mandated by the OAU to follow the Somalia peace process and to act on behalf of the organization. It was involved in aspects of the political negotiation, providing the forum for several of the meetings. But given the history of the relations between Somalia and Ethiopia, and between Ethiopia and some of the warring factions, Ethiopia could only play a limited role. In Somalia, the African and OAU commitment to the solution of the crisis was lacking. This denied the UN the value of the perspectives of those who were more familiar with the cultures, traditions and regional complexities neces-

sary to make a meaningful impact. Such knowledge would have influenced some of the choices made by the UN in trying to implement the peace process.

4. In Liberia, the command and control of ECOMOG remained largely vested in the hands of the force contributing states. There was no central military high command at the ECOWAS secretariat to co-ordinate the military operations. It was only in 1994 that the Chiefs of Staff of member states began to hold regular meetings. In real terms, the command of the ECOMOG operations was vested largely in Nigeria. That country deployed a major part of its military arsenal to the Liberian operation, carrying out punitive air strikes on factions that were considered recalcitrant, enforcing, in collaboration with the other contingents, a land and sea-based embargo, and asserting a military surveillance of the areas under ECOMOG control to prevent infiltration. To a large extent, ECOMOG did not operate with the style of a peace-keeping force but more in an assertive military policing style. Generally, ECOMOG operated with flexibility in the interpretation of its mandate, fluctuating between peace-keeping and enforcement without the political capital of having its mandate placed under scrutiny by a multi-national, security council-type organization. In Somalia, the determination of what the mandate allowed the multilateral force to do was problematic as many of the force contributing states would not allow their troops to be placed in offensive deployment. Additionally, UNOSOM lacked the resources, command structure and numbers required to carry out an enforcement action. Enforcement requires massive, surgical operations by forces with far superior fire power, the capability to mount a military headquarters and quick non-political decisions. Once an enforcement action is complete, another type of force must be employed to continue with the peace-keeping mandate in order to avoid confusing the people about the objectives of the new force. In the Somali context where military power was distributed throughout the entire society, some question the utility of large-scale enforcement action, arguing that the required force would have been impossible to mount. Others argue that if, as the Somalis expected, the factions had been disarmed from the beginning by UNITAF, which had the superior capability to do so, the task of policing the country and of peace-building would have been facilitated. However, in Somalia, unlike Liberia, UNOSOM tried to deploy its military assets and limited personnel to some of the zones it had identified as critical to the support of relief operations in the interior. The diffusion of the smaller force available to UNOSOM II made the security and sustenance of the supply lines to the zones very difficult.

This listing is far from exhaustive, but it may highlight a few of the salient issues around which a comparative analysis can be constructed. One major factor to be considered is that in the situation of a "failed state", what is probably most urgently needed is social and political reconstruction and institution building.

## A CONFLICT MANAGEMENT MECHANISM FOR AFRICA

The lessons learnt from the management of conflicts in Africa in the period since 1990 have led to the conclusion there is a need for the exploitation of a wide array of approaches:

1. by a variety of actors, either acting individually or collectively in a well coordinated fashion, and
2. to provide a hierarchy of responses in a given conflict situation.

This not to negate the central and primary role which the United Nations has to play in the management of international security problems. The African experience shows that each organization has its areas of comparative advantage and weakness in responding to a conflict situation. For the OAU, for example, the organization has played a relatively successful role in the mediation of conflicts, and if developed, may be able to play a larger role in conflict prevention. Since the adoption by the OAU of the Mechanism on Conflict Prevention, Management and Resolution in 1994, the Organization has sought partnerships with some of the UN agencies and some international organizations to facilitate the development of its operational capabilities.

One of the principal partners of the OAU in this regard is the International Peace Academy, a private international organization with experience in training and the study of issues relating to peace-keeping and conflict management. The OAU established, in partnership with the IPA, an IPA/OAU Task Force of eminent Africans, including senior military officers, to help identify those issues and areas that the OAU would require for the efficient operationalization of the Mechanism.[12] Some of the areas that the Task Force is examining include issues relating to the development of a wide range of preventative measures and the institutional mechanism within the OAU to carry these through. They include peace-keeping and peace making, the requirements and identification of the areas in which the OAU may have the comparative advantage to act, the areas for which it will have to depend on the UN and others, including the subregional organizations, and the development of the political organ, essentially the Central Organ and the OAU Secretariat, to carry out the functions that have been proposed.

---

[12] The International Peace Academy Update of the Africa Program, 1996.

## THE DEVELOPMENT OF THE OAU INSTITUTIONAL CAPACITY FOR CONFLICT PREVENTION THROUGH EARLY WARNING

The OAU has recognized the need to develop its institutional networks and capacity for the monitoring and analysis of evolving conflicts in Africa, especially since the organization, unlike the UN, which has regional offices (at least of most of its agencies in most member states), does not presently have political representation in most African countries. The OAU has itself recognized the need to develop linkages with several national institutions and individuals who can support its newly created early-warning mechanism. The paucity of the communication linkages affects the operational efficiency of those operating in Africa. Information getting to Addis Ababa late in turn hampers the ability of the Secretary-General to provide timely response to emergencies. On the other hand, it is assumed that because of their closeness to and understanding of the political and cultural environment in which the conflicts on the continent occur, the sub-regional and regional organizations should have the comparative advantage in taking the lead to prevent the escalation of conflict. This is accomplished by informing, coordinating from inception, and then bringing in the UN when the conflicts escalate beyond their resource capability.

To be effective partners with the UN in international security management, the OAU has identified the need to develop an early-warning capability which will collect and analyse information on African countries in order to provide the organization with the capability of acquiring knowledge of impending conflict situations in advance of their eruption.[13] The most important function of any early warning capacity should be the ability to enhance preventive action and to effectively exploit the appropriate entry points of intervention, especially in intra-state conflict situations. The follow-up of this information with appropriate preventive action should be seen as an integrally linked process between early-warning and timely prevention.

The difficulty in reacting to African crises was often not the lack of information on the specific conflict situations, but often the failure to respond early enough before they escalated into major crises. Experience shows that in most conflict situations the problem most often lies in the political will of states, in both the region and the international system, to agree to invest the necessary and appropriate resources for timely action.[14] In internal conflicts, the search

---

[13] Plans for the construction of an early warning capacity for the OAU are already being implemented with funding from the United States Government. See Summary Record of the Seminar for the Establishment, within the OAU, of an Early Warning System on Conflict Resolution in Africa, Addis Ababa, Ethiopia, 15–18 January 1996.

[14] The more recent developments in Burundi provide a clear example of this at the international level. For months, the Secretary-General of the UN argued for the preparation of an intervention force, under Chapter VII of the UN Charter, to stop another round of massacres in Burundi. The idea was neither supported by the Security Council members, who were reluctant to commit the necessary resources, nor by Burundi itself, whose dominant army objected to an international intervention that would have restricted its powers.

for an acceptable point of entry is often a politically delicate task for the regional organization as states are particularly sensitive to the impression that they have lost control of the situation within their boundaries. In Liberia, at the beginning of the crisis in 1989 for example, there was a general presumption by the governments in the region that the Liberian situation could be easily contained. In Sierra Leone, while the government led by Valentine Strasser sought the assistance of the OAU to encourage the RUF (Revolutionary United Front) to come to the bargaining table, the insurgents were reluctant to accept the regional initiatives until it became clear, following the successful conduct of democratic elections in Sierra Leone, that they would be completely marginalized if they refused to mainstream their movement with other political groups.

In developing its early-warning systems, the OAU needs to have three levels of information. Firstly, it requires comprehensive and standard information on each of its member states, covering issues such as the demography, population distribution and changes and movements, information on the political developments, the armed forces, their structure and facilities available to support regional security, defence spending, military acquisition, agriculture and food security, urban violence, information on social trends, educational institutions and trends, labour, employment and other vital economic indicators that would provide a broad profile of the general state of security of the member states, without compromising the vital security interests of those states. Secondly, more specialized and focused information will be required on those states in which conflicts are already in ferment, and thirdly even more detailed and regular monitoring of fully blown conflict situations to inform the organization of the developments on the ground and the potential for escalation. Contrary to the expectation that regional organizations would have more accurate knowledge of countries in its neighbourhood, experience shows that this is often not the case. When the ECOMOG states were preparing to mount their operations in Liberia, for example, for a long time they were hampered by the inability to get accurate operational maps of the country; nor were the military forces sufficiently briefed on the political complexities and on the people. However, being African forces with similar cultures, they were able to adapt relatively quickly.


PREVENTIVE ACTION

The OAU has traditionally employed several methods of preventive intervention. These have included mediation methods such as the use of Good Offices Missions, Special Envoys, Political and Military Observer missions and more recently, election monitoring. In many cases, the OAU still has the comparative advantage over the United Nations in assuming the initiative in these areas as has been shown both in Rwanda and Burundi. Intervention by brotherly African countries, appealing to the sentiment that what happens in the neighbourhood is everybody's business, the OAU Secretary-General is often successful in convincing states to accept a quiet facilitation of their crises. If the OAU can successfully establish a system of such mediation and facilitation, which is backed by an institutional technical facility such as a team of political officers from the OAU, communications equipment manned by a trained technical team and a comfortable budget, the OAU can then develop its capabilities in this respect. Often important initiatives are compromised or cannot be developed because of the lack of the necessary resources. For example, the OAU Special Envoys to both Liberia and Burundi have not been able to establish an effective presence in those conflict zones to provide a regular and on the spot input and assessment. During the Chadian operations in 1982, the OAU Force Commander had no means of direct communication with the OAU Secretariat. The same was true of the OAU observer mission that was deployed to Rwanda and withdrawn in 1993. The OAU can be assisted to develop the capacity to do the following in the area of conflict prevention:

1. Maintain a data bank of resource people, eminent persons and "friends of the Secretary-General", civilian-diplomatic, academic, military and a pool of technical support staff who can be called upon at short notice for deployment to politically tense situations and are able to establish a small field office with direct communication links with the OAU Secretariat. The United Nations and Africa's "strategic allies" could provide the financial and technical support for such missions. The OAU political missions will be similar to UN special political missions deployed to countries such as Sierra Leone and Burundi. They will form part of an early warning and intervention system. The objective is to develop the facility to monitor events closely as they develop and to suggest options for intervention, while providing a platform for early action.

2. Maintain in advance of a crisis the technical capability and logistical support to deploy and operate a mission of a limited, pre-determined size for the performance of either a political intervention mission or a military observation mission. This will necessitate the ear-marking of troops from member states that would be pre-trained and equipped for deployment at short notice. It will also necessitate collaboration between the UN, OAU and sub-regional organizations for the identification, needs assessment and training of both the political and military teams of observers. It will also necessitate the maintenance, with the collaboration of the UN, of an optimum level of logistical stores. The OAU is already in the process of developing and assembling in Addis Ababa a logistical store and equipment adequate for the outfitting and deployment of a team of at least 100 military observers at the shortest possible notice into a conflict zone.

3. The development of the concept of using the civilian police and a Pan-African team of professionals for the restoration of law and order and for institution building in collapsed state systems or in countries where the social structures have been badly weakened or destabilized.

PEACE-KEEPING AND MULTILATERAL MILITARY OPERATIONS

The experience of the ECOWAS intervention in Liberia and the tremendous cost of that operation seem to suggest that the mounting of such missions integrally by the sub-regional organization or by the OAU may lie beyond the capability of the regional bodies. For example, by June 1995 the Nigerian government said it had spent about $4 billion on peace-keeping in Liberia; this is discounting the amount spent by the UN and the contributions to the Special Fund for Liberia. It is clear that the Liberian peace process can only be successfully concluded with the extensive collaboration and financial support of the three tiers of actors and the international donor community. The Liberian experience suggests the importance of a multi-level coordination of management strategies between the UN, the regional and the sub-regional organizations. At the continental level, the OAU's capacity should be developed to coordinate the sub-regional initiatives in the areas of planning, the development of doctrines, mandates and common operational procedures, and to organize periodic joint training at designated centres.

The UN certainly has the comparative financial and logistical advantage in the area of multilateral military operations in Africa, especially in peace-keeping. However, the experience of the past events in Rwanda and also in Liberia, show that there is still tremendous scope for OAU action as well as initiatives at various levels by the sub-regional bodies similar to the ECOMOG intervention in Liberia, SADC intervention in Lesotho, and Angolan intervention in Sao Tome and Principe. The most realistic option for the OAU at this time is to perform the coordinating role in the preparation of African military and political forces for UN-sponsored military intervention in African crises. To perform these roles effectively, the OAU would have to develop its capacity in the following areas:

1. Development of the institutional framework at the OAU Secretariat level for the effective management of its OAU Mechanism for Conflict Prevention, Management and Resolution. Apart from the early-warning system earlier discussed, the capacity for political analysis of crises and the establishment of a well developed military component at the OAU Secretariat to co-ordinate military operations and training have to be developed. Appropriate manning of the Secretariat is necessary, either through secondment from member states or through the recruitment of its own staff. In the short term, the secondment, especially of serving military officers as well as the recruitment of a few retired ones, would probably be the best option. The Conflict Management Division at the OAU has developed tremendously in the last few months, especially following the development of the early-warning system.

2. The development of a statutory and regular meeting of the Chiefs of Staff, the Chiefs of Defence Staff, or the appropriate head of the armed forces of African countries, as they are variously designated, similar to the periodic

meetings of the Chiefs of Staff of ECOWAS member states, would facilitate the co-ordination of planning for joint operations. The sub-regional bodies would continue with their regular co-ordination and meetings while the regional meetings would occur maybe quarterly. The Chiefs of Staff would discuss the ear-marking and operation of contingents for UN military operations, assess the existing assets of their member states and review the needs of their various forces. They would also deliberate on issues such as the doctrine that should govern the utilization of their forces, the concepts of operation and the various types of mandate that would be required. The first of such meetings ever to be held took place in Addis Ababa in June 1996 and agreed to the coordination of some of the activities designated above. The next challenge would lie in the development of the appropriate mechanisms within the Secretariat itself to manage the military aspects of its operations.

3. The OAU would co-ordinate with the United Nations and Africa's strategic allies for meeting the needs of the African contingents for UN operations. Along lines suggested in the Nigerian/British initiative, the UN could be facilitated to create forward deployed logistical stores in strategic regions of Africa, stockpiling the full range of non-lethal supplies and equipment for mounting an expanded peace-keeping operation, including the possibility of supplies for humanitarian support activities and for minimal peace enforcement.[15] These stores would be designed to service a minimum size of operation, such as one or two brigade size, or smaller, and the stores would be owned by the UN and manned by UN employed personnel. The emphasis in the proposal is the development of a partnership between the UN and the regional organizations in which the UN will retain the primary responsibility for international security.[16]

THE CENTRAL ORGAN OF THE OAU

The Central Organ was created as the central decision-making body of the OAU Mechanism. The idea was evolved to provide a political frame for the member states to review issues of peace and security on the continent on an on-going basis and to back the activities of the OAU Secretary-General. The Central Organ is composed of the Bureau (the current chair of the OAU, the immediate past chair and the in-coming chair) and states representing the five regions of Africa. Currently, the Central Organ consists of 16 states. The initial conception was for a body that would perform a Security Council type of mandate, review

---

[15] Nigerian/British Initiative, Conflict Prevention and Peace-keeping in Africa, April 1995.

[16] These ideas are well explained in the recent Anglo/Nigerian proposal. The proposal suggests the establishment of mobile logistics units of the UN that would visit troop contributing states to enhance their capacity, especially in the area of heavy equipment and armoured personnel carriers. Another alternative is the establishment by potential troop contributing states of partnerships with countries that can provide equipment.

the security situation in Africa, decide on a course of action, approve the appropriate mandate for action and provide the required resources. The Division of Conflict Prevention, Management and Resolution serves as the Secretariat of the Mechanism and its implementing agency.

While the establishment of a standing committee of heads of state has solved the problems encountered in convening special summits whenever there is a problem on the continent, the number of countries represented in the Central Organ is quite large, 16 of 52 member states, and decisions taken by the body are still by consensus. This means that for every situation, all members must agree to a course of action and one dissenting vote is enough to present a stalemate. The discussion whether the OAU should support intervention in Burundi was stalled because the Burundian government opposed intervention. The difficulty in generating the political will to act also affects the credibility of the OAU. The member states often fail to act in support of conflict management in Africa, partly as a result of their inability to agree on the appropriate course of action and also as a result of the lack of appropriate resources and financial support to initiate collective action. In the last few months, however, there has been greater evidence of decisive moves by some of the sub-regional states to act collectively to restore regional security. Apart from the West African initiative in Liberia and the pressures of the Southern African states against military intervention in Lesotho, the countries of the Great Lakes have instituted a collective punitive blockade against the military supported government in Burundi. To the surprise of some sceptics, Uganda and Rwanda have joined in the boycott.

It is too premature to conclude that the reticence of African countries to allow entry by the regional organization into threatening internal crises has been abandoned. While successful collective pressure has been mounted against smaller and militarily weaker states, similar pressures against more powerful states, such as Zaire, Zambia and Nigeria, have not been as successful.

# Conflict Resolution in Africa—A New Role for the Organization of African Unity?

*Chris J. Bakwesegha*

## INTRODUCTION

Conflicts constitute one of the greatest challenges currently facing the African continent. Issues of identity, governance, resource allocation, state sovereignty and power struggle, sometimes coupled with the personality question, have all conspired not only to cause staggering loss of human life, destruction of property and environmental degradation but also to saddle Africa with the unenviable record of hosting the biggest number of uprooted communities in the world: 7 million refugees out of the global total of 17 million, as well as close to 20 million internally displaced persons.

It is a truism that conflicts in Africa have existed since the beginning of recorded history. Indeed, most of the good things the African people normally cherish in life such as power, glory, love, and wealth as well as democracy tend to generate conflicts as people strive to acquire them. It is also true that throughout the Cold War period, the world witnessed many events that threatened peace, security and stability in many African countries due to super-power rivalry. However, the end of the Cold War has brought to the fore a new path-stream of conflicts and domestic tension which has seriously hamstrung the African development process in almost all respects. Today, while increased cooperation between various states in Africa has fortunately helped to reduce the tempo of inter-state conflicts considerably, unfortunately the post Cold War period has ushered in its wake an upsurge of conflicts not only across regional, ethnic and religious divisions, but also along clan and even sub-clan lines within some nations.

From Liberia to Somalia, the world has seen some African nations almost disintegrate. From Angola to Burundi and, of course, to Rwanda, one has witnessed death, outright carnage and the destruction of property and traditional institutions which used to contain domestic tension and conflicts, as well as environmental decay as a result of conflict and instability.

As the African people celebrate their undoubtedly tremendous achievement in the area of liberating their continent, they should not forget that their collective failure to identify the roots of instability and underdevelopment, and their failure to redress them meaningfully, casts a long shadow on Africa's achievement in the field of liberation.

As the twenty-first century approaches, the imperative for Africa to take a hard look at the scourge of conflicts and to design viable mechanisms for conflict resolution and management capacities becomes more pressing. Put most simply, for Africa to remain relevant in the new international order, the peoples of Africa, through their continental political body, the Organization of African Unity (OAU), must fill the vacuum left by Cold War engagements.

Conflicts by their nature do not disappear simply through the invisible hand of God. Their causes and effects are always many and varied, their histories more complex, their solutions more challenging than a remote observer could ever imagine. It should also be understood that a conflict is usually the playing out of human needs and fears in society. In other words, a conflict is driven by the unfulfilled needs of the people be it in terms of autonomy, sense of justice, identity, basic needs, rights of individuals, or whatever. Most of these needs are of a collective character, and are more often than not provoked by official neglect, persecution, denial of human rights, insensitivity or egoism as well as by the arrogance of power on the part of some of the African leaders. These significantly contribute to the escalation of conflict. It is these felt needs that can create resistance to change. In fact, societies have always been in potential or actual conflict because some segments of the population yearn for change to fulfil their needs and fears, while others fear change and its threat to their interests.

Most fundamentally, because change in many instances is not merely inevitable but also desirable, the conflict resolution process is effective only to the extent that parties to a dispute are helped to cost accurately the consequences of their resistance to change.

The above information is provided in the spirit of demonstrating the imperative necessity for all those concerned to remain sensitive to the scourge of conflicts and to strive to analyze critically through solid and objective research the issues and options involved in conflict management in Africa, in order to assist governments, which often find themselves party to the conflict in question, and all concerned in formulating meaningful policies relating to crisis management.

It is here recognized that in the preamble of the OAU charter, the heads of state and government speak as if the OAU is their exclusive domain rather than something which belongs to all the peoples of Africa. Indeed, they assert: "We, the Heads of State and Government...," rather than: "We, the peoples of Africa..."[1] But this should not, in any way, be interpreted to mean lack of interest in the OAU by the rest of the African peoples. For questions could be asked: if, indeed, Africa must all rise to the challenges of the twenty-first

---

[1] Organization of African Unity, *OAU Charter and Rules of Procedure*, Press and Information Service of the OAU General Secretariat, 1 August 1992, Addis Ababa, Ethiopia, p. 1.

century, especially that of management of transition, are the Africans sufficiently knowledgeable or informed of the work of the OAU? Are they really disposed to learn something about the OAU? How many of them have ever taken interest in reading and understanding the fundamentals of the OAU, namely:

— the OAU Charter, of 1963;
— the OAU Convention on Refugees, of 1969;
— the Lagos Plan of Action, of 1979;
— the African Charter on Human and Peoples' Rights, of 1981;
— the African Charter for Popular Participation in Development and Transformation, of 1990;
— the Declaration of the Assembly of Heads of State and Government of the Organization of African Unity on the Political and Socio-economic Situation in Africa and the Fundamental Changes Taking Place in the World, of 1990;
— the Abuja Treaty establishing the African Economic Community, of 1991;
— the Declaration of the Assembly of Heads of State and Government on the Establishment, Within the OAU, of a Mechanism for Conflict Prevention, Management and Resolution, of 1993?[2]

The present paper, therefore, first of all attempts to analyze the evolving role of the OAU in conflict prevention, management and resolution, in the context of the political evolution of Africa. The thrust of the paper is that conflict resolution and the issue of peace, security and stability have been a major concern of the OAU from its inception, in 1963. It is true that the Commission of Mediation, Conciliation and Arbitration, which was set up as the official organ charged with the responsibility for peaceful settlement of disputes among member states, never became fully operational. It is equally true that other ad hoc arrangements later put in place to deal with interstate disputes and conflicts were not without limitations. However, they had a positive impact on stabilizing conflict situations among Member States.[3]

It should also be noted that for the first 30 years of the existence of the OAU, the organization was preoccupied with interstate conflicts, rather than intrastate conflicts. The latter had been left as the business of each individual Member State, as attested to by the provision of the principle of "non interference" in the internal affairs of other member states in the charter of the OAU. It was after 1990, when intrastate conflicts began to gain the upper hand, that it became necessary for the member states also to embrace the issue of intrastate conflicts; and to intensify and consolidate their activities relating to conflict situations in Africa, as outlined below. But all the same, it is not

---

[2] All the above-cited documents are available with the Press and Information Division of the OAU General Secretariat.

[3] See also Bakwesegha, Christopher J., 1993, "The Need to Strengthen Regional Organizations: A Rejoinder", *Security dialogue*, 24(4), pp. 377–381.

necessarily correct that the issue of resolving conflicts in Africa constitutes a new role for the OAU.

Secondly, the paper argues that strictly speaking, and for those who have been following closely the activities of the OAU, the OAU of today is essentially quite different from the OAU of yesterday. Today's OAU has clearly become more flexible and more sensitive to the needs of the Africans than the OAU prior to the disappearance of the Cold War, especially in so far as matters relating to the principle of sovereignty are concerned. Clearly the African collective leadership has demonstrated a positive response to the dramatic events that have been taking place in the world as they have been affecting Africa's development patterns since the end of the Cold War.

Thirdly, the paper advances the view that the OAU, as a continental political body, should remain in the vanguard of conflict containment and conflict resolution in Africa, while working in close cooperation and collaboration with other international organizations like the UN on the one hand, and/or sub-regional entities like the Inter-governmental Authority for Development, the Economic Community of West African States, the Maghreb Union, the Southern African Development Community and the Economic Community of Central African States, on the other hand. This, clearly, is the heart and soul of the newly established OAU Mechanism for Conflict Prevention, Management and Resolution.


THE OAU'S ROLE IN RESOLVING CONFLICTS

Toward the turn of the 1980s, a succession of dramatic events began to take place world-wide reflecting the then changing character of east–west relations. African leaders immediately came to realize that unless they prepared themselves to respond appropriately to those events, the continent could easily find itself marginalized by the rest of the world in the post Cold War era.

Therefore, at their twenty-sixth ordinary session, which took place in Addis Ababa from 9 to 11 July 1990, and having taken a critical review of the political, social and economic situation of Africa as presented in the "Report of the Secretary-General on the Fundamental Changes Taking Place in the World and their Implications for Africa: Proposals for an African Response", adopted a Declaration on those changes entitled: "Declaration of the Assembly of Heads of State and Government of the Organization of African Unity on the Political and Socio-Economic Situation in Africa and the Fundamental Changes Taking Place in the World."[4]

By that declaration, the heads of state and government pointedly expressed their determined effort to transform Africa politically, socially and economically and lay a "solid foundation for self-reliant, human-centered and sustainable development on the basis of social justice and collective self-reliance."

---

[4] Organization of African Unity, 11 July 1990, Conflict Management Division.

Indeed, in article 10 of that declaration, the heads of state and government succinctly stated as follows:

> We are fully aware that in order to facilitate this process of socio-economic transformation and integration, it is necessary to promote popular participation of our peoples in the processes of government and development. A political environment which guarantees human rights and the observance of the rule of law, would assure high standards of probity and accountability particularly on the part of those who hold public office. In addition, popular-based political processes would ensure the involvement of all including in particular women and youth in the development efforts. We accordingly recommit ourselves to the further democratization of our societies and to the consolidation of democratic institutions in our countries. We reaffirm the right of our countries to determine, in all sovereignty, their system of democracy on the basis of their socio-cultural values, taking into account the realities of each of our countries and the necessity to ensure development and satisfy the basic needs of our peoples. We therefore assert that democracy and development should go together and should be mutually reinforcing.[5]

With that declaration, the African leaders set out on the first step of the long and arduous journey towards meeting the biggest challenge since the struggle for liberation and decolonization, namely: economic integration and development as well as conflict prevention, management and resolution. Africa's determined effort to promote economic integration and development resulted in the signing, in Abuja, Nigeria, in 1991, of a treaty establishing the African Economic Community,[6] while her commitment to the issue of peace, security and stability culminated in the establishment of the Mechanism for Conflict Prevention, Management and Resolution in Cairo, Egypt, in 1993.[7] This, however, had been preceded by the creation of a Division of Conflict Prevention, Management and Resolution within the OAU General Secretariat in 1992.

The decision to establish the said Mechanism within the OAU had been reached against the background that there was no way Africa could improve its socio-economic performance in the years following the end of the Cold War in an ocean of wars, conflicts and domestic tension. The heads of state and government, saw in the establishment of such a mechanism the opportunity to bring to the process of dealing with conflicts on the African continent a new institutional dynamism, enabling speedy action to prevent or manage and ultimately resolve conflicts when and where they occur.

In establishing such a mechanism, the African heads of state and government were guided by six principal considerations:

— Firstly, that the United Nations with its cumulative experience, expertise and greater resources than the OAU should remain the pre-eminent international

---

[5] Ibid, Article 10.

[6] For further treatment of this subject, contact the Economic Development and Cooperation Department of the OAU.

[7] See Organization of African Unity, Declaration of the Heads of State and Government on the Establishment, Within the OAU, of a Mechanism for Conflict Prevention, Management and Resolution", June 1993, Conflict Management Division.

authority with the responsibility for dealing with international peace and security, as well as internal crises which threaten regional stability, particularly in Africa, taking on board the fact that all African states are members of the United Nations.

— Secondly, that the United Nations together with regional and sub-regional organizations and arrangements should form or maintain a partnership, and act decisively and expeditiously in framing new approaches to crisis prevention, management and resolution in this post Cold War era.

— Thirdly, that those new approaches to international or regional peace and security should be framed in a manner that transcends the traditional politico-military approaches, embracing, as they should, economic, environmental, humanitarian as well as human rights issues, as these tend to impact heavily on conflict situations on the continent.

— Fourthly, that regional and sub-regional organizations, on the one hand, and the United Nations system, on the other hand, should endeavour to share proportionately the burdens of maintaining peace, security and stability, world-wide.

— Fifthly, that there was an imperative need for regional organizations such as the OAU to develop and maintain formal and explicit capacities with which to ensure that the United Nations Security Council remains seized of matters of concern to those regional organizations, matters such as democratization or management of transition, socio-economic transformation and regional integration, if only to avoid marginalization in the post Cold War world.

— Finally, for it to take the primary ownership of its own problems, especially those relating to the issue of peace, security and stability, has never been more imperative than in this post Cold War period. The African heads of state and government recognized that unless Africa took the issue of conflict containment more seriously, African countries would continue to shoulder such costly humanitarian undertakings relating to the flow of refugees and internally displaced persons, as well as continue to bear witness to heavy losses of human life and destruction of property, as has been the case in both Rwanda and Somalia recently.

Therefore, the African heads of state and government declared that the mechanism so established would have as a primary objective the anticipation and prevention of conflicts. Indeed, in the declaration which they adopted in June 1993, establishing the mechanism, the African heads of state and government stated as follows:

> In circumstances where conflicts have occurred, it will be its responsibility to undertake peace making and peace building functions in order to facilitate the resolution of these conflicts. In this respect, civilian and military missions of obser-

vation and monitoring of limited scope and duration may be mounted and deployed.[8]

It is important to make a distinction between the two objectives of the mechanism. The first and overriding objective is that of anticipating and preventing situations of tension from turning into fully-fledged conflicts. The second objective concerns situations where conflicts have already occurred and which, in turn, call for the undertaking of peace-making and peace-building functions in order to facilitate the resolution of those conflicts. It is also important to emphasize that in setting up those two objectives, the heads of state and government were fully convinced that prompt and decisive action in situations of conflict would, in the first instance, prevent the emergence of full-blown conflicts; but where by force of circumstances conflicts inevitably do occur, the prompt and decisive action could stop them from degenerating into intense or generalized conflicts.

Furthermore, it was observed that emphasis on anticipatory and preventive measures and concerted actions in peace-making and peace-building would obviate the need to resort to complex and resource demanding peace-keeping operations, which African countries find difficult to finance.

The heads of state and government also directed, in paragraph 16 of the Declaration establishing the Mechanism, that: "... in the event that conflicts degenerate to the extent of requiring collective international intervention and policing, the assistance or where appropriate the services of the United Nations will be sought under the general terms of its Charter."[9]

In such situations, African countries would examine ways and modalities through which they can make practical contributions to such a United Nations undertaking and participate effectively in peace-keeping operations in Africa.

The mechanism as provided for by the declaration establishing it has, in brief, the following structure:

— It is built around a Central Organ, composed of the states which are members of the Bureau of the Assembly of Heads of State and Government, elected annually, with the Secretary-General and the Secretariat as its operational arm. It convenes every month at ambassadorial level, twice a year at ministerial level, and once a year at the level of heads of state and government.

— Under the authority of the Central Organ, the Secretary General, in consultation with the parties involved in the conflict, is mandated to focus efforts on conflict prevention, peace-making and peace-building. In this regard, the Secretary General may, in consultation with the authorities of their countries of origin, and relying heavily on their cumulative experience and deep-seated knowledge of African historical, socio-economic and cultural

---

[8] Paragraph 15 of the "Declaration of the Heads of State and Government on the establishment, Within the OAU, of a Mechanism for Conflict Prevention, Management and Resolution."

[9] Ibid, para. 16.

conditions, also resort to the use of eminent African personalities, special envoys or special representatives and dispatch fact-finding missions to conflict areas.

— Within the mandate of the mechanism, the OAU is required to coordinate its activities closely with African regional and sub-regional organizations and to cooperate, as appropriate, with neighbouring countries with respect to conflicts arising in the different parts of the continent, it being understood that these regional and sub-regional organizations and countries are more familiar with the local issues.

— Similarly, the OAU has been mandated to cooperate and work more closely with the United Nations, not only with regard to issues relating to peace-making but also, and more especially, those relating to peace-keeping. In like manner, the Secretary-General is mandated to maintain close cooperation with other relevant international organizations.

An OAU Peace Fund, governed by the relevant OAU financial rules and regulations, has been established as a permanent organ for the purpose of providing financial resources on a regular and continuous basis to support exclusively OAU operational activities relating to conflict management and resolution.[10] The fund is made up of financial appropriations of five per cent of the regular budget of the OAU, voluntary contributions from member states, as well as from other sources within Africa. The Secretary-General may, with the consent of the Central Organ and in conformity with the principles and objectives of the OAU Charter, also accept voluntary contributions from sources outside Africa.

Specifically on regional organizations, if these must take the primary responsibility of taking care of their own problems, especially those relating to peace and security, then the strengthening of those organizations becomes an imperative. The reasons behind this argument run as follows:

— Firstly, strengthening regional organizations which, in any case, are members of the United Nations, will make that world body stronger and more relevant to world problems.

— Secondly, given its current struggles to find resources with which to meet the challenges of the steadily growing number of regional conflicts, especially those relating to peace-keeping, the question of the United Nations sharing the burden of conflicts with regional organizations is an issue that cannot be questioned.

— Thirdly, by the logic of things, and as the United Nations Charter stipulates, regional problems should, ipso facto, have regional solutions. For one thing, mainly due to their cultural affinity and common social and historical configuration, the people in the region normally have more intimate knowledge

---

[10] The document on the "OAU Peace Fund" is available from the Conflict Management Division of the OAU General Secretariat.

of the evolution and political sensitivities of the conflict in question. For another, their sense of general solidarity, arising out of their common histories, experiences, geographic contiguity and cultural compatibility can play a central role in the process of consensus building, which is so crucial in times of crises.

Conflict management in its comprehensive form, however, should be seen and appreciated as a system, which at every stage involves not only many actors acting and reacting against one another, but also a range of activities in the areas of conflict prevention, peace-making, peace-building and peace-keeping. It follows, therefore, that as much as one would like to see an effective partnership between the United Nations and the OAU as a regional organization put in place, the base of that partnership should be the sub-regional organizations which, in the case of Africa, will help to enhance OAU's conflict management capability. For us at the OAU, this is our clear vision.

One may wish to recall that currently there are five main sub-regions in Africa: one in the East, one in the West, one in the North, one in the South and one in the Central part of the continent. Each of these sub-regions currently hosts a sub-regional organization: with the Inter-governmental Authority for Development (IGAD) in the East; the Economic Community of West African States (ECOWAS) in the West; the Maghreb Union in the North; the Southern African Development Community and the (SADC) in the South; and the Economic Community of Central African States (ECCAS) in the Central African sub-region.

While the main focus of the existing sub-regional groupings in Africa is economic development, experience has revealed that intra-regional competition and squabbles between their member states have impeded their pace of integration and development. In addition, the rising tide of domestic tension and conflicts has also placed a negative impact on their economic performance. Moreover, apart from the present initiative of ECOWAS in Liberia, these sub-regional groupings have tended to rely heavily on the facilities of the OAU and the United Nations in addressing the situations of crisis within their member states. There is, therefore, a pressing need to restructure and strengthen these sub-regional organizations, which have no meaningful tradition in getting involved in conflict resolution, so that they become an integral part of the partnership of the United Nations, as a world body, and the OAU, as a regional organization, in the fostering of peace and security on the African continent, without being seen to duplicate that which is being done by the OAU and the UN.

In graphical terms, and for the purposes of conflict management, the partnership between the United Nations and the Organization of African Unity together with its corresponding sub-regional organizations should be akin to a pyramid. At the top of that pyramid should be the United Nations as a world body, and as the supreme organ for ensuring peace and security world-wide. At the bottom of that pyramid should be the sub-regional organizations together with civil society; and between those extreme ends should be the OAU.[11]

The biggest advantage of a sub-regional approach to conflict management in Africa is that neighbours are more familiar with each other's problems than outsiders. Neighbours usually have a common culture, a common social identity, a common history and similar experiences. As such, they should always be the first port of call in situations of internal crisis. The disadvantage, however, is that close proximity sometimes generates tension and reduces the spirit of impartiality between the neighbours to the extent that sometimes they become part of the problem, rather than part of the solution.

Be that as it may, a sub-regional approach is possible, as long as neighbours sharing borders are excluded from certain conflict management situations affecting each other. On the other hand, combining the principle of neighbourhood with the principle of distant impartiality to create mixed teams of peace-makers or peace-keepers would be another possible solution. Recent examples include the case of Liberia, where peace-keepers from Tanzania and Uganda were at one point in time dispatched to become an integral part of ECOMOG, and the case of the OAU mission in Burundi, where officers have been drawn from African countries, further afield. However, in general terms, keeping neighbours entirely out of each other's problems carries the risk of creating avenues of suspicion and new resentments.

For purposes of emphasis, between the United Nations, standing at the apex of the pyramid, and the sub-regional organizations and the civil society sitting at the bottom of the pyramid, should lie the OAU as a regional entity for conflict management. The biggest advantage of having the OAU mid-way up the pyramid is that the organization is neither too far from, nor too close to, the theatre of conflicts. It is, therefore, in a position to coordinate all the activities relating to conflict management, as performed by the various entities which lie above it or below, with a relatively high degree of impartiality.

Since the adoption of the mechanism, the OAU through the Central Organ of the mechanism, has expended a lot of energy in ensuring that the mechanism takes off and becomes fully operational. The organization cannot presume to have achieved much in its efforts to operationalize the mechanism since its adoption, nor can one assume that the mechanism as it is today is without shortcomings. However, the OAU has received a lot of encouragement from many circles of the international community with regard to what it has so far accomplished in operationalizing the mechanism.

One of the areas relating to the mechanism in which the OAU has scored highly has been election observing. Even before the adoption of the mechanism, in 1993, the OAU had already started to respond to invitations from member

---

[11] See also Salim, Salim Ahmed, 1996, "Localizing Outbreaks: The Role of Regional Organizations in Preventive Actions." Paper presented to a Symposium on Preventive Diplomacy: Therapeutics of Mediation. Organized by the Center for International Health and Cooperation, United Nations, New York, 23–24 April 1996.

states to send teams of people to observe elections. So far OAU has been able to observe well over forty elections and referenda in more than 40 member states, including South Africa. In most of these cases, potential conflicts have been diffused as in the case of Lesotho, Togo, Congo and Gabon; while actual conflicts, on the whole, have been resolved as in the case of Namibia, South Africa, Mozambique and the Comoros. It can also be assumed that in a similar fashion, the conflict in Angola, which has played such havoc on the lives of the people of that country will be resolved sooner than later. But this will very much depend on the willingness of the parties to the conflict to negotiate and honour the terms and conditions of the Lusaka Protocol. It will also depend on the extent to which the international community can bring pressure to bear on UNITA to remain committed to the Lusaka Protocol.

It must be emphasized that prior to 1990, nobody ever imagined that any member state of the OAU would ever invite the OAU Secretary-General to send a team of people to observe elections within its sovereign borders. Today, there is a growing number of member states which are inviting the OAU not only to merely observe elections but also to supervise them. One may see this as a new dynamism and commitment, on the side of member states, to the current democratization process of the continent.

However, one should not minimize the problems member states are still facing in the management of transition through the electoral process. There is still room for some African heads of state and government to realize that there is still life after the "state house"; and that even if they lose out in an election, they still can do other duties for their respective populations. The second problem is that the ordinary citizens who have remained subjects of brutal dictatorships seriously need to be exposed to civic education before participating in an electoral process. Due to lack of civic education, some of the electoral processes which the OAU has observed have been far from perfect.

The third problem relating to the electoral processes the OAU has been observing is that due to financial constraints, the number of OAU election observers has remained too symbolic for large countries like the Republic of the Sudan to come out with a fair verdict of the outcome of the elections. Still due to financial constraints, OAU election observers have invariably arrived on the political scene rather too late, and have also departed after the elections rather too soon.

The fourth problem has been that quite often member states concerned do not realize that elections in themselves are not an end per se but rather the beginning of a long process towards good governance, in the course of which the elected governments and their people need to establish democratic institutions capable of absorbing conflicts and domestic tension. Be that as it may, Africa has started off rather well on its arduous journey to democratic transition through the electoral process since so far the Africans have been spared such absurdities as the incumbent winning an election by 99.99 per cent!

Conflict resolution in Africa has also been handled effectively by the OAU through the concept of preventive diplomacy which has taken many forms, including the use of the good offices of the Secretary-General, the use of eminent persons, the use of special envoys, representatives of the Secretary-General, direct contacts between the OAU and the government of the country concerned, as well as missions from the General Secretariat to the country in question.[12] Such field missions as those which have been undertaken to the Congo, Gabon, Sierra Leone, Somalia, Rwanda, Burundi, Sudan, Nigeria, Cameroon, Lesotho, and the Comoros, just to cite a few, have been aimed at facilitating the process of mediation between the parties at conflict; or assessing the conflict situation obtaining on the ground, with a view to reporting to the Secretary-General and/or to the Central Organ for further action.

Still within the area of conflict resolution, and using mediation as a tool for resolving actual conflicts obtaining on the ground, the OAU has been at centre stage in countries like South Africa and Mozambique, the Congo and Liberia, Gabon and Sierra Leone, as well as Burundi and Rwanda. As an example, in the case of Rwanda and Burundi, the Arusha peace agreement between the government of Rwanda and the Rwandese Patriotic Front which was duly signed by the parties concerned in August 1993, despite the unfortunate events of April 1994, together with the observation mission deployed in that country by the OAU while the negotiations were going on, were the outcome of an African initiative through Africa's regional body, the OAU, at mediation. Similarly, the OAU military and civilian mission currently in Burundi is aimed at building confidence and working for the promotion of dialogue between the government and the social, political, and civilian components of the Burundian society.

Other African initiatives at mediation through the OAU can also be cited. In the case of Liberia, the OAU has been very supportive of the ECOWAS initiative to restore peace and stability in that country. The Secretary-General, in fact, personally attended the meeting whose proceedings culminated in the creation of ECOMOG. Similarly, the Secretary-General appointed professor Canaan Banana, former President of the Republic of Zimbabwe, as the OAU's special envoy for the Liberian crisis to assist ECOWAS to resolve the Liberian conflict. Of course the current developments in Liberia, precipitated by the intransigence on the side of the parties to the conflict, have caused great concern in the OAU and the international community at large. But while ECOMOG has been blamed in certain circles for not asserting itself in averting the current events, ECOMOG cannot simply change its mandate on its own. More fundamentally, ECOMOG is currently suffering from lack of financial resources and logistics, hence cannot even fulfil its mandate as it is today. ECOMOG has been let down

---

[12] For further treatment of the subject, see Christopher J. Bakwesegha, "Mission to the United States of America in Respect of the OAU Mechanism for Conflict Prevention, Management and Resolution". Back-to-Office Report (Confidential), Addis Ababa, November/December 1994, pp. 6–23, Conflict Management Division.

by the international community which has failed to provide the necessary financial resources and logistics, which it has often pledged in its declarations.

In the Congo, when a crisis arose between the government and opposition around the time when the OAU mechanism for conflict prevention, management and resolution was being adopted in Cairo, in July 1993, the OAU moved in quickly and played a central role in the mediation process for bringing normalcy to that country.

In like manner, when a crisis developed between the government of Gabon and some members of the opposition party, the OAU was immediately called upon by the President of that country to help in diffusing the crisis.

Furthermore, SADC played a leading and successful role in the Lesotho crisis of last year, as well as in the crisis that developed between the Frelimo government and Mr. Dhlakhama in Mozambique, just before the elections were held. More recently, and as a way of curbing mercenary activities in Africa, when the Islands of the Comoros were invaded by a group of French mercenaries, the OAU, through its Central Organ, acted speedily and expeditiously to prevent the conflict from degenerating into an uncontrollable situation.

Recently, due to the stalemate in the conflict situation in Burundi, Julius Nyerere, former President of Tanzania, was approached to launch a peace initiative for Burundi. This peace initiative which should be encouraged by Africa and the international community at large, is already underway. But while the Nyerere initiative should be emulated by other African statesmen like former presidents Canaan Banana (currently the OAU Secretary-General's special envoy for the Liberian crisis) of Zimbabwe, General Amadou Toumani Toure of Mali as well as former Secretaries-General of the OAU, sight should not be lost of the lesser known personalities like local chiefs and religious leaders who may be quite knowledgeable about the dynamics of a given conflict. One point that deserves special mention is that it does not matter how many statesmen Africa does have. As long as the parties to the conflict are not ready to negotiate with each other, peace in countries like Burundi, Liberia, Angola and Somalia will remain elusive. Indeed, the OAU as such does not impose peace. It only facilitates the peace process through mediation.

Turning now to the constraints facing the OAU with regards to the operationalization of the mechanism, OAU's experience since the adoption of that mechanism clearly reveals two fundamental short-comings. The first short-coming is OAU's inadequacy to fully operationalize the mechanism in the area of preventive diplomacy and peacemaking, due to lack of speedy exchange of information on conflict situations obtaining within member states, as well as shortage of resources.

Quite often, the Secretary-General has sought information on new developments relating to conflict situations within member states, only to discover that it is not possible to obtain such information as would enable him to take the necessary political action. Additionally, OAU has experienced serious difficulties and constraints in managing its missions in the field or consulting with

African leaders in the various national capitals and the civil society including the intellectuals at universities and research centres, about conflict situations obtaining in different parts of Africa, due to communication problems. Thus, delays in communication have impeded the decision-making process of the organization in the field of conflict management.

The second shortcoming that the General Secretariat has faced in operationalizing the mechanism lies in the area of peace-keeping. Once again the OAU's experience so far with the mechanism demonstrates the increasing reluctance on the side of the United Nations, especially the major powers, to get more involved in peace-keeping operations directly.

The OAU no doubt recognizes the fact that the bulk of activities within the realm of conflict management should be in the field of prevention, since it is cheaper to prevent than to put out the flames of war. At the same time, however, and given the realities obtaining in Africa, the organization believes that the time has come for Africa to be prepared to take some degree of responsibility in peace-keeping, in collaboration with her external friends and operational partners.

Moreover, since the adoption of the mechanism, ideas have been emerging both within and outside the OAU, on the place of peace-keeping as part of the work of the mechanism. Several significant developments have also taken place in respect of peace-keeping, including the establishment of an OAU military observer mission in Burundi (OMIB), all of which demonstrate that while the OAU should no doubt focus its work on the prevention of conflicts, exigencies of the time dictate that the organization cannot continue to underrate the importance of peace-keeping.

In addition, there have been several other initiatives of the OAU's external partners which include what is now known as the British and the French initiatives. The British proposal ranges from early warning to post-conflict peace-building in what is referred to as "wider peace-keeping support operations." The French proposal, on the other hand, deals with the setting up of an African intervention force, to be established at sub-regional level, but placed under the political direction of the OAU and/or UN.

The British government, in pursuit of its initiative, has in the recent past organized a series of seminars and workshops which came up with a number of conclusions on peace-keeping which for lack of space cannot be reproduced here.

It must, however, be emphasized that while those initiatives are not African, they are about Africa, and therefore member states have generally taken interest in them. The only unresolved issue is how these and other initiatives can be synchronized with the work of the mechanism so that Africa and her allies outside the continent can achieve greater coordination and avoid duplication of efforts. That is why at its sixty-second ordinary session, the OAU Council of Ministers, on the strength of the report submitted to it by the Secretary-General on those parallel initiatives adopted a number of measures on the way forward. Chief among those was the directive for the Secretariat to prepare for the holding of a meeting of the chiefs of staff of member states of the Central Organ to deal with the technical issues relating to peace-keeping by the OAU. At the time of inviting, the meeting had been scheduled to take place from 3 to 5 June 1996, in Addis Ababa, Ethiopia.

Going back to preventive diplomacy as a tool for restoring and maintaining peace, security and stability in Africa by the OAU, the process of preventive diplomacy and its attendant functions fall under the joint jurisdiction of the Secretary-General and the Central Organ. These two need to be fed with relevant information and data speedily and regularly through the active participation and cooperation of member states, sub-regional organizations, the UN and its specialized agencies, non-governmental organizations, the media, as well as academic centres and research institutions.

However, for preventive diplomacy to succeed, the process must be predicated on the early warning signals relating to crisis situations or incipient conflicts on the continent. During the thirty-first summit of the African heads of state and government, a decision was taken for the establishment of an early warning network based on a coordinating facility to be located in the Conflict Management Centre which is now being constructed at the OAU headquarters, and which will be equipped with a crisis management room.[13] It is here that a core of officers, both civilian and military, will monitor electronically on a 24-hour basis, crisis situations in Africa receiving, synthesizing and analyzing the relevant information and data on the basis of which recommendations will be made to the Secretary-General and the Central Organ on the options open for early political action.[14]

CONCLUSIONS AND POLICY RECOMMENDATION

It must be stressed that much as the OAU is doing its best to address conflict situations on the continent, a lot remains to be done. One should not lose sight of the obvious fact that conflicts are, by their nature, multi-layered and therefore call for multi-layered solutions. The thinking that conflicts must always be solved solely through government to government efforts is simply a mirage. Durable solutions to Africa's conflicts will have to come not only from the top in the form of governments, international organizations and agencies, but also from the grassroots and/or from local non-governmental organizations and associations. In other words, the civil society must be prepared to join hands

---

[13] The Construction of the Conflict Management Centre at the OAU Headquarters was completed at the end of June 1996. It is hoped that the Centre will become operational by the end of 1996 or beginning of 1997.

[14] The Appendix to this paper gives a Summary of the background and outcome of the Seminar hosted by the OAU in January 1996, on the prospects for establishing an Early Warning Network of the OAU Headquarters.

with the government concerned to address conflict situations in Africa more meaningfully.

Furthermore, it would appear that most situations of instability in Africa stem from violent protests against the way power is exercised, national resources are allocated and human rights issues are handled. It follows that good governance, justice and fair play are clearly the most fundamental ingredients for building and sustaining African capacities in conflict prevention. However, what constitutes the notion of good governance is an issue which not too many people in Africa, especially the policy makers and academics, seem to agree on. It is this and other related issues which Africans need to address with seriousness of purpose, and a sense of urgency.

# Appendix

## Seminar on the establishment within the OAU of an early warning system on conflict situations in Africa.

Cognizant of the crucial role an early warning network, matched with an early political action, can play in conflict situations, the OAU hosted from 15 to 18 January 1996, a seminar which examined the prospects for establishing such a network within the OAU.

The primary objective of the seminar was to provide an opportunity for exchange of information with a view to exploring the modalities for establishing within the OAU an early warning system on conflict situations in Africa. To this end, the seminar examined the ways in which the capacity of the mechanism in data collection, collation and dissemination could be strengthened to promote its function of anticipating and preventing conflicts. The seminar also explored ways and means of enhancing the capacity of the decision-making organs of the OAU mechanism in responding in a timely and decisive manner to crisis situations in Africa.

The second objective of the seminar was to identify actors within the OAU member states, sub-regional organizations, UN Secretariat and UN specialized agencies, the media, research centres and academic institutions as well as other institutions which could serve as focal points for the work of an early warning network.

The third objective was to examine infrastructural needs and logistical requirements for the putting in place of such a network.

The fourth objective was to establish a framework for determining the human resource requirements and training for the staff in early warning techniques.

The final objective of the seminar was to provide an opportunity for public awareness-building and information about the OAU mechanism, particularly its preventive responsibilities and its efforts towards establishing an early warning network.

Thus, the seminar drew participants from the member states of the OAU, sub-regional organizations, academic institutions and research centres, UN and its specialized agencies, NGOs, the media as well as eminent personalities from various parts of Africa.

More than 350 participants deliberated a wide spectrum of issues relating to the Seminar. At the end of their deliberations, the participants took note of the need to mobilize strategic constituencies and to build national platforms for preventive action, and recommended that peace missions to conflict areas should be organized on a regular basis by the OAU. The OAU is in the process of publishing a comprehensive record of the proceedings, conclusions and recommendations that emerged out of the seminar.

It should also be pointed out that for purposes of augmenting the mechanism particularly in the field of understanding the underlying causes of crisis situations in Africa, a data base which will store information and data relating to political and socio-economic conditions in Africa is now being set up. The data base will also be used to store information and data on:

(a) personalities who can serve as special envoys or special representatives of the Secretary-General in crisis areas;
(b) the OAU's involvement in election observing within member states;
(c) the effects of conflicts in Africa, i.e., refugee flows and internal human displacement, environmental degradation, and so on;
(d) major decisions of the Central Organ relating to its work;
(e) successful as well as unsuccessful stories on conflict resolution in Africa; and
(f) conflict profiles within member states.

# UN Peace-Keeping in Rwanda

*Astri Suhrke*

## INTRODUCTION

The history of UN peace-keeping in Rwanda is a history of failure. The main points are well known: The organization failed to read early signs that plans were being made to eliminate the Tutsi minority and enemies of the regime of Juvenal Habyarimana. When the plans became a reality in April 1994, the United Nations Security Council responded by withdrawing most of the peace-keeping force that in late 1993 had been deployed to help implement the Arusha peace accords. About a month later, the Security Council reversed itself, recognized an obligation to protect civilians—who by that time were being slaughtered at the rate of thousands a day—and authorised sending 5,500 peace-keepers into the mayhem. The peace-keeping force, known as UNAMIR II, did not start arriving in Rwanda until late July, by which time the killings were all but over.

The main reasons for this incoherent response also seem clear. Most fundamentally, they were rooted in a structural mismatch between institutions and interests in the contemporary state system. Revitalised by the end of the Cold War, the United Nations in the 1990s rapidly expanded its peace-keeping operations throughout the world. Rwanda was added to the list in October 1993. The framework for peace-keeping, however, was set by the distribution of power in the Security Council, which in form still reflected the world as it was half a century ago. Except for France, the major powers on the Council were basically uninterested in a small Central African country that was marginal to their economic or political concerns, and peripheral to international strategic rivalries. Through their power of veto and financial commitments, these states also controlled the peace-keeping or enforcement operations of the United Nations. Preoccupied with crises elsewhere, especially in Bosnia and Haiti, and haunted by the memories of Somalia, they decided not to engage in Rwanda until it was too late. The United States, which exercised a double veto over the UN's peace-keeping operations by virtue of being assessed 31 per cent of the costs, was at the time recasting its policy towards peace-keeping operations in a

This chapter draws on material presented in Early Warning and Conflict Management. Study 2 of the Joint Evaluation of Emergency Assistance to Rwanda by Howard Adelman and Astri Suhrke, with contributions by Bruce Jones. Copenhagen: 1996.

much more restrictive direction. Rwanda was effectively defined as an outside case that did not merit a commitment.

Since the late and hesitant response from the United Nations reflected the strategic marginality of Rwanda to the major powers, it lies near to ask whether greater involvement of the Organization of African Unity (OAU) and the regional powers could have made a difference. Counterfactual analysis must necessarily remain speculative, but it is instructive to review the record of regional and sub-regional involvement in the Rwanda conflict and draw out the implications for African participation in conflict management.

FROM INVASION TO ARUSHA

The regional history is one of both failures and successes. The 1994 disaster in Rwanda had its immediate roots in the events of 1 October 1990 when an armed refugee movement, the Tutsi-dominated Rwandese Patriotic Front (RPF), invaded Rwanda from southern Uganda. The invasion was itself the culmination of previous strife of a type frequently seen in Africa: victims or losers in a conflict seek refuge in a neighbouring country, which then becomes a base for invading the homeland.[1] In this case, members of Rwanda's Tutsi minority, who had been the principal victims of political violence in Rwanda after decolonization transferred political power to the majority Hutu community, fled to the surrounding countries, with large numbers settling in southern Uganda.[2] Repeated efforts by the refugees to return had been of no avail until a generation of Rwandans born in exile launched a new invasion in 1990. The objective was to permit full and free settlement in Rwanda—a demand consistently denied by President Habyarimana—and to force the regime to accept power sharing arrangements that would give the Tutsi significant political representation in the government. The attack was propitiously timed to take advantage of support from Uganda's President Museveni and a decline in the political and economic fortunes of the Habyarimana regime.[3]

The principal external parties to the conflict were regional states—with Zaire and Uganda lining up behind the government of Rwanda and the RPF respectively—and two European powers which were engaged by virtue of colonial ties (Belgium) and continuous aspirations to play a major role in Africa

---

[1] By now a commonly phenomenon, it is also known as "refugee warriors". See Zolberg, Aristide, Astri Suhrke and Sergio Aguayo, 1989, *Escape from Violence*, pp. 275–278. New York: Oxford University Press.

[2] Khiddu-Makubuya, E., 1994, "Voluntary Repatriation by Force. The case of Rwandan Refugees in Uganda", in H. Adelman and Sorensen (eds.), *African Refugees*, pp. 143–158. See also Watson, Catherine, 1991, *Exile from Rwanda. Background to an Invasion*. Washington DC: US Committee for Refugees.

[3] Newbury, Catherine, 1989, "Rwanda: Recent Debates Over Governance and Rural Development" in Goran Hyden and Michael Bratton (eds.), *Governance and Politics in Africa*, pp. 193–213. Boulder: Lynne Rienner.

(France). The Mitterand government supported the Habyarimana regime through special development funds and military training agreements of the kind normally given to French ex-colonies in Africa,[4] and marked its interests by sending a small number of troops to help the government when the RPF invaded. Given French concerns to keep francophone Africa as a sphere of influence; Paris viewed the RPF as particularly worrisome because of the movement's ties to anglophone Uganda. Formal denials notwithstanding, it was commonly known at the time and subsequently confirmed that Uganda served as a rear base for the RPF. The military leader of the RPF during most of the civil war, Major General Paul Kagame, was close to Ugandan President Yoweri Museveni, and many RPF soldiers came from posts in the Ugandan army (NRA) which they deserted, taking along guns, trucks and all, often with the tacit support of their commanding officers. For Museveni, supporting the RPF enabled him to repay the Rwandan refugee leadership, many of whom had fought by his side in the early days of his own rebellion. By 1990, there was also growing resentment among Ugandans against the refugees; were the RPF to achieve victory, many would presumably leave for Rwanda.

None of the large powers had been engaged in this part of the Great Lakes region during the Cold War, nor was the one remaining superpower afterwards. Even during the years of globalised superpower rivalry, the United States had no military presence and quite limited interest in this small Central African country. It is indicative that the CIA did not begin tracking the country situation systematically until after the RPF invasion in 1990.[5] Among top officials in Washington, only the Under-Secretary of State for Africa, Herman Cohen, took more than a passing interest in the civil war, in keeping with his general efforts to engage the Department in conflict resolution in Africa during his tenure. After he left office (1993), Washington's tendency to assign Rwanda to a French sphere of interest resurfaced.

The October 1990 invasion triggered an extraordinary diplomatic activity that demonstrated the vitality of international mediatory structures on several levels.[6] Just two weeks after the invasion, Tanzania called a regional meeting of the Heads of State of Rwanda, Uganda and Zaire to discuss the situation, and, fearing further refugee flows, remained actively involved and became host as well as "facilitator"for the subsequent peace talks. The OAU Secretariat was also active in recognition of the organization's principle that African states had a primary responsibility to address regional conflicts. Soon other levels were informed or engaged—the (informal) Economic Community of the Great Lakes Region, the European Union and more peripherally the UN. Also the governments of Belgium, France and the United States at various times helped to

---

[4] Prunier, Gerard, 1995, *The Rwandese Crisis (1959–1994): From cultural mythology to genocide.* London: C. Hurst.

[5] Interview, Washington DC, 22 March 1995.

[6] Jones, Bruce, 1995, Background report for Study II of the Joint Evaluation of Emergency Assistance to Rwanda. London.

move the process forward. The Belgian government became actively involved within days of the invasion, pushing forward a regional mediation process which achieved a first cease-fire within four months.[7]

The initial success of regional diplomacy was short-lived. A formal cease-fire signed at N'Sele, Zaire on 29 March 1991 lasted only to mid-April, when fighting resumed. The limits of regional diplomacy were further revealed when a second cease-fire broke down in early 1992. It required a push from France— supported by more limited but parallel diplomatic suasion by the US Under Secretary of State, Herman Cohen—to move the conflicting parties to the nego-tiation table.[8] Also the European Union, Canada, Switzerland, the Catholic Church and others counselled peace talks. The result was Arusha talks, launched in the summer of 1992 and concluding in a comprehensive settlement signed in August 1993.

The Arusha process brought together the RPF, the Habyarimana regime, and opposition parties which had grown up during the period of civil war. Supporting the negotiations were international organizations which had a stake or a role in Rwanda, including prominently the OAU and, more belatedly, also the UN, and the major donor countries. The Tanzanian government formally acted as a "facilitator", and undertook a sustained and skilful mediating effort that was critical in bringing about an agreement.

It required a decisive push on the battlefield, however, to finalise the agree-ment. In February 1993, the RPF launched a major offensive to break Habyari-mana's opposition to the power-sharing formula tentatively negotiated in Arusha. The offensive shocked Kigali and threw the government forces into disarray. Rebel troops fought to within 23 km of the capital, demonstrating the Front's military superiority. The offensive deepened the French engagement as Paris dispatched a small military reinforcement to stiffen the government side. In New York, the UN system responded to the disruption of the peace process as well: The Secretary-General sent a goodwill mission which helped bring the parties back to the negotiating table, and the Security Council approved a mili-tary observer mission to monitor the Uganda-Rwanda border. Designed to stop Ugandan supplies flowing to the RPF which had dug in northern Rwanda, the small mission (UNOMUR) was pitifully inadequate for the task, however.

As the negotiations neared completion, the role of the peace-keepers was extended. The Accords called for the deployment of a Neutral International Force to oversee the implementation of the agreement, the principal feature of which was the creation of a transitional government encompassing some ele-ments of the Habyarimana regime, the RPF, and various opposition parties that had grown up during the negotiation period. A new national army composed of units from both sides in the civil war was to be formed; the rest would be

---

[7] Braeckman, Colette, 1994, *Rwanda. Histoire d'un génocide*. Paris: Fayard.

[8] Jones, Bruce, 1995, "Intervention without Borders: Humanitarian Intervention in Rwanda", *Millennium: Journal of International Studies*, 24(2), pp. 225–249.

demobilised. Invoking Chapter VI of the UN Charter, the UN Security Council voted to deploy a UN Assistance Mission in Rwanda (UNAMIR) to oversee the installation of the transitional government and other parts of the peace agreement, in particular, to assist in disarming and demobilising the two armies.

FROM ARUSHA TO GENOCIDE

Yet the signing of a peace agreement in August 1993 and the deployment of UNAMIR two months later—i.e. the initial success of what may be characterized as preventive diplomacy[9]—set the stage for a new conflict. The Rwandan conflict was transformed from a simple civil war into a genocide with a resumed civil war attached. The escalation in casualties after April 1994 speaks for itself: from roughly 6,000 deaths during three years of civil war, the toll was estimated to roughly 800,000 deaths from April to mid-July 1994.

The genocide—as it was later recognized to be by the UN human rights institutions—was planned and to a large extent controlled by a tightly organized group of extremists from within the Habyarimana power structure: members of the ruling MRND party, leaders of the Presidential Guard, the *interahamwe* and *impuzamugambi* militias, and members of the hard-line political grouping, the *Comité pour le defense de la république* (CDR).[10] In the first days of the killings, this group massacred the Tutsi population of Kigali and wiped out the ranks of moderate politicians and civil society leaders, most of them Hutu. Over the next three months, unchecked by any international force, the extremists systematically slaughtered Tutsi populations across the country, killing hundreds of thousands of people before the RPF's victory on 17 July 1994 drove them into final retreat.

The essential motive for the genocide was to retain political power and all that went with it. Given the history and ethnic structure of Rwanda, the political contest over who would control the state machinery had developed along a deepening majority-minority divide. Members of the Hutu majority community which planned, organized, and directed the genocide stood to lose power as a result of the power-sharing arrangements negotiated in Arusha. Alternately, many feared that the RPF would use its legitimised entry into national politics and foothold in the new national army to engineer a coup. In either case, the Tutsi were perceived as the winners. The fear which this prospect generated among the Hutu population—and which took extreme forms among some of the power-holders and their followers—must be understood against the historical memory of Tutsi overlordship before and during the colonial period, and the practice of treating power transfer as a totalistic, zerosum game and a "winner-takes-all" attitude. As the civil war neared an end and power-sharing

---

[9] In Boutros Boutros-Ghali's *Agenda for Peace* (1992) preventive diplomacy includes in its purview efforts to contain conflicts which are underway and to prevent escalation within them.

[10] African Rights, *Rwanda: Death, Despair and Defiance*. London, rev. ed. 1995.

was on the horizon, Hutu extremist ideologues deliberately exploited this fear to whip up a frenzy of ethnic hatred. Just after the peace agreement was signed, Hutu fears were powerfully reinforced by events in neighbouring Burundi, where the ethnic structure also consisted of a Hutu majority and Tutsi minority. In October 1993, Burundi's first elected Hutu president was assassinated and tens of thousands of Hutu were killed in the ensuing violence in which the Tutsi army was implicated. The Hutu extremists in Rwanda portrayed the events as a warning of things to come in their own country, and gained ground.

Events in Burundi had a special impact since the Hutu would also lose control over Rwanda's army as a result of Arusha Accords. After the RPF demonstrated its military superiority in the February 1993 offensive, the government was eventually forced to accept a scheme that split positions in the joint command 50–50, not only at the high command level but all the way down to field level, and narrowly favoured the government in a 60–40 distribution of troops. Over 20,000 government troops would be demobilised, more than twice the figure for the RPF.[11]

For several months before the genocide was launched, information accumulated that would have allowed the main states involved, as well as the UN Secretariat, to anticipate a massive escalation in violence. Indeed, the UN Secretariat and the French, US and Belgian diplomatic missions in Rwanda received clear warnings to the effect that the closer the Arusha Accords came to being implemented, the more the extremists were prepared to unleash a death campaign against supporters of the Accords and the entire Tutsi minority community. Key African embassies in Kigali, including the Tanzanian one, and the OAU resident representative, were also well informed and reported frequently on the increasingly violent and organized resistance to Arusha Accords. However, the impact of the warning signals were diminished because the states that had taken on peace-keeping responsibility in Rwanda had very limited interests in the country, and the UN as a collective actor was unable to rise above the restraints set by the major powers in the Security Council. The African actors which arguably had more direct interests, were either operating in a partisan fashion (Uganda and Zaire), or constrained to play a limited diplomatic role (Tanzania and the OAU).

A closer examination of the diplomatic and military strategies formulated by the international community towards Rwanda helps to explain why this division of labour came about.

---

[11] This is based on the figures in the report of the UN Reconnaissance Mission to Rwanda in August 1993. If the higher figures sometimes cited of FAR having 30,000 men and RPF 15,000 are more accurate, the difference in demobilization requirements becomes even greater, i.e. about 24,000 on the government side and 9,000 for the RPF.

DIPLOMATIC STRATEGY: THE ARUSHA POLITICAL NEGOTIATIONS

The main objective at Arusha was to end a civil war and construct a post-war peace agreement in a situation short of total victory and absolute defeat. This required a formula for immediate power-sharing as well as agreement on a broad range of issues: the nature of the future political process, rules for demobilization and integration of the respective armies, and a system to facilitate the return of refugees and internally displaced persons. The closer the Arusha process came to end the war and to define the protocols that would structure future politics, the closer—most participants believed—they had come to achieve peace. In this calculus, the primary criterion for success was to obtain the signatures of both parties on a peace agreement. As it turned out, the historical dynamic worked in the opposite direction: the closer the Arusha agreement came to be realized, the more determined became the extremists to derail it by means of a coup and mass murder.

As the RPF and the domestic opposition drove home their demands on all key points, Habyarimana pulled back from the negotiating mode. He would not this "piece of paper", as he disparagingly referred to the Accords in November 1992. The Accords, then, did not rest on a new-found political consensus created by defeat, exhaustion or the emergence of new political forces but represented *une paix militaire* as André Guichaoua aptly has phrased it.[12] Of critical importance, Accords also left the losing side with access to the state apparatus in an interim period, and hence the means for obstructing the implementation of a political order that was decidedly unfavourable to its interests. To implement a peace agreement of this kind required a quick implementation process and a peace-keeping force with a robust mandate.

The need to neutralise the potential spoilers of the peace agreement was recognized by many of the Arusha negotiators and reflected in the Accords. Ambitious—in part also unrealistic—clauses called for almost immediate deployment of a powerful international peace-keeping force. With international presence and rapid installation of the transitional government, supporters of the agreement expected that the extremists could be controlled and contained. Delays in establishing a transitional government would increase the likelihood that the entire peace agreement would be derailed, the UN was told by several regional diplomats and the Rwandese parties to the agreement just weeks after it was signed.

---

[12] Communication with the authors 27 November 1995. For an excellent collection of documents and analysis of the Rwandan conflict, see André Guichaoua (ed.), 1995, *Les Crises Politiques au Burundi et au Rwanda, 1993–94*. Université des Sciences et Technologies de Lille.

MILITARY STRATEGY: THE UN AND THE OAU

The Tanzanian and OAU architects of the Arusha Accords had envisaged a Neutral International Force (NIF), as it was referred to in the Arusha texts, which could enhance security and facilitate the formation of the transitional government before the forces of opposition had time to consolidate. Reflecting this concern, the Arusha Accords stipulated the deployment of NIF within 37 days of the signing of the agreement. Moreover, the Accords envisaged a mandate that in important respects went beyond a classic Chapter VI peace-keeping operation of the UN, and beyond the mandate eventually given to UNAMIR. The Arusha Accords called for a neutral international force to "guarantee overall security of the country"(B(1)), which in the UN resolution authorisation UNAMIR (Res.846/1993) became "contribute to the security of the city of Kigali *inter alia* within a weapons-secure area established by the parties in and around the city"((3(a)). The Accords have two strong provisions for confiscating illegal arms, the UN resolution has none.

The sense of urgency that emanates from the Arusha Accords was lost in the UN Security Council's authorisation for a peace-keeping operation. Instead of quick deployment of an international force with teeth and a robust mandate, Rwanda got a small force, haltingly deployed and with a mandate that was not only conventional, but interpreted cautiously by the UN Secretariat when the Force Commander in the field wanted to stretch the terms.

It was not a foregone conclusion that the Neutral International Force (NIF) envisaged by the Accords would be a UN force. Since early 1993, OAU Secretary-General Salim A. Salim had pursued the idea of strengthening the small group of military observers fielded by African states in Rwanda through the OAU (NMOG). The RPF offensive and resultant cease-fire in March 1993 had expanded the buffer zone to be monitored. The OAU Secretariat felt that a rapid response was necessary to stabilize the cease-fire and pave the way for a larger international presence as the prospects for a full peace agreement drew near. The present NMOG of only 50 men could not effectively monitor even the smaller buffer zone, but OAU was unable to raise funds for a larger force.[13] Turning to the UN for assistance in March 1993, Salim twice pursued the matter in letters to the UN Secretary-General, personally presented the case to Security Council members and presented a detailed proposal to a special envoy of Boutros-Ghali who visited Addis Ababa. His goals were modest: the maximum option was for an OAU force of 500 men at an estimated cost of US$ 2.5 million per month. After preliminary discussions with the Security Council, the response of Boutros-Ghali was that the request for UN logistics and financing "could only be entertained if the operations were under UN command and

---

[13] By its own account, NMOG was much too small to carry out its mission. The head of field operations, the Nigerian Col. Ihekiré, told a UN good-will mission sent to Rwanda by the Secretary-General in early March 1993 that he needed at least 400 men to do the work effectively.

control". [14] This went against the OAU's wishes to develop a field presence so as to complement its mediatory efforts in Arusha, and demonstrate that African states indeed took an active part in solving African problems.

Finances were not the only issue. The larger question concerned the role of the respective organizations in an eventual peace-keeping force in Rwanda. Since late 1992 the French ambassador to the UN had started to lobby the Security Council for a post-war UN military presence in Rwanda. In early 1993— and especially when the RPF offensive in February pushed Rwandese government forces back—French efforts had become so insistent that it was "a standing joke in the Council", according to one ambassador present. From a French perspective, such a force would at best check the RPF's advance and provide a breathing space for the government both by positioning itself between the two belligerents and by monitoring the border between Uganda and Rwanda. At the same time, a UN force would be an answer to increasingly insistent demands from the RPF that French forces withdraw, as had been stipulated already in the 1991 N'Sele agreement. With a UN force in Rwanda and a French veto on UN peace-keeping operations in the Security Council, Paris could still exercise some influence after its own troops were gone.

The government of Rwanda, which had been elected to the Security Council, was generally ineffective, but on this issue vigorously supported France. The OAU was, with some reason, regarded as partisan towards the RPF and at any rate unable effectively to monitor or maintain the military status quo. By the same logic, and because France was promoting a UN force, the RPF wanted an OAU command.

Travelling to Dar-es-Salaam for a summit meeting on 5–7 March 1993, Salim nevertheless obtained approval from both the Rwandese parties to move ahead with an expanded OAU monitoring force. Two days later, the initiative was effectively upstaged in the UN Security Council. France introduced a resolution proposing a UN peace-keeping force for Rwanda, operating "in conjunction with" the OAU. (S/25400(1993)). Non-aligned members of the Security Council and some European states cautioned that French efforts might be viewed as an attempt by Paris to salvage its influence in Rwanda and warned against sidelining the OAU. While the language of the resolution subsequently was softened, the signals given to OAU became clearer as every effort by Salim to increase even the monitoring function of NMOG slightly, was rebuffed.[15] Boutros-Ghali sided with his own organization, despite formal deference to the

---

[14] Report of Meeting between H. E. Dr. Salim Ahmed Salim, Secretary-General, and Mr. James Jonah, UN Under Secretary-General for Political Affairs. OAU Headquarters, Addis Ababa, 25 May 1993, p. 2. See also Tekle, Amare, 1995, *The OAU and Conflict Prevention, Management and Resolution.* Report prepared fro Study II, Asmara.

[15] The US, Belgium, and the UK suggested to the UN Secretariat that they were ready to support the OAU on a bilateral basis. France was said not to be enthusiastic, making reference to the UN role in Rwanda. The OAU Secretariat, for its part, was sceptical. Earlier promises of bilateral assistance to NMOG and its predecessor MOT had either not been realized, or funds were tied to conditionality that prevented their disbursal. Report of Meeting, Addis Ababa 25 May 1993, op. cit.

importance of regional initiatives in conflict resolution. Apart from insisting on UN command and control, he added that any discussion of UN assistance would have to await the outcome of the Arusha talks. In the meantime, plans for a UN peace-keeping force went forward.[16]

In face of these discouraging messages, OAU abandoned efforts to play a significant role in the monitoring and implementation of the Arusha peace agreement. NIF was realized in the form of UNAMIR.

Deliberating on the strength, mandate and deployment schedule of UNAMIR, the UN Security Council and the Department of Peace-keeping Operations in the Secretariat (DPKO) settled for a small, interpositional force of the kind the UN was familiar with. UNAMIR was tailored it to an optimistic scenario of future developments in Rwanda . The signals coming in were mixed, and both the Security Council and the Secretariat highlighted the rosy parts. To a UN which collectively looked for relief from the mounting troubles facing the peace-keeping force in Somalia at the time, "Rwanda seemed like a winner", as the Force Commander, General Romeo Dallaire, later commented.[17]

Financial considerations worked in the same direction. Being assessed 31 per cent of the costs of UN peace-keeping, the United States insisted on a minimal force. Emphasising the bright aspects of the Rwandan situation, the cost-conscious US delegation in New York suggested in September that a token mission of some 500 men would suffice.[18] The French mission in New York recommended a small force of around 1,000 men, noting that the French contingent in Kigali was merely 600–700 men. In the end, the Security Council authorised a force of 2,548, which was clearly more than a token contingent and at that time considered quite acceptable by the Force Commander-designate,

---

[16] Letter to Salim A. Salim dated 1 April 1994. Boutros-Ghali did not mention that, on the very same day, he had effectively upstaged his OAU counterpart by ordering his top military advisor, General Maurice Baril, to travel to Rwanda and Uganda to prepare for a UN monitoring force in the border area. The Baril mission resulted in the establishment of the United Nations Observer Mission Uganda-Rwanda (UNOMUR), as approved by the Security Council on 22 June (Res. 846(1993)). NMOG for a while limped along and monitored the cease-fire within Rwanda, and—thanks to Salim's continuous efforts—increased its capacity slightly. It was later folded into UNAMIR, as was UNOMUR.

[17] Interview, Montreal, 23 February 1995.

[18] UNAMIR was authorised at the time of a Washington review of peace-keeping, which had started out in mid-1993 on the premise that UN peace-keeping was a valuable instrument of US foreign policy, but soon took a critical course. Announced in May 1994, Presidential Decision Directive 25 (PPD 25) held that the United States needed to apply stringent criteria of national interest before supporting UN peace-keeping operations, whether or not this involved US troops (National Security Council, The Clinton Administration's Policy on Reforming Multilateral Peace Operations, Washington: May 1994). The increased activities of UN peace-keeping after the end of the Cold War had dramatically increased the assessed US contributions, from a range of US$ 29–47 million in 1985–89, to a sizeable US$ 460.4 million in 1993, the latter figure representing an increase of 370 per cent from the previous year. Under a new procedure laid down by PPD 25, the costs of all Chapter VII operations plus those in which US troops were involved would be charged against the Pentagon's budget, which inclined the latter to oppose such operations. Rosner, Jeremy, 1995, *The New Tug-of-War: Congress, the Executive Branch and National Security*, pp. 65-91. Washington DC: The Carnegie Endowment.

although his preferred option had been almost twice that size. UNAMIR was estimated to cost about US\$ 10 million a month, a very modest amount compared to larger UN peace-keeping operations.[19]

Despite a speedy start,[20] the deployment of UNAMIR did not fully meet the schedule laid out by the Reconnaissance Mission or the Arusha Accords. The first UNAMIR battalion entered Kigali in late November, more than two months later than the admittedly unrealistic deadline for deployment specified in the Arusha texts. Putting together the rest of the mission also proved difficult. The force never received all the equipment authorised (including an armoured unit and helicopters).[21] UNAMIR's budget was subject to the standard, lengthy UN decision-making process and was not formally approved until 4 April 1994.[22] As a result, the mission was constrained by numerous shortcomings in personnel, equipment and disbursable funds (including petty cash), and even basics such as ammunition. Repeated field requests to New York to bring the Mission up to authorised strength were of no avail. UNAMIR had weak or no capacity in two areas that were significant for its operation. With only a small civilian police unit and no human rights cell, the mission had very limited ability to investigate violent incidents. The force also lacked an official

---

[19] At the very high end was the UNTAC operation in Cambodia which had an international staff of 22,000, including 16,000 blue helmets, whose cost was estimated to US\$ 60–70 million per month. United Nations Peace-keeping Operations. UN Department of Public Information, 1995.

[20] The Arusha Accords were signed on 4 August. The UN Reconnaissance Mission (DPKO/DPA/DHA) travelled in Rwanda during the last two weeks of August. Upon its return, it prepared its report, had it translated, and submitted it to the Security Council on 24 September. Authorisation for deployment was received on 5 October (S/Res. 872). General Dallaire arrived in Kigali with an advance party on 22 October.

[21] No country came up with an armoured unit with Armoured Personnel Carriers (APCs), as UNAMIR plans approved by the Security Council called for. As a result, the DPKO had to search for left-overs from other UN operations (and did scrounge 8 APCs from Mozambique); the rest had to be obtained through civilian contracts. Since the commercial market for APCs was limited, and UNAMIR's budget at any rate was not fully approved until 4 April 1994, the force never got its armoured unit. The 8 APCs assembled from the UN operation in Mozambique rapidly broke down, and UNAMIR had no repair facilities. A similar fate befell the small helicopter unit authorised by the Security Council. No country offered even half a helicopter squadron; a commercial contractor who eventually was found withdrew the equipment in April when violence broke out.

[22] The mission had a temporary budget until the end of 1993. The first formal budget proposal was released by the Secretariat (DAM) on 3 January 1994 (A/48/837), translated into 16 languages, passed to the Fifth Committee sub-committee dealing with budgets (Advisory Committee on Administrative and Budgetary Questions), which began consideration of the budget and released it on 17 March (A/48/828 Add. 1). Member states received requests for contributions on 18 April 1994. The process has since been speeded up. Previously the Secretary-General could spend no more than 10 million dollars per year without an approved budget from the General Assembly, an then only with approval of ACABQ. Now, the Secretariat can go straight to the ACABQ for a temporary budget of \$50 million once an operation is set up. Formal budgets are prepared for fiscal years rather than mandate periods (annual budgets for stable periods and 6-months budgets for less stable periods), which harmonize better with regular national and UN budget processes. See A/49/375 and A/48/945, and also Durch, William, *The Evolution of Peace-keeping*. New York: St. Martin's Press.

intelligence unit, a fact that was deplored by the Force Commander and led to some improvisation on the ground.

The stepmotherly treatment of UNAMIR reflected the overarching restraints of the nation-state system on the peace-keeping activity of the UN as a collective actor. Without critical support from Security Council members or other potential troop contributing countries (TCC), the Secretariat had virtually no capacity for outfitting a force. Thus, when no member state came up with the authorised armoured unit and helicopters, the DPKO had neither budgetary recourse nor ready suppliers of such equipment to compensate. The indifference of member states, in turn, reflected the strategic marginality of Rwanda to all but one of the major powers on the Security Council, and France—recognising the changing political landscape after Arusha—had positioned itself in a secondary role. The neutrality of a UN peace-keeping force, moreover, made it difficult for France to help out UNAMIR, as the French delegation was quick to point out.

With no political patron in the Security Council and no institutional-bureaucratic "safety net" to catch it, the case of Rwanda fell into a yawning crack of neglect. It remained so even when the situation clearly worsened in early 1994: the transitional government was not installed, civil violence mounted, and Kigali was "awash in illegal weapons", as a visiting Belgian Minister of Defense told the press in mid-March. In face of the non-implementation of the Arusha Accords, the only contingency planning made for UNAMIR in New York was to withdraw the entire force, thereby indicating the UN's chosen strategy in a future worse-case scenario.

Just as the terms of the peace agreement laid down some tracks for the post-Arusha period, so the strategy of mounting a barebones force in the interim period had consequences for the evolution of the conflict. UNAMIR had little ability to project power and deter violations of the Accords. Instead, and—as we shall see—particularly in some key decisions immediately preceding the genocide, UNAMIR signalled inaction and limited presence. Moreover, when the situation radically changed after 6 April the force had minimal capacity to respond. Lacking defensive equipment and being thinly spread out, UNAMIR units could not even move securely through the city and were stopped at road blocks manned by para-military thugs. Weakness on the ground, in turn, became a major argument for withdrawing the entire force once widespread violence erupted

CRISIS RESPONSE

The two weeks following the shooting down of the plane carrying President Habyarimana and associates on 6 April 1994 constituted a critical decision-making phase in the international response to the conflict. If there were any chances of reducing the scope of the genocide before it fully unfolded, this was the time. Recent analysis by a leading US scholar on Rwanda, Allison Des

Forges, suggests that the coup and simultaneous genocide was launched before the coup-makers were fully prepared, hence the uneven tempo of the killings during he first week. Not until mid-April was it decided to extend the killings to Butare and the rest of the southern region. The decision, according to Des Forges, was taken at the highest level by members of the "Crisis Committee" in Kigali, and an important one factor in their decision was the failure of the international community to respond forcefully to the initial killings in Kigali and other regions.[23] Divisions within the military, moreover, suggested that a more determined international response against the extremists would have found allies within. The strategy attempted by the UN Force Commander before April 6 and his retrospective analysis reflects a similar assessment: a forceful response at the outset would have been a warning to the extremists and—at best—stop them in their tracks.

Deployed as a barebones peace-keeping mission, and not strengthened despite signals of a worsening situation, UNAMIR had no capacity to respond forcefully. The weakness of the force—a mere 2,5 battalion for the whole country, of which one (the Ghanaian) was deployed outside the capital, plus some military observers—was graphically depicted by General Dallaire in a cable to DPKO on 8 April: his force was spread out and extremely short of ammunition, fuel and water. Without resupplies, it could only function in a limited and highly defensive manner. Resupply was, of course, a technical possibility. The Kigali airport was initially secure, and several UN members had the means to intervene decisively, as France, Belgium and also Italy showed by launching efficient airborne operations soon after April 6 to evacuate their expatriates. The immediate response of the UN, however—both as a state system and collectively in the form of the Secretariat—was to emphasise the security of expatriates and the UN peace-keepers and preparing to evacuate both. The signals given were thus clear: Rwanda was abandoned to its fate.

Until the middle of April, there were open divisions in the Security Council on the issue of UNAMIR's future. The non-aligned states, led by Nigeria, argued for strengthening UNAMIR, and on 13 April circulated a draft proposal to that effect. By then, however, it was too late and the option was not backed by offers to contribute. The draft resolution was not even tabled. The day before, the Belgian government had told the Secretary-General that, following the murder of the 10 Belgian peace-keepers in Kigali, the entire Belgian UNAMIR contingent would be withdrawn, The decision was communicated to the Security Council the next day. The decision deprived UNAMIR of its strongest unit, and put the rest of the force in a precarious position. The Secretary-General made the point bluntly in a letter to Security-Council members on 13 April. Belgian withdrawal will make it "extremely difficult for UNAMIR to carry out its task effectively... In these circumstances, I have asked

---

[23] Conversation with Allison Des Forges, June–July 1996. The argument is presented in more detail in Des Forges' forthcoming book on the genocide, to be published by Human Rights Watch (New York, Washington), 1996.

my Special Representative and the Force Commander to prepare plans for the withdrawal of UNAMIR".[24]

Having decided to withdraw its own contingent, the Belgian government lobbied hard to persuade the Security Council that conditions in Rwanda necessitated withdrawal of UNAMIR as a whole. The stance was widely seen as an attempt to legitimize its own withdrawal, but the Belgians were pushing on an open door.[25] They were strongly backed by the Americans;[26] the UK and France, though less vocal, also favoured withdrawal. No country came forward with troop contributions, and the Secretariat claimed later that informal canvassing at the time had produced negative results.[27]

The formal decision to withdraw was taken by the Security Council in the context of a choice between three options formulated by the Secretary-General. In reality, all but one option had already been ruled out in the informal and officially unrecorded consultations in the Council and its communications with the Secretariat, probably de facto almost a week earlier. In this situation, the language used by Boutros-Ghali when he presented the reinforcement option to

---

[24] Letter from the Secretary-General to the President of the Security Council, 13 April 1994. The letter was not well received by the Council, where some members saw it as an attempt by Boutros-Ghali to place the responsibility for UNAMIR withdrawal squarely on the shoulders of Belgium. In a letter to the Security Council the same day, the Belgians had publicly pointed to the "chaos in Rwanda". The Belgian government concluded that it was "obvious that under these circumstances the continuation of the UNAMIR operation has become pointless ... and it is imperative to suspend the activities of UNAMIR forces without delay."(S/1994/430). DPKO reinforced this interpretation by telling the Security Council (13 April) that with the Belgians about to leave, the Force Commandeer could no longer guarantee the security of the airport or that of even his own men. DPKO did not relay to the Council the more differentiated appreciation of the situation made by the Force Commander in Kigali.

[25] Invoking NATO solidarity as well, the Belgian Foreign Minister phoned his counterparts in Washington, London and Paris to plead for withdrawal. "Willy Claes panicked a bit", a Belgian official later commented. Outcries from the public and the press over brutal murders of the Belgian soldiers had placed enormous pressure on Belgian political leaders to withdraw, similar to that faced by the Americans in Somalia half a year earlier.

[26] The United States had been traumatised by the Somalia crisis, which had been imprinted on American TV-screens in the picture of a mob dragging the body of an American soldier through the streets of Mogadishu. Although no American soldiers were in UNAMIR, the experience had given peace-keeping a bad name in the United States. Washington apparently considered total withdrawal as soon as the Belgian peace-keepers were killed. When the Belgian decision was known, the US position in the Security Council progressively favoured withdrawal. In the informal consultations on 12 April, the American ambassador expressed serious doubts about the viability of UNAMIR in the circumstances, noting that it could not carry out its original mandate and might even be a de-stabilizing factor. The next day he suggested withdrawing, leaving only a skeletal force. On the 14th, the US claimed that the Security Council needed a resolution for orderly evacuation of the force; on the 15th there was no doubt: the US delegation expressed firm opposition to keep UNAMIR in place (Adelman and Suhrke 1996, pp. 90–91).

[27] Reports from the informal consultations in the Security Council make no mention of such canvassing. It should be noted, however, that even Nigeria, which circulated a draft resolution to strengthen UNAMIR, did not itself volunteer troops. Although a major military power in Africa, and a contributor to other peace-keeping operations, Nigeria claimed it lacked logistics to send reinforcements. However, Nigeria had military observers in UNAMIR and made no move to withdraw them.

the Security Council on 20 April seemed prohibitive. The situation in Rwanda could only be changed by "immediate and massive reinforcement of UNAMIR ... [which would] require several thousand additional troops and UNAMIR may have to be given enforcement powers under Chapter VII"(S/1994/470. par. 13). The alternative of complete withdrawal also seemed difficult. Given the "dimensions of the violence and mass killings over the last two weeks... the consequences of complete withdrawal, in terms of human lives lost, could be very severe indeed."(par 19). That left the middle alternative of reducing UNAMIR to about 270 military personnel. These would take on a diplomatic role by promoting a cease-fire and, when feasible, assist in the resumption of humanitarian relief. On 21 April the Security Council approved this option over the recorded doubt, but with the votes, of its non-aligned members (S/PV.3368, 1994).

By this time, the Security Council and the Secretariat had ample information by mid-April to the effect that the killings in Rwanda were both massive, and organized. As noted above, information suggesting genocidal massacres had been coming in for some time prior to April. After April 6, detailed information about mass killings was pooled in the DPKO's Situation Centre, and the UNAMIR Force Commander reported already on April 8 that "a very well planned, organized, deliberate and conducted campaign of terror" was under way. The Nigerian draft resolution that circulated in the Security Council on 13 April expressed shock over "the death of thousands of innocent civilians".[28] The decision to withdraw was thus taken with considerable knowledge of the likely consequences on the ground.

The impact of the Somali experience is again important as a cognitive filter that shaped the assessment of the situation and the attendant risks and costs. Viewing Rwanda in the Somali lens, the UN delegations to the Security Council, particularly the US and the UK and also senior officials in the Secretariat (DPKO) by this time perceived the situation as civil war combined with anarchic, or "mindless violence"(Res.912/1994), and took that to mean an all-or-nothing response: a forceful Chapter VII operation or withdrawal. What the decisions-makers did not see was the systematic killings of civilians, organized by a small but determined group of coup-makers and carried out by lightly armed thugs and civilians. To respond effectively to the latter situation need not necessarily require a massive intervention armed with a Chapter VII mandate, but a smaller force inserted to with a mandate to protect civilians in designated sites. A mandate of this kind was in fact later drawn up and given to UNAMIR II when political pressure mounted for the international community to "do something" to mitigate the killings of civilians, thousands of whom were murdered daily in April and May.

Evidently recognising that it was falling into a decision-making trap in early April, the Security Council commented critically on the failure of the Secretariat

---

[28] Cited in Adelman and Suhrke, p. 42.

to come up with options other than an all-or-nothing response. The Security Council wanted options to go beyond the classic framework of Chapter VI versus Chapter VII, or a Somalia-type engagement versus withdrawal, as the British ambassador said on 13 April.[29] But the Secretariat, labouring under enormous pressure of time and scarce resources, and lacking decisive leadership from the Secretary-General during the first week of the crisis, failed to innovate under stress.[30] Instead, standard concepts and procedures prevailed. The genocide was not distinguished from the civil war, and the latter over-determined the analysis. Options to reinforce UNAMIR were always put in terms of a classic enforcement operation with full Chapter VII mandate, suggesting intervention between the two armies, rather than maintaining or increasing troop strength to protect civilians. The Security Council, for its part, did not strike new directions on its own, and the political signals by the second week were clearly in direction of withdrawal, particularly from the United States.[31] This constrained the Secretariat further.

Withdrawal became a means to salvage a UN peace-keeping operation that had been tailored to a situation that had never really existed. But by largely absenting itself from the conflict in April the UN simultaneously lost leverage to influence its future course—on the ground and diplomatically. External conflict management essentially came to a halt. When the UN subsequently reversed itself by authorizing on 17 May reinforcement and reconstitution of UNAMIR into a Chap. VI force that would primarily protect civilians, re-entry proved slow, difficult and fundamentally too late. The point was fully understood by the UNAMIR officers who discussed options in the middle of the madness that was Kigali on 21 April. Reducing the force to 270 men, which the Security Council was about to decide, meant "we can do little", and "we will really not be able to come back", the Ghanaian Deputy Force Commander scribbled on a notepad.

CONCLUSIONS

Regional states played important roles during the first phases of the Rwanda conflict related to the invasion, the first civil war and the Arusha process. The regional contributions served both to promote peace and to fan the forces of war permitting—or even supporting—a militarisation of the conflict. By late

---

[29] The Secretariat came back on 14 April with two options. Both were premised on a cease-fire, an assumption that the Security Council found unrealistic. The logic apparently was to threaten withdrawal of the entire force unless the RPF and FAR agreed to a cease-fire. That threat would hardly persuade any of the parties to stop either the wars or the killings.

[30] During the first week of the crisis, the Secretary-General was travelling at a brisk pace in the former Soviet Union and Europe. Even when returning to New York, Boutros-Ghali did not take a high-profile position on Rwanda until late in April, in particular on 29 April, when he urged the Security Council to take "forceful action".

[31] Reports from the informal discussions (op. cit.) in the Security Council are revealing.

1993, however, the regional actors almost disappeared from the conflict management scene as the United Nations moved in.

In retrospect, the formation and deployment of the United Nations Assistance Mission in Rwanda, UNAMIR, represented a critical juncture in the evolution of the conflict. A more decisive and robust demonstration of international force at that time might have restrained the extremist forces directly, and at any rate sent signals to the effect that the international community was fully behind the peace accords. Whether that would have been sufficient to avert the course of events which followed cannot be known, but it clearly would have heightened the stakes and costs to those seeking to undermine the agreement, as the architects of the Arusha Accords, various diplomats in Kigali and the Force Commander argued at the time, and as retrospective analysis tends to confirm.

We have showed why the letter and spirit of the Arusha Accords were not followed by those who authorised and deployed the force. A combination of organizational competition, the demonstrated weakness of the OAU, and partisan political interests ensured that NIF was realized in the form of UNAMIR. In the process, the understanding of the significance of the international presence and of the extremist threat to Accords which had been evident at Arusha was partially lost. An organizational disjuncture, so to speak, opened up between the mediation and the implementation phase. It turned out to be a critical gap between a peace agreement that moved key players out of power, and a peace-keeping operation that had neither mandate nor capacity to tackle the potential spoilers.

The Rwanda case raises important questions concerning the appropriate working relationship between the UN and the OAU. OAU admittedly had limited experience in peace-keeping and had problems fielding even a small military observer group. It was wholly dependent upon the UN to provide logistics and finance. Yet it was effectively discouraged by the UN and key Security Council members from taking a larger role. This is particularly ironic given the demonstrated inefficiency of the UN to deploy and develop the peace-keeping operation it had so aggressively sought.[32] When the crisis later erupted, on 6 April 1994, it was the European battalion of UNAMIR that withdrew and crippled the future options of the force; the African battalion stayed. The political instinct among the veto-wielding members of the Security Council was to abandon the mission. Prima facie, there is no reason to think that the OAU would have performed worse.

---

[32] The other Rwandese operation mounted by the UN was UNOMUR, designed to monitor the supplies going to the RPF across the Rwanda–Uganda border. Also UNOMUR had a checkered efficiency record. Established by a UN resolution in June 1993, UNOMUR had only 81 military observers and lacked equipment for aerial surveillance of the 150 km long border between Rwanda and Uganda. The Security Council evidently made cost a primary consideration when deciding that UNOMUR would focus its control and verification activities on main roads and tracks (Res. 846(1993)). American military experts regarded the force as largely symbolic.

# The Lessons from Peace-Keeping Operations

*Henry Kwami Anyidoho*

## INTRODUCTION

The complexities of peace-keeping operations in the immediate past and the dilemma in which peace-keepers continuously find themselves have made it imperative for scholars and practitioners to dedicate some time for a study of the situation with a view to finding better ways of handling conflicts all over the world and particularly in Africa, the continent that has seen the most of such conflicts. United Nations Operations in Somalia (UNOSOM) were almost a failed mission. The United Nations Angola Verification Mission (UNAVEM) which was established in January 1989 degenerated into a quagmire when UNITA and Angola Government forces resumed fighting. It was not until November 1994, when the Lusaka Accord was signed between the two parties, that UNAVEM operations regained momentum and even then at a very slow pace. In Rwanda, the United Nations Assistance Mission was reduced to a ridiculously low level at the outbreak of the civil war in April 1994, only to be expanded when the situation degenerated into genocide. In the case of Liberia, the ECOWAS Monitoring Group (ECOMOG) was launched into Liberia by the West African States without even the tacit approval of the UN. Nor was any proper reconnaissance carried out by the military team. Even current operational maps on Liberia were not available. Nevertheless the ECOWAS Heads of State could not look at Liberian civil war as a distant misery when the UN was slow in initiating the required action in that country. After all, the Organisation of American States (OAS) intervened and restored stability to the Dominican Republic in 1965.[1] The most recent UN peace-keeping operations in Africa have certainly had some setbacks. As these peace operations continue to have a chequered history, many nations in Africa are embedded in protracted conflicts that may eventually necessitate the employment of UN peace-keeping forces. Sierra Leone and Burundi already have representatives of the UN Secretary-General. Cameroon and Nigeria resumed fighting over the Bakassi Peninsula on Saturday, 3 February 1996. Sudan has been engulfed in a civil war for decades and settlement prospects are remote. Most of Africa seems numb with the sufferings of its people. Sensitivity is disappearing into the distance. What is

---

[1] Cilliers, Jakkie and Greg Mills, *Peace-keeping in Africa*, p. 132.

wrong? Cruelty and war have continued to leap a harvest of hatred and mistrust on the continent. Certainly the African case needs a careful analysis if future operations are to attain the set goals. The discussions that follow will also analyse the role of the international community in regard to peace and security and how this role has been applied in Africa and other geographical areas of the world.

## RESPONSIBILITY OF THE UNITED NATIONS

Article 24 of the United Nations Charter clearly states that the primary responsibility for maintenance of international peace and security is that of the Security Council. This article stems from the fact that the international community, having seen two world wars, is not prepared to descend again to that depth of human loss, genocide and holocaust. It is in conformity with its role that the UN has tried over the years of its existence to intervene in all areas of conflict that clearly go beyond the solution of the parties involved. The aim is to save lives. Do recent events in Africa and elsewhere prove that lives have been saved? Was the UN able to prevent genocide in Rwanda or has it been able to prevent the carnage in the former Yugoslavia? Is the international community only wringing its hands over the world's conflicts? Can there be better approaches that will help eliminate some of the bottlenecks that have continued to frustrate peace-keeping operations? This last question points to the reason why lessons learned from Africa's past and current operations will be most useful.

## AFRICA'S HISTORY

In order to understand Africa's lingering conflicts, there is the need to look at its history. Following the Berlin Conference of 1884, at which the European powers carved the African continent among themselves, boundaries were drawn through homogeneous states, ethnic and tribal groupings that had lived together for years. In the process, different cultural values and foreign languages were imposed on Africans. After many years of colonial domination, peoples that were once brothers began to look at each other differently. Western education made them literate in the various European languages to the extent that some languages in Africa today are not even written though they are spoken. Language is the basic way of communicating. Anyone who succeeds in taking your culture and language from you succeeds in enslaving you. That was exactly what colonialism did. This unfortunate history was to account for some of the problems associated with conflicts in Africa today. However, whilst colonial rule persisted, there was relative peace among African nations because in most cases, force was used to suppress any anti-colonial sentiments. European authority was obeyed without question until the desire for self-rule began.

Following Ghana's independence in March 1957 as the first black African state south of the Sahara to free itself from colonial rule, the wind of decolonization swept across the whole of the African continent. Liberation struggles were therefore intensified everywhere, resulting in the independence of most African nations from colonial domination. The last to join the group of independent states was South Africa, which finally got rid of apartheid in 1994. The early days of decolonisation witnessed inter-state African conflicts as the newly independent nations struggled to assert their authority of statehood. That was also the peak of superpower struggle. The era of the Cold War therefore kept such conflicts under control as the major powers struggled to maintain their spheres of influence in various parts of Africa. The end of the Cold War, however, created a new form of conflicts in Africa—so-called intra-state conflicts. They arise as a result of various ethnic, tribal and religious groups struggling for identity and authority. Paradoxically, the origin of former head of state of Zambia is now being questioned. Kenneth Kaunda however ruled Zambia for over twenty years. We now hear of warlords, religious fundamentalism and ethnic affiliations. Africa has therefore continued to witness interstate and intra-state conflicts that have involved the deployment of UN, OAU and sub-regional peace-keeping forces.

COMMENCEMENT ON PEACE-KEEPING OPERATIONS IN AFRICA

The UN Operations in the Congo (ONUC), later Zaire, were the largest third party peace keeping effort ever to be authorised by any international organisation in the sixties. During its four years of operation from 1960 to 1964, a total of 93,000 men from thirty-five countries served in ONUC. The operation took a death toll of 126 men and an equal number of wounded and at a total cost of US$ 411 million.[2] To deploy peace-keepers in a country the size of Western Europe and to be able to support them administratively and logistically was no mean task.

The case of the Congo started with the emergence of nationalist movements towards independence. The resistance on the part of Belgium to realising that time was due for colonisation to be terminated in Africa exacerbated the internal conflicts. The fact that Belgium did not anticipate leaving the Congo and that colonial power's unwillingness to grant self-rule, led her to fail to prepare the Congolese people to administer their own country. In the public sector and in the security forces, the Belgians dominated the hierarchy. For example, at the time of independence, the Force Public (later to change its name to Armée Nationale Congolaise (ANC) had a strength of approximately 28,000 men who were officered by 1,100 Europeans, of whom the great majority were Belgians. No Congolese held a rank higher than that of a warrant officer.[3] This unfair

---

[2] Rikhye, Indar Jit, Michael Harbottle and Bjørn Egge, *The Thin Blue Line*, p. 71.
[3] Ibid.

treatment by colonial powers were also to account for subsequent disorders in other parts of Africa. Naturally, mutiny and disorders spread throughout the country soon after independence and the Congolese Government had to cable the UN Secretary-General on 12 July 1960 for the urgent dispatch of military assistance to protect the national territory of the Congo against the Belgians. Indeed, it was Prime Minister Lumumba who himself appealed to the United Nations for assistance in restoring law and order to a situation largely brought about through the breakdown of discipline within the ANC.[4]

It must be noted that the Congolese authorities requested assistance from the United Nations. This is an important ingredient of UN peace-keeping operations. In order to ensure full co-operation a request must be made by the country in distress to the UN. The absence of this factor derailed some of the recent peace-keeping operations in Africa even though humanitarian considerations sometimes drove the world body to take certain decisions, the UN operations in Somalia (UNOSOM) being a typical example of UN going in without the consent of the parties. When the request was made by the Congo, the initial estimate of troops indicated that about 3,000 men could restore law and order in a reasonably short time but this expectation faded in the face of continued violence and political conflict throughout the Congo. Tunisian and Ghanaian troops were the first to arrive in the Congo only forty-eight hours after the resolution establishing ONUC had been approved by the Security Council.[5] What was significant here was the quick response of African countries to a sister country in distress. The need for an OAU peace-keeping force was then identified. President Nkrumah of Ghana, while proposing the proclamation of a cease-fire, also suggested that the OAU should maintain a peace-keeping force when he became disappointed with the UN operations in the Congo.[6]

After the Congo crisis, the struggle for the liberation of the rest of Africa continued with its attendant problems. In the course of pursuing freedom, more than one liberation movement emerged in some of the colonial territories, creating fertile grounds for confusion and distrust after eventual attainment of independence. For example, in January 1975 Portugal had to sign an agreement with three Angolan liberation groups for elections to be held before independence on 11 November of that year. Fighting soon flared up between the three groups.[7] As it eventually transpired, Angola eventually had to receive a UN peace-keeping mission. In like manner, Alfonso Dhlakama's fight against President Joaquim Chissano's government in Mozambique took its roots from the colonial past. Mozambique subsequently had a UN mission established on its territory. In all these cases, the UN Security Council sanctioned the operations.

---

[4] Ibid p. 73.

[5] Ibid p. 76.

[6] OAU Information Publication, *Resolving Conflicts in Africa—Implementation Options*, p. 36.

[7] Hume, Cameron, *Ending Mozambique's War*, p. 6.

The timely passing of Security Council Resolutions and the quick response of member nations are important preconditions for successful Peace-Keeping Operations. UN Security Council resolutions give the mandate of the mission, whereas member states support the mission by providing troops and the necessary administrative and logistics support. A close study of some of the Council's resolutions will reveal some difficulties that practitioners in the field have had to contend with.

SECURITY COUNCIL RESOLUTIONS

It is resolutions of the Security Council that normally give birth to peace-keeping operations. These resolutions are constructed in a particular order and are worded or phrased in such a manner that a short background to the conflict is stated and subsequent efforts made by the UN and other mediating bodies are summarised, then the concern of the Council is expressed as to the deteriorating situation for which a decision is to be made. When I was under pressure in Rwanda during the civil war of 1994, the catch-words I always looked for were "decides that". I had very little time to go through all the beautiful words in the preamble so I looked out all the time for the decision of the Council. That was what I needed to work with.

Security Council resolutions are wordy and in certain cases not exactly to the point. For example, one of the clauses embodied in the Council's Resolution 918 of 17 May 1994, which expanded our mission in Rwanda (United Nations Assistance Mission for Rwanda, UNAMIR), stated its objective as being: "To protect civilians at risk". The UN force level was established at 5,500. There was no way that this force could protect all civilians at risk in Rwanda at a time when sporadic killings were common place and the force had to deal with an overwhelming number of internally displaced people while trying to restore a modicum of confidence and peace all over Rwanda—another former territory of Belgium like the Congo. From its very onset that particular mission, UNAMIR, had clauses in its mandate that could not be executed with the number of troops available. Resolution 872 of 5 October 1993, which established the mission, called for 2,548 troops made up of essentially three contingents provided by Bangladesh, Belgium and Ghana. The Ghanaian contingent, for example, was to be deployed in the entire demilitarised zone between the Rwandese Government forces and the Rwandese Patriotic Army. How could one battalion of 800 men cover a space of several kilometres in length and breadth? All we did was to give the sub-units areas of responsibility which they patrolled from time to time with the military observers in support. In like manner, the Bangladeshi and Belgian battalions of about 500 each could not effectively maintain security in Kigali, a city that was designated by the UN as a "Weapons Secured Area".

The UN operations in Somalia suffered a similar fate. It was ironic and ill-omened that the Unified Task Force (UNITAF), a multinational force which was set up under the direction of the Security Council with great power and a limited mandate, handed over operational responsibility to UNOSOM II, which had far less power and a much broader mandate. It is a known fact that UNITAF, with all its resources, operated only in part of Southern Somalia while UNOSOM II with much more limited resources was expected to cover the entire country. What the Security Council should have done in that case was to have revised its objectives set up in the mandate for UNOSOM II.[8] Instead, the force was left to interpret and wade its way through all the uncertainties which eventually made the mission impossible with only very minimal success. On the other hand, the United Nations Transition Assistance Group in Namibia (UNTAG) was a successful mission because of its clear and practicable mandate, in conjunction with the consent and co-operation of the parties.[9]

It cannot be over-stressed that all successful UN operations depend on clear and unambiguous mandates that equally provide the resources to support the mission. If things go in the right order, some reconnaissance and detailed planning will have been carried out prior to the passing of the Security Council resolution. Closely linked with the mandate is also the authority given to the various individuals that command the hierarchy of UN missions. The organisational structure as pertains in most UN peace-keeping missions seems unfair to those placed in authority to ensure that such missions are accomplished. The various levels of control are examined in the succeeding paragraphs.

## ADMINISTRATIVE CONTROL

The key appointment holders are often the Special Representative of the Secretary-General (SRSG), the Force Commander (FC) and the Chief Administrative Officer (CAO). Whilst the SRSG is the head of the mission, the Force Commander commands the many officers and men that form the contingents. These contingents are those that actually execute the various tasks that are deduced from the Mandate. Ironically, neither the SRSG nor the FC has the control over the finances of the mission. It is the CAO that controls the "purse". This state of affairs renders the two men at the top powerless. Instant decisions concerning minor expenditures that could go a long way to boost the morale of troops or enhance their operational efficiency cannot be effected because of long and bureaucratic procedures in the UN system.

For example, in Rwanda, when the civil war broke out, the Force Commander needed to get some food and water for the troops immediately. These are basic necessities of life but his staff could not make any procurement from the nearest point of availability. The CAO was relocated in Nairobi and could not have the same sense of urgency as the Force Commander. To worsen the

---

[8] From a Department of Peace-keeping Operations Report of the Seminar on Lessons learned from UN Operations in Somalia.

[9] The Blue Helmets, *A Review of UN Peace-Keeping*, p. xvii.

situation, the CAO was in an acting capacity and therefore did not approach his assignment with the required confidence. A nasty and heart-breaking incident took place when vehicles that were transporting water for our troops were believed to have been involved in an accident somewhere between Kampala, capital of Uganda and Mbarara, a southern city of Uganda. Meanwhile, water was available in Kabale also a southern city of Uganda which lies only a few kilometres from the Rwandan border. The FC had no petty cash or expendable imprest to buy even water. Giving a command of thousands of men to a commander without the means with which to look after them is something a professional military officer is not used to. The troops' welfare is the commander's foremost priority if his orders are to be executed to the full.

Another sore point in the administration is staffing. In selecting the various categories of the civilian staff that man and provide the support services to the mission, great care must be exercised to ensure that the individuals chosen are qualified for the jobs assigned to them. UNAMIR and UNOSOM were administered by makeshift staff. For example, a staff member who was responsible for building management in Rwanda before the civil war became a procurement officer when he was re-deployed to Nairobi. It was not surprising that at times the mission had 40 days' reserve of water with only a day's reserve ration.


OPERATIONAL CONTROL

Whilst administrative control plagues almost all UN missions, operational control is another area of concern. The commander on the ground analyses the UN mandate and decides which tasks he must give to his subordinate commanders in his operational orders. As a rule, he must contact New York—Department of Peace Keeping Operations (DPKO) to clear his pending operations before arriving at the final decision. He may or may not receive the approval for an operation he considers very crucial to the attainment of his mission. For example, a commander may decide to conduct a cordon and search in a part of a peace-keeping area which is designated a "Weapons Secured Area" as was the case of Kigali before the civil war of April 1994. The approval of such an operation may not be granted by the DPKO in New York particularly because of the failures of such operations in Somalia.

Another area of operational difficulty is the control of home governments over their contingents in the mission area. Normally, all contingents have radio, telex, facsimile and telephone communication with their home governments. When emergencies develop, some commanders tend to look back before carrying out the Force Commander's orders. The subordinate commanders do so when they anticipate that they are likely to take casualties in a pending operation. Before I delivered my orders to the battalion commanders for the cordon and search operations of KIBEHO internally displaced peoples camps in South Western Rwanda during December of 1994, I had to ask my "Orders Group" whether any of them had an objection to participating in the pending operations. Fortunately the answer was spontaneous "No objection, we are with you". I then went ahead with the orders. I was very pleased with the co-operation of those diligent commanding officers.

That cordon and search was of course one of the most significant achievements of UNAMIR during its immediate post-civil war mandate. It was an operation that DPKO also sanctioned. Had we not received the approval, we could have missed an opportunity of demonstrating to the Rwandese government that we were professional soldiers. For that operation to succeed, UNAMIR gathered a lot of information and carried out a detailed reconnaissance. These were possible because our troops were then deployed in the camps. Had it not been so, lack of information about the area would have been a major handicap.

## INTELLIGENCE/INFORMATION

In a purely military sense, commanders require intelligence upon which operational plans are made. The UN resists using the phrase intelligence gathering since it connotes spying on its member states. Whichever terminology is used, there is the need to have information upon which plans could be formulated and executed. The absence of an intelligence or information gathering system within UN missions created a gap that was filled in certain cases by unreliable and non-co-ordinated news from NGOs and the news media. It is gratifying to know that at least a Situation Room has now been created within the DPKO at UN headquarters in New York. From that level, information collection, collation and dissemination should go down to the missions in the field. Funds will have to be set aside for this purpose. Hitherto Military Observers and individual commanders at the battalion level have been spending their own moneys in getting information from the communities in which they operate.

Apart from operational control and lack of intelligence gathering capability, some of the difficulties take their root from fragile logistics support for individual battalions or for the mission as a whole.

## LOGISTICS PROBLEMS

The most nagging of all the difficulties that a field commander faces on peace-keeping operations is that of logistics. Military history shows that it is upon sound logistics that any operation depends for success. For this reason, it is the policy of the DPKO that all contingents deployed with UN missions should be self-sustaining for the first sixty days. Experience, however, shows that most of the contingents from third world countries hardly ever arrive in any mission with that degree of self support. The reasons are not difficult to establish. Most of the developing countries have very fragile economies. They can hardly look after their own domestic problems let alone stock-piling stores and equipment for peace-keeping operations. Contingents from such countries therefore often arrive in the mission area with only personal gear, weapons and first-line ammunition. In some cases they could manage a little office equipment, cooking pots, and field cookers. However, the major and expensive items such as vehicles, communication equipment, night vision aids, armoured personnel carriers, plants and engineering equipment are above the economic means of these contingents. They have the men trained professionally and are always ready to be launched into peace-keeping operations anywhere in the world but the logistics support is lacking. Specifically, because of the atrocities committed against American servicemen in Somalia, the United States and some Western European nations have been unwilling to participate actively in peace-keeping operations in Africa (even though they are willing to go to Bosnia where similar atrocities were committed against peace-keepers). That was the reason a typical developing country such as Bangladesh offered to provide a logistics battalion to UNAMIR and it was virtually impossible to take up the offer.

Under such circumstances, the UN contacts its members in the developed world to provide the much needed logistics support for the contingents on deployment. Experience has shown that even though a response may be received from some of the developed countries to support these contingents, the help is either slow in arriving or sometimes much needed stores and equipment may not arrive in the mission area at all. For example, Security Council Resolution 918 of 17 May 1994 expanded the UN Mission in Rwandan from 270 to 5,500 all ranks. This was a period when the Rwandan civil war was at its peak and immediate deployment of troops was crucial to stop the genocide. The Secretary-General, Dr. Boutros Boutros-Ghali, appealed to all the UN members with a special message to the African governments to provide troops immediately for the expanded force level under the mandate. The response from African heads of state was immediate for availability of troops but with the limitation on logistics support. The United Nations Secretary-General then turned to the Western World to support the African contingents. Some countries accepted to provide the items but in reality what did we see in Rwanda? The African contingents were hurriedly flown to Kigali for immediate deployment but they were to operate on a shoestring for a very long time under very trying conditions. By the time the American Armoured Personnel Carriers (APCs) arrived in Rwanda, there was really no need for them. There is a popular saying among those of us from traditional peace-keeping countries that with United Nations operations the equipment and stores arrive when the mission is winding-up.

The case of Rwanda was peculiar. That mission was given no money to purchase any major item of equipment. We were to receive almost everything from Cambodia or Somalia. Whilst troops were deployed to guard a large number of vehicles in Cambodia against theft, we were in dire need of just a limited number of the same type of patrol vehicles and troop carriers. UNAMIR had no transport aircraft of its own. We had to depend on the United Nations Operations in Somalia (UNOSOM) to carry out medical evacuation and re-supply for over eighteen months of the mission's existence. UNAMIR saw no prefabricated accommodation in a country in which the authorities continuously took back buildings that had been repaired by the UN. So bad was the logistics support for that mission (UNAMIR) that we felt we were abandoned.

The case in point here is that whilst logistics items are expensive and therefore difficult to come by, the United Nations lacks the right organization and expertise in its distribution system. Some equipment could be in excess on one mission whereas others may not have even a limited number to keep their assignments on course. These lapses in logistics support perhaps more than any other factor account for the failures recorded on most United Nations Missions. Why did I come to that conclusion? I did so because early deployment of troops depends so much on how quickly these stores and equipment are made available. Lack of them create delays and delays in turn result in loss of lives. In the case of Rwanda it was not only loss of lives but the world witnessed a genocide. The UN Mission for the Referendum in the Western Sahara (MINURSO), established in September 1991, never had its logistics battalion deployed. The small observer group had to improvise its own support system in the Sahara desert. In like manner the UN Peace-Keeping Mission to Nicaragua from 1989 to 1992 also lacked effective logistics support.[10] The UN Observer Mission in Uganda-Rwanda (UNOMUR) had no capability for monitoring the common border. For future United Nations Missions to succeed, the problem of logistics must be addressed. The on-going debate on the pre-positioning of logistics items for immediate distribution to contingents from Africa must be vigorously pursued. In the same vein, the OAU's own effort in identifying and ensuring the sub-regional stand-by forces must not become a forgotten dream. Instead the idea must of necessity be a reality.

FINANCIAL SUPPORT

Closely linked with logistics support is the willingness of the member states of the UN to honour their obligations financially. It is obvious that funds continue to dry up and there is donor-fatigue in support of peace-keeping operations. There is, however, no other way these operations could be supported other than from contributions of all members of the UN since by itself the UN is not a sovereign state.

---

10 Cilliers, Jakkie and Greg Mills, *Peace-keeping in Africa*, p. 121.

## TRAINING

Even though UN peace-keeping operations have been on-going for years and have indeed multiplied several fold, more and more new nations are becoming troop contributors. There are therefore different standards of performance and attitude in the same mission area. The desirable thing is for all contingents to have a standard knowledge in the role of the peace-keeper. It is even more crucial for the staff officers that man the mission headquarters including the Operations Room. Regional and sub-regional training is essential for the success of future operations. Programmes for training should include the essential principles such as mutual respect, impartiality, credibility, transparency, military/civil co-operation, flexibility, use of minimum force etc. The appropriate standing operating procedures which are available from the UN could be adapted to suit every situation.

## PSYCHOLOGICAL AND CIVIL AFFAIRS

Analysis of the failure of past operations clearly indicates the absence of psychologists and civil affairs experts. Trained staff in these disciplines will be invaluable.

## THE MEDIA

In spite of many complaints and accusations against the press, the news media play a very important role in awakening the conscience of the international community to draw its attention to needy peoples and exposes the plight of peace-keepers.

## THE OAU

As the United Nations grapples with its organizational and response problems, the Organisation of African Unity (OAU), an organisation with Byzantine complexity, has its own inadequacies that have become so obvious that the role of the organization in the maintenance of peace and security on the continent has been criticised by Africans and the world at large. As much as the OAU is adequately covered in a separate chapter, the lessons learned on recent United Nations peace-keeping operations will be incomplete if the OAU is not discussed here. The Organization of African Unity played a very useful role in the early days of peace efforts in Rwanda and in Somalia. For example, the OAU sent its own observers to Rwanda long before the United Nations Mission was established in that country but when the civil war broke out in April 1994, the organization did not appear equally active in the subsequent events. Whilst some of the African countries willingly contributed troops, political will was lacking. As the Secretary-General of the OAU and his immediate staff struggled to generate support for the Kigali government, spontaneous support did not come from the African governments in the political process. Tanzanian's support for the peace process in Rwanda before the civil war was strong and such support was equally needed from all the immediate neighbours during and after the civil war.


NEIGHBOURS

Rwanda's immediate neighbours, Tanzania and Zaire received large numbers of refugees on their territories and were humane enough to keep them but the political process through which Rwanda could be assisted to come out of the quagmire was completely ignored. Even when a meeting of the Heads of State of the region was organized in January 1995 in Nairobi, Kenya, specifically to discuss the situation in Rwanda with a view to finding solutions to the problem, the President of Zaire was absent. Yet it was Zaire that had the highest number of refugees on her territory. That summit really did not record any success. If the heads of states that are contiguous to a country that is in deep conflict are unable to meet at a conference table, how can they help in such a situation and in turn return peace to their sub-region? Southern African nations, notably South Africa and Zimbabwe, demonstrated this resolve in the Lesotho uprising in 1995. It must be emphasised that even though UN peace-keeping troops might be deployed into a conflict zone, in the final analysis it is politics that will have to take its course.


SALE AND SMUGGLING OF WEAPONS AND AMMUNITION

Another issue worthy of discussion is the sale and smuggling of weapons and ammunition through neighbouring states to the one in conflict. In a land-locked country in which airports are closed, the re-supply of weapons can only come over land. Africa's many conflicts witnessed a continuous flow of weapons and ammunition which in turn prolonged such conflicts. For example, after Mozambique achieved independence in 1975, she became tragically trapped in the futile contest between the exiled African National Congress (ANC) and the South African Defence Force. By the mid-1980s, sustained South African destabilization efforts in Mozambique had slipped into a brutal civil war that thrived on external involvement and on the many inadequacies of its incumbent government.[11] Who have been responsible for the production and sale of the variety of weapons, ammunition and the overwhelming number of landmines that have been planted all over Africa? Why should such a situation be encouraged?

---

[11] Hume, Cameron, *Ending Mozambique's War*, p. x.

Is Africa really looking for peace? Does the international community wish to see peace prevail in Africa?

Whilst the UN and the OAU have their responsibilities as international organisations, some specific organisations have been at the forefront of providing relief for the population in conflict areas. These include UN agencies, the International Committee of the Red Cross (ICRC) and Non-Governmental Organisations (NGOs). The performance of these organisations also requires some reflection if they are to be of more concrete support to future peace-keeping operations.

## UN AGENCIES

The UN High Commissioner for Refugees (UNHCR) is one agency of the UN that features very prominently in conflict areas of the world even though experience in Rwanda gave a lot of credit to the United Nations Children's Fund (UNICEF) which stayed with the peace-keeping forces throughout the civil war months. UNHCR, as the name clearly states, is responsible for refugees. A refugee is a person who has been compelled by circumstances in his/ her own country to live in another country under emergency conditions. This interpretation makes UNHCR field officers concentrate their attention on refugees and tend to ignore the plight of internally displaced people.

However, one would think that if internally displaced people could be assisted in their own countries to resettle, they would not have become refugees to start with. Interpretation of the various charters under which UN agencies operate therefore needs critical examination for the field officers to be able to use their own initiative and react to situations as they develop.

## INTERNATIONAL COMMITTEE OF THE RED CROSS (ICRC)

This is perhaps the organisation that is the most resilient in the face of danger. The heads of the delegations to many conflict areas often refuse to yield to the pressures of the warring factions and press on with their role in saving lives. As much as every organisation has its strength and weaknesses, I feel the ICRC has a lot that other similar organisations can learn from.

## NON-GOVERNMENTAL ORGANISATIONS (NGO'S)

The NGOs are those I describe as partners to the peace-keeping forces despite the occasional difficulties of co-operation due to differences in culture. People in distress, locked up behind warring factions or internally displaced in their own countries as a result of civil war need a lot of support from sympathetic organisations. These are the NGOs that support the UN agencies and the ICRC to provide food, medicine, clothes, water, shelter and the lot for the afflicted population. Who are the needy? Mostly women and children form the majority of the world's refugees, internally displaced population or those locked up in prisons subjected to asphyxia. These are people who have nothing to do with the conflicts. They do not aspire for power, they don't necessarily hate each other but they are often the victims of war. In principle, the affliction of the world's refugees should be a rebuke to all civilised peoples. It was pathetic to see children huddling under tarpaulins for warmth and their heads hanging down dejectedly and hopelessly in camps in Rwanda, Tanzania and Zaire as a result of the Rwandese civil war of 1994.

These are the categories of people that the NGOs try to reach to deliver the needed support. During the civil war in Rwanda, Medicins Sans Frontières (MSF) and Adventist Development Relief Agency (ADRA), both NGOs, stayed and worked in full co-operation with the UN mission. Immediately after the war, over 170 NGOs came to Rwanda. However, these NGOs refused to be registered and they operated haphazardly all over the country. Whilst some of them chose to go to areas they perceived to be safe, and without the presence of UNAMIR troops, others preferred working only where troops were deployed. Most NGOs did not want to have any co-ordination with UNAMIR or Rwandese government authorities. This state of affairs led to political confusion in that country. NGO operations in Somalia was even more grotesquely disorganised.

Again whilst some of the NGOs employ professionally qualified individuals, many others make do with non-professionals. Using non-professionals in a volatile situation where people's patience had dried up only led to some of the NGOs being expelled from Rwanda. Whereas undue interference from any government will lead to suspicion in NGO operations, it is my considered opinion that co-ordination is needed at some point if such operations are to achieve the desired results. There is also the need to set professional standards for the NGOs so that they will have some code of ethics. The idea must be for the UN agencies and NGOs to strengthen government machinery by providing humanitarian aid whilst political structures are put in place.

THE ROLE OF THE CHURCHES AND CHURCH PEOPLE

In close co-operation and collaboration with the NGOs is the role played by churches and individuals within the churches whilst peace-keeping operations are in progress. Church people can help build bridges between people separated by conflict and help reconcile adversaries, thereby creating communities between former enemies.[12] For much of the active mediation phase in Mozambique, the mediation "team" comprised a Mozambican archbishop, an Italian

---

[12] From International Alert Workshop Hand-out on Conflict Resolution, Dakar, Senegal, December 1995.

socialist parliamentarian and a former diplomat, and two key leaders of Sant'
Egidio, a Catholic lay order based in Rome's Trastevere district.[13]


RECONSTRUCTION

A necessary impetus to peace-keeping operations is reconstruction. Peace-keepers do not have access to humanitarian aid. Peoples in devastated areas and
"failed states" require reconstruction of their country. What use is a batch of
soldiers with blue helmets to a community that is very badly in need of food,
water, clothing, hospitals and schools for their children? What about a government that has no infrastructure whilst all banks have been looted? The presence
of the troops gives the population the sense of security but if nothing is done
quickly to repair the ruins of war, the population, sooner than later, loses confidence in the peace-keepers and begins to question their usefulness. In the past,
the peace-keepers have on occasion given out their rations and first aid drugs to
the communities in which they worked. However, those were very limited and
the inability to sustain such a gesture only generated anger against the blue
helmets. When the international community urges a failed state or a country
that has passed through a bitter civil war to respect human rights and for the
internal factions to reconcile, it is incumbent upon the same world body to help
in reconstructing such a country. It is only when practical sympathy is demonstrated that new governments or warring factions can show their reciprocity in
conforming to the norms of society.


SUMMARY AND RECOMMENDATIONS

The United Nations organisation has the ultimate responsibility for maintaining
peace and security on every continent, including Africa. Whatever regional or
sub-regional organisations do will only be in support of the UN. Co-ordination
is therefore the keyword. Despite the difficulties of the colonial past, Africa
with the help of the United Nations should look forward into the future with
positive thinking. Instead of always looking at the past as a handcuff to limit us,
Africans should view their history as a handrail to guide them in steep places.
The international community must give its whole-hearted support to UN peace-
keeping operations and stop hiding behind the UN.

The obvious lessons that have come out of the peace-keeping operations in
Africa include the following:

— Former colonial masters must stop interfering in the internal conflicts of
  African states, especially when such conflicts have already degenerated into
  bitter civil wars or inter-state wars.

---

[13] Hume, Cameron, *Ending Mozambique's War*, p. x.

— A successful peace-keeping operation requires a clear, unambiguous and practicable mandate with the consent of the factions in the conflict. Preferably the operations should follow a peace accord.

— The mandate must be supported by all members of the UN financially and morally. When the international community fails to act in a conflict situation, all governments find it convenient to blame the UN. This is unfair and dishonest. The Security Council should also create a balance in all regions of the world.

— Coherent planning as a result of available useful intelligence and thorough reconnaissance will ensure the successful take-off of peace-keeping missions. Ad hoc approaches to peace-keeping should give way to a professional approach.

— The organisational structure of the UN missions needs to be redefined. Those placed in authority should have direct control over the finances of the mission. In brief, a unified command is essential.

— The UN must reach out for competent staff. Whatever the present recruitment procedures are, due cognizance must be taken of the professional competence of the individual. A makeshift staff will only aggravate peace-keeping operations that are in themselves complex in nature.

— The operational control of the field units requires a clear definition. To my mind, I strongly feel that the Force Commander's decision should be the final. This being the case, a careful consideration must be given to the selection of the commander. Having selected such a commander, the Peace-Keeping Department must give him full backing in whatever he does. This does not prevent him from seeking advice. Neither should liaison and co-ordination stop taking place. What is being advocated here is for the commander to take charge of his troops and discharge his responsibilities with confidence in the secure knowledge that he has the support of the authorities in New York.

— Contingents, once assigned to a UN mission, should be loyal to their Force Commanders. Certainly, consultation with home governments will take place but battalion commanders deciding to "chicken out" of crucial operations should stop.

— Logistics support as an essential element of any UN peace-keeping operations cannot be over-stressed. Without it, the contingents will always feel abandoned and cannot operate at their optimum. In this regard, the proposal for the pre-positioning of essential logistics items in the sub-regions of Africa is in the right direction.

— Stand-by forces in the various sub-regions of Africa must become a reality.

— Training is an essential prerequisite for any successful operation. It is even more crucial for peace-keeping operations which are not the normal orientation of a soldier. Since peace-keeping is obviously the soldier's battle for the future, the principles and procedures must be taught in military institutions throughout Africa. Sub-regional centers for peace-keeping training are being established. These centers need the support of the developed nations in formulating the appropriate doctrine for peace support operations.

— The roles of the media, psychological operations and civil affairs teams must be duly recognized.

— The OAU's mechanism for prevention, management and resolution of conflicts must be vigorously pursued with the support of UN and individual countries in the developed world. It is gratifying to note that many western countries are already willing to assist. African armies must also persist in trying to keep themselves better prepared for the future.

— Political will is of utmost importance in any peace-keeping operations. Africa's political leaders need to give total support to the OAU in honoring their obligations. Political naivety should be overcome.

— The role of neighbours to a conflict-torn state is so important that it cannot be over-stated. The flow of arms and ammunition must be stopped. Readiness to provide genuine and sympathetic refuge to refugees should ultimately help in providing the necessary political stability to enable such refugees return home.

— The developed world and third world countries that produce arms and ammunition should stop escalating conflicts by ending the sale of such items to conflict zones.

— There is definitely the need for co-ordination between UN agencies, NGOs and peace-keeping troops. It must be realized that there is a cultural difference between the military and those organizations. Through joint seminars and combined training some skills can be shared. In addition, the charters of UN agencies and NGOs need to be re-examined in order to achieve better results. I suggest that the NGOs be more selective in deciding upon those who work for them.

— The role of churches, individuals and other respectable organisations must be recognized even though peace-keepers might have been deployed.

— Reconstruction of a state that has been ravaged by war needs no further emphasis. Help is required from the international community.

REFERENCES

## Books

Cilliers, Jakkie and Greg Mills, 1995, *Peace-keeping in Africa*. Institute of Defence Policy and the South African Institute of International Affairs.
Hume Cameron, 1994, *Ending Mozambique's War*. Washington DC: United States Institute of Peace.
OAU Information Publication, *Resolving Conflicts in Africa*. Implementation Options series (II) 1993.
Rikhye, Indar Jit, Michael Harbottle and Bjørn Egge, 1974, *The Thin Blue Line*. New Haven and London: Yale University Press.
The Blue Helmets, *A Review of UN Peace-Keeping* 1990.

## Additional Sources

Department of Peace-keeping Operations; Report of the Seminar on Lessons Learned from UN Operations in Somalia.
International Alert Workshop Hand-out on Conflict Resolution held in Dakar, Senegal December 1995.
United Nations Security Council Resolutions on the Mission in Rwanda.

# African Governments—African Conflicts

*Bethuel A. Kiplagat*

The role of African governments in African conflicts is not straightforward. They have been involved directly or indirectly in conflicts at all stages: pre-conflict, conflict and post conflict. Their role has varied from instigation and support to the resolution of conflicts. Often policies pursued, the fear of reprisals and the manipulation of power all contribute at some stage to the outbreak of conflict. In any case, conflicts serve varying purposes to different players; thus African governments have sustained conflicts internally or in neighbouring countries to serve their own interests.

African governments in the early days of independence made use of the newly created Organisation of African Unity (OAU) to deal with the emerging inter-state conflicts usually caused by unresolved border problems. The OAU got involved in bringing together around the table the heads of state of Morocco and Algeria to settle their differences on the question of borders. A lot of time and resources were invested in the Chadian conflict, including the sending of a peace-keeping force. Although the Congo may have been a disaster, the OAU was nevertheless a concerned party alongside the UN. The efforts to resolve the Nigerian civil war and a host of other events show African governments as very active on the conflict scene whether acting independently, jointly or through the OAU. It is interesting to note that they did not take any initiative on the Ethiopian conflict. This may have been due partly to the prestige and respect enjoyed by the Emperor and the non-interference clause of the OAU charter which hampered it from getting involved in the internal affairs of a country.[1]

The approach and involvement of African governments through the OAU had to follow established rules. One of the aggrieved member states would raise the issue on the agenda of the Council of Ministers and an extraordinary session would be convened. The parties would be asked to present their position after which a mediation committee consisting of a number of countries would then be formed to look into the problem and help the parties to come to an amicable solution. Although heads of state were involved, the bulk of the work rested on the shoulders of the ministers of foreign affairs. It is amazing

---

[1] See the discussion on liberation in Amate C.O.C, 1996, *Inside the OAU: Pan-Africanism in Practice*. London: Macmillan Publishers.

how much was actively achieved considering the cumbersome structure used and the costs involved. Nigeria alone spent upwards of US$ 50 million in Chad and their total outlay for involvement in ECOMOG has been around US$ 3 billion! What Africa has spent on conflict resolution comes to a staggering figure even without adding the costs of shuttle diplomacy. When heads of state get involved, there are the additional costs related to normal presidential travel. The contribution of African governments towards conflict management is most interesting. Kenya for example hosted the Ugandan peace talks for four months and contributed substantially to the Mozambican Peace Initiative and now to IGADD. This contribution by Africa must not go unnoticed.

The purpose of this paper is not, however, to praise Africa, nor is it to submit an inventory of Africa's involvement in conflicts. This has been well covered elsewhere. The paper will attempt to show that conflicts which might give a first impression of being isolated are actually part of a system which we shall term a "conflict system" for lack of better terminology. If one were to accept that premise, then it would no longer be possible to talk of internal or external conflicts or even boundaries as these would not have meaning or validity. It would also mean that conflicts could not be dealt with satisfactorily in isolation.

A lasting solution can only come by a holistic, or comprehensive, approach taking into account not only the geographical dimension but also the more subtle and complex psychological, ethnic and perhaps ideological dimensions.

A conflict system has certain common characteristics and patterns. The geographical location groups countries or regions together, yet these may not share much linguistically, racially or religiously. They may also belong to the same ideological system, be bound together by creed, by their degree of development or underdevelopment or by historical ties. On the hole, however, it would be difficult to define a system that is mutually exclusive. Elements of one system will be found in another. Our purpose is to look at specific conflicts and determine how the concept of a system exacerbates or enhances the opportunities for resolving the conflict. It is within that system that we examine the role of governments.

The example we shall look at is that of what is now termed the "Great Lakes". The countries that belong to the Great Lakes are Tanzania, Zaire, Uganda, Burundi and Rwanda. Uganda can be considered to be at the core of the conflict system. Kenya and Sudan are on the periphery of that system. To examine the role of governments satisfactorily would require a consideration of their political history. Each of the countries of the Great Lakes Region has suffered enormous political instability. Mobutu of Zaire came to power through a military coup in 1960. He went on to rule with an iron fist, turning his mineral-rich country into one of the poorest on the continent. His government has done little to invest in infrastructure. Were it not for the popularity of her musicians, little good could be said of Zaire. The government of Zaire, however, received immense Western support which helped entrench Mobutu's personalised rule. It is only when the wind of change was ushered in by the collapse of the Soviet

Union that Mobutu's government faced a real threat to its survival. Until then, the government had been a willing conduit for conflict, e.g. in the Angolan civil war.

Uganda has been through a number of coups, including the one that brought the infamous Idi Amin to power. Uganda is only now recovering from the effects of the war that began with the ousting of Amin and the capture of power by the incumbent President Yoweri Museveni. Museveni benefited during his "days in the bush" from the support of exiled Rwandese who had been plotting a return to the homeland. That the Rwandese Patriotic Front (RPF) was launched from Uganda came as no surprise. There were, however, Hutu communities settled in Zaire and as the conflict in Rwanda and Burundi have flared up, Zaire and Uganda have been key players. Rwanda and Burundi, carved out of the same Belgian colony of Rwanda–Urundi, are tied by similar ethnic, linguistic and historical roots. Both have a history of ethnic discrimination and the post-independence policies of the governments have been exclusionist.

To consider how the governments of the region have handled conflict, it may be useful to look briefly into their political history.

In 1966, President Milton Obote of Uganda decided to resolve the political crisis which was brewing up between the Kingdom of Baganda (the most important kingdom in the country in terms of history and size) and the central government through both a constitutional and a palace military coup.[2] The President went ahead and forced parliament to pass a bill amending the constitution to abolish the kingdoms in Uganda. realising the possibility of major resistance in Baganda, Obote ordered the army to storm the palace, the headquarters of the Kingdom of Baganda. The king was forced to flee the country through Rwanda to exile in Britain where he subsequently died a poor man. The anger and bitterness among the Baganda ran deep. The Baganda subsequently became a thorn in the flesh of Obote's government which was later successfully exploited.

Uganda as a country had a long tradition of importing labour from Rwanda for menial tasks like working in the coffee plantations and as herdsmen. There was therefore an old migrant workers' community in Uganda from Rwanda and to a limited extent from Burundi who spoke the same language.

Rwandese also had a system of kings. After independence, and the subsequent revolution which deposed the king, a large exodus of Rwandese crossed the border into Uganda. Before long this Rwandese community became a liability in the eyes of the Obote government which started making things difficult for them. It was made quite clear to the Rwandese that they were not wanted and that they should go back to their own country. This was extremely painful, particularly to the migrant workers who had settled in Uganda for generations. At home in Rwanda, the government had made it quite clear that they were not in a position to receive them back. The policies of the two neigh-

---

[2] See also Mwagiru, M., 1994.

bouring governments towards the Rwandese refugee community in Uganda were later to become the source of the greatest tragedy in modern history: the 1994 genocide. These policies created out of the exiled Rwandese a near "stateless" people. And so in a similar manner as the Baganda, the Rwandese in Uganda felt deep suspicion and hatred of the government of Obote. Rwanda did not feel comfortable with Obote as a neighbour either. The political utterances on the Rwandese emanating from the Ugandan government were seen as a danger signal. An explosive but latent opposition was thus put in place. The following players were at the centre of events: the governments of Rwanda and Uganda, the Baganda and the Rwandese in Uganda and the sympathisers in Rwanda. It was upon this force that Museveni was able to draw in his struggle for power a decade later, and it was this alliance that propelled the Rwandese Patriotic Front.

Obote did not last long in power and in 1971 he was toppled by a military coup engineered by his Chief of Staff, Idi Amin, who had earlier been used to storm the palace of the Kabaka, the king of Baganda. There was jubilation and rejoicing in Kampala and throughout Baganda. Obote and his followers were forced to flee to neighbouring Tanzania where they immediately began preparing for a comeback. Ironically, Obote was attending a Commonwealth Summit when he was toppled. Amin Dada turned out to be a ruthless dictator, who went out of his way to eliminate any influential persons not only of the Baganda but wherever they were to be found. Thousands went into exile as refugees. Tanzania was a welcoming neighbour and many of them fled there. It must be noted here that Tanzania and Uganda under Obote had at least some ideological similarities: Tanzania with its Ujamaa type of socialism and Uganda with its common man's charter. Obote did not have time to implement his ideology, which was inspired by that of Tanzania. The two leaders had a common understanding of the problems and development of the region and were politically close. Obote was given a red carpet welcome in Tanzania where he took up asylum. It was even reported in the press that he was allowed the privilege of flying the Ugandan flag at his residence in Dar-es-Salaam, signifying that he was recognised as a "government in exile".

With Amin's dictatorial policies and threat to neighbours, the region became very tense. The Ugandan exiles, particularly those in Tanzania, exploited the situation and utilised it to support their objective of overthrowing the regime in Kampala. They did make a number of incursions but were repulsed by Ugandan forces. Amin decided to teach Nyerere a lesson and he launched an attack deep inside Tanzanian territory arguing that his forces were pursuing rebels. A counter-attack was launched by the Ugandan rebels with the support of the Tanzanian army and they went all the way to Kampala and overthrew the regime of Amin Dada, who in turn was forced to flee into exile. The government of Tanzania supported the successful return to power of Obote.

The Ugandan rebellion led by Museveni started within a short time of Obote's regaining power. it was strategically launched in the Southwest, an area close to the border with Rwanda and inhabited by people of Museveni's ethnic group and the "stateless" Rwandese. It was not long before the major war theatre moved to the Ruwero triangle in the heartland of the Baganda. There could not have been a better strategy for using natural allies: the Baganda still nursing their humiliation and the Rwandese engaging in a cause which they could identify with. The grievances of these groups had never been addressed by their respective governments.

It has been suggested that the National Resistance Movement/Army (NRM/A) gave an undertaking to the Baganda about the restoration of their kingdom and also to the Rwandese about returning home. Coupled with the mistrust for Obote from the government in Rwanda, Museveni found fertile ground for support from these groups. The Rwandese in Uganda joined his army and in fact took control of it. The Baganda population in Ruwero and elsewhere gave him support: intelligence, food and soldiers for the front. The Rwandese government allowed some supplies to be channelled through its territory and granted safe passage for the rebels who needed to get out of the country. In the later days of the war when the NRA occupied virtually all the coffee growing region, they were able to export the coffee through Rwanda. Museveni had indeed perfected the Byzantine diplomatic tactics: my neighbour's enemy is my friend.[3] Little did the Rwandese government ever imagine that it was digging its own grave. And even when it looked necessary for the governments to address the compelling issues for potential conflict, they preferred to look the other way and beef up their personal security. This turned out to be an exercise in futility.

With concerted military pressure and propaganda, the government of Obote fell and the two Okello generals took power. Tito Okello became head of state and Basilio the head of the army. For a while the NRA acted as if it were in concert with the power changes in Uganda but it soon became evident that their objective for ruling Uganda was still on the Agenda.

Diplomatic pressure began to gather momentum for a negotiated settlement. It is, however, not clear who actually took the initiative to approach Kenya to arrange peace talks between the government of Tito Okello and the NRM. Be that as it may, talks started which later were widened to include the majority of the political forces in Uganda. After intensive negotiation, which at times were close to a breaking point, the diplomatic skills of President Moi of Kenya and the support of other officials led to the signing of the Nairobi peace accord in November 1985. Implementation was to start immediately but the accord was never given a chance. Museveni and his high command had other plans and by 25 January 1986, NRA forces were in Kampala and Museveni was sworn in as President the following day. The Ugandan army, at least the section from the east and the north, left, carrying with them a lot of military equipment. The Acholi in particular, under the army commander General Basilio Okello,

---

[3] Hamilton, K. and R. Langhorne, 1985, *The Practice of Diplomacy*. London: Routledge.

crossed over into the Sudan to prepare themselves for a comeback. It is the remnants of this group that are now the subject of conflict in Northern Uganda.

A tactic for conflict had been established: that of exploiting differences among governments to obtain support for attacking the "offender". In Uganda, one group would move in while the other retreated to the bush to fight their way back. Recognising that, the new NRM government seized the opportunity to approach President Moi of Kenya to use his good offices to plead with President Mobutu of Zaire not to allow his territory to be used to attack Uganda from the west. There was this fear that Mobutu might in fact destabilise Uganda by helping rebels to attack from the west flank. President Moi acted immediately by sending a message to Mobutu who was on a state visit to Rwanda. Mobutu agreed to meet with Moi across the border in Goma. He brought his host the President of Rwanda with him. They were later during the day joined by the newly sworn in President of Uganda Yoweri Museveni who had not been invited. The three heads of state took up the issue of security and stability of Uganda. They expressed concern that the region had suffered immensely and in particular Uganda. They agreed and pledged to give every support to the new regime in Uganda. Mobutu of course vehemently refuted the allegation that he was preparing to attack Uganda. To assure the Ugandan government of their commitment and goodwill, the three heads of state decided to create a kind of forum at summit level consisting of all the neighbouring countries of Uganda: the four founding members—Kenya, Rwanda, Zaire and Uganda—plus Sudan, Tanzania and Burundi. The main objective for the forum was to deliberate on issues related to security. Unfortunately, as they went on to meet, the issues broadened and the question of security faded into the background. They had altogether four meetings—Goma, Kampala, Nairobi and Khartoum—but due to differences between them, they ceased to meet.

In time, the security in the region deteriorated and so did the relationships between states. The security forum that had been put in place could not be sustained due to the suspicion and mistrust entertained by leaders. There were intermittent and sometimes sustained tensions between Uganda, Zaire, Rwanda, Kenya, and later, Sudan. Relations between Kenya and Uganda deteriorated to the extent that Kenya was forced to take drastic action and declared the High Commissioner of Uganda persona non grata while the Zairian ambassador in Kampala was implicated in a coup attempt. Relations with Rwanda, however, remained on a better footing.

In 1990, while Museveni was away attending the UN General Assembly in New York, a large section of his army, consisting of the Rwandese who had fought with him, launched an attack on Rwanda from Uganda. The statements of the Ugandan leadership on the invasion were vague and non-committal, thereby confirming suspicions of complicity. The Rwandese refugees and migrant workers had fought with Museveni and he had achieved his goals. A promise to enable the Rwandese to return home was quite conceivable. Given the hardening of positions over the years of the policies of the then Rwandese government on the return of refugees, the option for an armed return found easy prey. The Rwandese government had publicly stated in 1985 that refugees living in Eastern Africa could not come back home because the territory was too small to accommodate returnees. The government resisted with the help of Zaire and France but they were later unable to ward off the advancing soldiers of the RPF.

At the peak of the war, there were more than one million displaced people living in camps inside Rwanda. The conflict situation became worse by the day. Sensing a need for intervention, Tanzania took the initiative and brought the parties to Arusha for peace talks. All the major political forces in Rwanda discussed and worked out a political arrangement for the country. The result was the Arusha Peace Accords of October 1992 and January 1993.[4] Like the Uganda case, these Accords were never given a chance. The shooting of the plane bringing back the Presidents of Rwanda and Burundi, both Hutu, unleashed a massacre and created a huge refugee population across the borders and particularly in Zaire and Tanzania. The national army, predominantly Hutu, crossed over into Zaire along with displaced or fearstricken Hutu. As happened in Uganda, this group found its kin in Zaire. Again a cycle of had been repeated: the former officials and army have found a possible re-launching ground in a neighbouring country. Unless old scores are settled, we can expect to see another cycle of conflict, with governments in the region playing either a supporting or restraining role. For now, in the case of Rwanda, we can see some political alignments, viz. Uganda and Rwanda and Zaire with the former officials. These alliances do not indicate a conducive environment for managing conflict.

Burundi is the mirror image of Rwanda, having the same ethnic groups, a similar social and ethnic structure which is almost cast-like, where the Tutsi, though a minority, have traditionally been the ruling class, The revolutionary changes that overthrew the Tutsi domination in Rwanda have never succeeded in Burundi. every attempt by the Hutu in Burundi to bring change has been countered by the Tutsi-dominated army, resulting in death and massive displacements of people. The pattern has been for most refugees to cross over to the neighbouring countries of Zaire, Rwanda and Tanzania. Tanzania and Zaire have borne the greatest burden of refugees from Rwanda and Burundi. The present conflict has already cost more than 100,000 lives. It is surprising that the international community is not so very much alarmed by the extent of the massacre perpetrated by extremists in Burundi, which could explode on the same scale as that of Rwanda. The problems of the two countries are so closely interlinked, that attention focused on one should not omit the other. The current

---

[4] Three documents were negotiated and signed. These were: i) The Peace Agreement between the Government of the republic of Rwanda and the Rwandese Patriotic Front. ii) Protocol of Agreement on Power-sharing within the framework of a broad-based transitional government between the Government of the Republic of Rwanda and the Rwandese patriotic Front. iii) Continuation of the Protocol of Agreement (ii above) signed in January 1993.

crisis is particularly serious because, since independence, it is the first time that the two governments and the armies in particular have been dominated by the Tutsi. Both are faced by potential rebellion emanating from the Hutu operating either from inside the country or from outside. The political impasse in Zaire resulting in the weakening of central authority has created a conducive environment along the eastern border which has enabled those fighting the government to use the border areas as a launching pad for sporadic incursions into the two countries. Whatever happens in one country will have direct impact on the other.

Burundi, which did not have a direct link with the events in Uganda, continued to be plagued with internal strife. The loss of two Hutu Presidents had deepened the suspicion, tension and conflict between the Tutsi and Hutu communities with heavy losses of life on both sides. Reports indicate that more than a hundred thousand people died in the last year alone. The killings are perpetuated by extremist Hutu and the army, which is predominantly Tutsi. The former President Bagaza is active on the Tutsi extremist front. He used to have connections with both Uganda and Libya, where he spent most of his exile days. He also spent some of his time in exile in Uganda.

The outbreak of violence in Burundi can also readily be explained by factors within the conflict system. In Zaire, Mobutu has been holed up in Gbadolite, nursing his anger at the way the political situation is unfolding in Rwanda and Burundi. Zaire is trying to use the Rwandese refugees to make a point about its role and position in the region. Zaire demands that the refugees leave its territory in the full knowledge of the attendant political and social consequences. The only precondition one can make if the refugees return without proper arrangements and without adequate protection is that security in the region will worsen. Mobutu showed his displeasure by not attending the regional meeting called by Moi to look specifically at the refugee situation as well as the security of the region, apparently because he was not accorded due prominence as the "old man of the region". Follow-up meetings of this initiative never took place. Kenya, though on the periphery of the system, has also been affected by the events in Rwanda. Kenya was particularly angered by the invasion of the Rwandese Patriotic Front which, the Kenya leadership strongly believed, could not have happened without the support of Uganda. Moi's outburst that Kenya would not co-operate with the UN tribunal on Rwanda was a reflection of this deep anger. The further deterioration of relations between Kenya and Uganda did not just stop at Rwanda, but also had a negative effect on the Sudan regional peace initiative and the establishment of the East African Community. The elections in Tanzania and the coming into power of a new President has opened opportunities to revisit the issues of the East African Community and ultimately address tension within that conflict system. The border meeting between Museveni and Moi was largely the result of persistent diplomatic efforts by the President of Tanzania, Benjamin Mkapa. If this diplomatic trend of co-operation persists it may open opportunities for addressing the conflicts in the Great Lakes region and beyond. Mobutu may even be persuaded to play a more positive role in the management of conflicts within the system.

The foregoing suggests that the conflict system under consideration has historical roots which are exploited at different times in different places and by different persons and groups. The system reveals a web of conflicts which are settled only for fresh ones to erupt. Every country in the system is touched by the conflict although the theatres of war keep shifting. Take the case of Uganda, which could be considered as the country that provided the launching pad for this round of tension and conflict in the system. Fundamental problems are still there even if they appear somewhat obscure. The Acholi, and to a small extent the Langi, who formed the bulk of the then national army under Obote, are now waging violence in the North. They feel excluded from power, which they had enjoyed for a long time. On the other hand, there are former Rwandese leaders who feel that the Ugandan government was responsible for their ouster. They would naturally want the same medicine applied to Uganda.

There is another factor which needs to be considered and that is the political evolution in Rwanda. Presently, the political base is narrow and fragile. Can such a system withstand the political storms which could easily sweep across the region? If that were to happen, it would have a direct impact in the region and particularly on Uganda being the front-line state as it were. The two million Rwandese refugees across the border in Zaire constitute a social and political time-bomb. Their return would undoubtedly destabilise the system. The returnees who had fled the country in 1959 may well face another exodus. It is time to put pressure on the government to open up the political system so that there is freer and wider participation. The chances are that a more open and democratic system would offer some healing and restore the regime's credibility in the dispensation of a new political order and the resolution of the age-old conflict.

When one examines closely the phenomenon of a conflict system in this region, there is one recurring constant. The instability of the system is due to the problem of exclusion: a zero sum game where the winner takes all. When the Tutsi were in power in Rwanda, they excluded the Hutu and that is what still is happening in Burundi. When the northerners were in power in Uganda, the southerners were marginalised and today it is the northerners who feel that they are excluded. In all this, there has been a willing neighbour to provide launching ground for insurgency and dissatisfied elements internally to support rebellion.

What is becoming apparent in this analysis is that problems of conflict in this region must be looked at comprehensively. Tentative attempts have been made with the Carter and Nyerere initiative to bring together leaders from the region to address the Great Lakes problems. To resolve the problem effectively requires time and a long-term perspective, especially given the nature and scope of the problems. One cannot, for example, change the power equation in

Burundi without giving consideration to how such a change will impact on the situation in Rwanda or Uganda for that matter.

The time has come to look creatively at the most viable political structures which can take into account the history and more so the ethnic mix of the people of this region. This would include as a priority the overhauling and restructuring of the state machinery and its uses. And most of all, the resolution of any problem in the region must take into account the system in which one conflict webs into another. The governments in the region and indeed in Africa need to accept their responsibility in managing conflict and make a bold decision to stop fanning or supporting conflict.

## CONCLUDING REMARKS

Quite clearly, governments in the Great Lakes region play a central role in the conflicts. This role is, however, not always guided by a vision for a peaceful future. The development of a common vision for peace is necessary. It goes without saying that it is of vital importance to involve or to make all the parties feel that they are involved in the resolution process and not left out. The foregoing is important in analysing the role of governments in the conflict system under study.

Governments in the region have been prone to fan and fuel conflict for their neighbours were relations are not considered friendly. Secondly, the potential causes of conflict in one country have easily found breeding grounds elsewhere in the system as a result of the policies of the government. Thirdly, the governments have either singularly or jointly tried to manage conflicts peacefully, but their historical involvement in conflicts has been an impediment and a source of fresh conflict. Lastly, none of the governments has retained any semblance of friendship or co-operation for any reasonable length of time and this too has provided other sources of conflict: suspicion and mistrust.

The Great Lakes conflict system also shows that governments do not always learn the lessons of the past. The policies of exclusion have again and again produced conflict, yet governments continue to adopt them. The current Rwandese leadership is Tutsi dominated while the previous one was Hutu dominated. With or without the vicious ethnic rivalries, unless governments are determinedly accommodating, we can expect the cycle of violence to continue with only the intervals varying.

The governments have also played the ethnicity card not necessarily to end conflict but for propping up the leadership. In Uganda, the powers the Kabaka as the cultural head of the Baganda have been restored. What about other parts of Uganda and other groups as well? Museveni, himself an Ankole, has rejected the reinstatement of the Ankole Kingdom. This pattern of extending privileges to certain ethnic groups at the expense of others creates a basis for conflict in the long run. These populist gestures have made Uganda a haven of peace.

The question of the entry point in the conflict system also needs to be addressed. There are today many players in the field of conflict but the mechanism or method of getting involved can end up being counter-productive. This is due either to inadequate understanding of the problem, or to lack of focus or co-ordination. Governments in the region need to take up a leaching role in the management of conflict.

The region's stand on Burundi vis-à-vis the ouster of President Ntibantuganya may be the beginning of a new era in the common management of conflicts in the region. The resolve of the governments needs to be supported.

Given the pattern of conflicts occurring in a system the case for strengthening sub-regional and regional mechanisms for conflict resolution is very strong. That will be charged with the whole spectrum of issues and problems related to conflict management or resolution and post-conflict reconstruction. The co-operation of governments in Africa will be vital to this process.

REFERENCES

Brown, J. and M. Schraub, 1992, *Resolving Third World Conflicts: Challenges for a New Era.* Washington DC: Institute of Peace Press.
Clough, Michael, 1992, *US Policy Towards Africa and the End of the Cold War.* New York: Council of Foreign Relations Press.
Davidson, Basil, 1978, *Let Freedom Come: Africa in Modern History.* Boston: Little Brown and Company.
Harbeson, W. John and Donald Rothchild, 1991, *Africa in World Politics.* Boulder: Westview Press.
Houle, David, 1989, *Mozambique, a Nation in Crisis.* London: Claridge Press.
Munene, M. et al., 1995, *The United States and Africa: From Independence to the End of the Cold War.* Nairobi: East African Educational Publishers.
Mwagiru, M., 1994, *The International Management of Internal Conflicts in Africa: The Uganda Mediation, 1985.* Ph.D. Thesis. Canterbury: Rutherford College, University of Kent.
Oren, Nissan, 1992, *Termination of Wars: Process, Procedures and Aftermaths.* Jerusalem: Hebrew University.
*Politique Africaine,* Janvier 1981. Paris: Editions Karthala.
*Politique Etrangère,* 3188. Paris: Institut Français des Relations Internationales.
Zartman, William (ed.), 1991, "Resolving Regional Conflicts: International Perspectives", *The Annals of the American Academy of Political and Social Science,* 518.

# Civil Society and Conflict Management in Africa —A Re-emerging Role?

*Josephine Ajema Odera*

## INTRODUCTION

The end of the East–West tension has been marked by mixed signals on the conflict scene in Africa. While some conflicts have been settled or are showing encouraging signs of settlement, new ones have emerged and some old ones have eschewed settlement.

The end of apartheid in South Africa brought to a conclusion a long battle in which the international community had become as much an interested party as, for example, the African National Congress. The end of this conflict was important not only for South Africa but for Africa as a whole. It signified the culmination of the central agenda of the Organisation of African Unity (OAU): the political liberation of the African continent. Coupled with the disintegration of the Soviet Union, the attainment of majority rule in South Africa implicitly strengthened the tide towards a new political order elsewhere in Africa. Attempts to settle the internal conflict in Angola, which appear finally to be taking root, may be viewed against that background. Progress in the peace process may well indicate the opportunities for settlement of conflicts that have been provided by the end of the Cold War as well as the changed role of South Africa. On the other hand, the collapse of the state in Somalia and the anarchy still prevailing, three years after the fall of Siyad Barre, may be an indication of conflicts that have opened up after being concealed for years by the Cold War. Gurr (1994:262–265) defines some of these conflicts as power-transition conflicts which have only been "nudged" by the deconstruction of the Soviet bloc.

The failure of the state to protect people from want has exacerbated the insecurity situation and provided a rallying point for deprived groups to wage violence with varying intensity. Referring to such conflicts as identity conflicts, Regehr (1993:3) opines that "they emerge with intensity when a community in response to unmet needs for social and economic security, resolves to strengthen its collective influence and to struggle for political recognition... Behind ethnic or national identity struggles are basic economic and social grievances..." He looks at the 1994 ethnic conflicts in Ghana between the Konkombas, Dagomba, Nanumba and Gonja and concludes that they were essentially conflicts over land ownership.

Issues related to environmental degradation which in extreme cases of drought and desertification threaten or decimate the means of livelihood, point to a very real conflict for survival. Thus in trying to survive environmental disasters the pastoral groups in the Horn of Africa end up clashing with other groups when their itineraries collide.[1] In acknowledging the economics of conflict, there is an urgent need to rethink policy within a comprehensive security framework. Civil society has a role to play in initiating and guiding debate on policies and their implications for a peaceful society. There is no denying that misconceived policies and mismanagement of the economy are significant explanatory factors for conflicts in Africa (World Bank 1989).

On the whole, Africa approaches the next century in a state of turmoil and dilemma: freed from being a pawn in the Cold War struggles for power and influence, yet a prisoner of that legacy; freed from being a superpower battleground, and now a battleground for the challenges posed at the cross-roads. While the OAU struggles to find its appropriate role at the cross-roads, the myriad of internal problems within its membership seems to be on the rise: internal conflicts, demands for political and economic reforms, launching insurgency from neighbouring member territories... In the cases of both Rwanda and Liberia, decisions to support the Rwandese Patriotic Front or Charles Taylor appear to have been secret pacts at very high official levels thus hindering any effective preventive action from civil society.

One is, however, tempted to question the role of civil society in the period before the outbreak of violence, especially in the case of Rwanda. Was it simply inconspicuous or was it partisan? It is the intention of this paper to address some of these issues and to reflect on the need for African civil society to be its brothers keeper if conflict is to be avoided, managed or resolved. How can the organisation deal effectively, for example, with the conflicts in Rwanda and Liberia knowing the role its own members have played in aiding the conflicts? Of what use is civil society to regional organisations in managing conflicts? This paper will therefore consider the role of civil society in conflict management against the knowledge that there are a multiplicity of actors and issues to be addressed. We will also consider the following major issues:

— who constitutes civil society in Africa?
— what conditions favour or hinder an effective role for civil society?
— how, when and why does civil society become engaged?
— in what specific areas can civil society be involved for the ultimate management of conflicts?

These issues point to both theoretical and practical concerns and they will constitute the major focus of this paper.

---

[1] See the discussion by Ball on "The effects of conflict on the economies of Third World Countries" in Deng and Zartman 1992:272–291. She recommends international support for "the creation and nurturing of participatory political and economic systems" and the removal of the military from politics.

Elsewhere in Africa, two issues seem to be particularly problematic for conflict management: the democratisation process and religious fundamentalism. Both these issues touch on the configuration of power and influence internally and both seem to draw a strong external appeal. The management of these conflicts must thus address not only the power relations inside countries but also the force of religion in its dual role as a pretext or cause for conflict or as an instrument for peace (Johnston and Sampson, 1994). The well known cases of poverty and injustice as factors in conflict must also receive attention. The conflict in Sudan, for example, manifests itself as fundamentally religious or racial, yet it has the dimensions of poverty, injustice and indeed "the struggle for power and peace".[2] In Algeria, the continuing conflict between FIS and the government is a function of both the democratisation process and the force of Islamic fundamentalism. An attempt to address the dilemmas of political power through a democratic formula, the recent presidential elections, has not brought the expected calm and a new dispensation will have to be worked out. In the case of Sudan, a negotiated formula which resulted in the 1972 agreement was only able to hold the peace temporarily. In the words of Kok, the agreement suffered from "the absence of national consensus on the fundamentals ... of state and nation-building." In his assessment no "regime, military or civilian, and no social force or a combination thereof, has been hitherto strong enough or persuasive enough to forge or impose a national consensus (African Academy of Sciences: 1993: 33–65). The manner in which the agreement was abrogated in 1983 and the interplay of forces since then seem to justify such an assessment. The difficulties encountered by IGAD, the latest sub-regional mediator, further suggest that more than a third party mediation will be necessary for lasting peace.

Countries where conflicts related to the democratisation process have taken place include Kenya, Nigeria, Togo, and Zaire. If we take the examples of Kenya and Nigeria, we note that the manifestation of this conflict has been markedly different. In both cases, however, the response of civil society has been predominantly to challenge the use of state power in the pursuit of good governance. In Nigeria, when the election results were annulled and the military government reversed the transition to civilian rule, civil society mobilised itself to protest the turn of events. Trade unions, journalists and professional associations were active in trying to obtain a restoration of the democratic process but their efforts have not achieved that. In Kenya, the election process went on to its conclusion but that was not without incident. It was only after the nationals and the development partners had applied sufficient pressure for the repeal of Section 2A of the constitution (which forbade multi-party politics) that the ruling party reluctantly conceded to a new political order. However, the ethnic clashes which coincided with the democratisation process provided fresh

---

[2] Sub-title of Morgenthau's (1986, 1948) classic, *Politics Among Nations: The Struggle for Power and Peace.*

ground for conflict with the opposition and government accusing each other of setting the conditions for civil war. In Kenya, the resort to ethnicity to fight political battles, the many who are still displaced as a result of the clashes and the skewed development policy denying funds to "opposition strongholds" suggest that the conflict is far from resolved.

In both Nigeria and Kenya, civil society has been present and active. In both cases again, the governments have also penetrated civil society through favours, threats, arrests and at the very worst death. The hanging of Ken Saro Wiwa and others is an extreme reflection of the risk that a true and faithful civil society can encounter in the task of pursuing peace with justice. These examples show that when civil society is pitted against the government, its effectiveness can be determinedly obstructed. In other words, in a situation where the exercise of power tends towards dictatorship, the power of civil society is dependent on the ability to mobilise not only the citizens but also to rally international opinion behind the cause of peace. The two examples also reveal some paradoxes in the role of civil society. On the one hand, civil society can be relied upon as an effective instrument for conflict management but on the other hand it can be persuaded to shun this role. The examples also shed some light on the momentum of civil society in managing conflicts. They suggest that civil society is strongest and most conspicuous in the period preceding and immediately after the crisis. As time progresses, passivity sets in either by force, fatigue or internal dissent. Thus in assigning roles to the civil society in conflict management, it may be necessary to do so against the life cycle of a conflict.[3]

Elsewhere, internal conflicts under the banner of ethnicity have occurred in Ghana, Congo and Rwanda. Rwanda was the scene of the deadliest conflict[4] in 1994 where up to a million people are believed to have been massacred between April and July, that is in a space of three months. The subsequent take-over of power by the Rwanda Patriotic Front (RPF) and the exodus of an estimated 2 million people as refugees suggest a serious challenge to the settlement of that conflict.

The international community has shown a keen interest in the management of African conflicts. At the United Nations level, for example, almost 40 per cent of the 16 peacekeeping/enforcement missions in 1994 were in Africa (Western Sahara, Chad, Liberia, Angola, Mozambique, Rwanda). Despite the interest in managing African conflicts, the stakes in conflicts in Africa eschew clear-cut categories while a sustainable, constructive and creative strategy for containment remains elusive. Perhaps it is the "competition for power, resources and prestige" (Otunnu 1995:4) defying an equilibrium that ultimately confers the

---

[3] See for example, Lund (1994:54–58). The life cycle of a conflict has been theorised to go from peace to rising tension, confrontation, outbreak of violence, ceasefire, settlement, rapprochement, reconciliation and back to peace. The means used to address the conflict thus depend on the stage of the conflict.

[4] Project Ploughshares (1995) *Armed Conflicts Report 1995*.

intractability status on conflicts in Africa. These conflicts clearly indicate that no one formula is sufficient for managing the conflicts in Africa.

DEFINING THE CIVIL SOCIETY

The understanding and application of the term civil society is quite varied among politicians, scholars, practitioners and ordinary citizens. Some scholars suggest that the importance of civil society has risen through the democratisation processes (Ekeh:1992) or what some have termed the second liberation.[5] To test the perception of the term, I inquired from a sample of people their understanding of the term civil society. The most common responses were:

— Civil society is that part of society between the government and the grass-roots.
— Civil society is a conceptual approach which represents values such as good governance, accountability and transparency.
— Civil society is that society that has civil leadership.
— Civil society is that group of people that influences public opinion although it is located outside both the government and political parties.
— Civil society excludes the military

Although my sample could hardly pass the statistical requirements for representation, it indicates the gaps in perception which are also evident in the allocation of tasks to civil society. In a general manner, the term must be conceived as a social force that derives momentum from convictions on the well functioning of society as a whole.

Hutchful (1995) in his article "The civil society debate in Africa" examines the application of this term by scholars. From his article, civil society may be identified either functionally or through association. This would include:

i) the participation in socio-economic and political processes through standard or rule setting;
ii) activities or functions that exercise restraint on either the excesses of the state or the society, i.e. they exact a moderating influence on society;
iii) non-formal participation in the just government of people or agitation for the same;
iv) a coalition of various classes pursuing their interests while being autonomously organised;
v) institutions such as the church, trade unions, political parties, the media and professional associations, which are sometimes referred to as platforms of civil society.

---

[5] The wave of democatisation in Africa has variously been referred to as the second liberation or the second independence "marking a new" political order.

Bloomfield (1996) defines civil society as "what occupies the space between governments at the top and the atomised mass of individuals at the bottom." Bloomfield also distinguishes between a functioning and a non-functioning civil society. Hesees the role of a functioning civil society as providing relevant information to create an open society, pursuing a commitment for the peaceful settlement of differences and strengthening the moral and political fabric of society.[6] Bloomfields discussion fits in quite well with the perception that civil society has a moral and political role in the promotion of a just and peaceful society. In other words, the functioning of the civil society is dependent not just on how it is organised but on the values it pursues.

Simone (1992:159–164) refers to civil society as "a vast array of both formal and informal community organisations, religious institutions and movements, voluntary associations, trade unions and guilds, cultural institutions, co-operatives, fraternal and ethnic associations and human service delivery systems." He suggests that a comprehensive definition of civil society must include those outside the official economic and political structures. Simone sees civil society as a melting point of Western influence and African resistance. Because of this juxtaposition of influences, civil society "becomes a space of reformulation, mutation and realignment of social bodies, individual capacities and desires."

The UNDP (1992:26–33) seems to identify civil society as those groups and institutions that have fought for freedom and kept the struggle for democracy alive while recognising that the ballot box is not an end in itself.

A summary of reports on the reconstruction of Rwanda[7] implies that civil society comprises civilians who are outside both the government and political parties and who enjoy the confidence of the regime as well as that of the refugees and ordinary citizens. In this respect civil society is accorded various tasks in the reconstruction:

— a mediating role in the return of the refugees;
— acting as the political point of contact with ordinary citizens;
— supervising the reconstruction on behalf of the citizens.

Quite clearly, a definition of civil society whether in Africa or elsewhere has this overriding feature of a segment of society that has some degree of organisation to enable it to pursue defined objectives deemed good for society and inherently for itself. A functioning civil society is able to articulate these values and exert pressure for their attainment. In Africa, it is reasonable to assume that civil society has become conspicuous mainly against major political processes. The decolonisation experience and the history of the Pan-African[8] movement

---

[6] See the discussion by Bilello (1996) where she traces the rise of civil society in Mexico. Its re-emergence is against violent confrontations with the state.

[7] *Traits d'Union Rwanda: African Points of View on the Reconstruction of Rwanda*, Special Issue No. 5 November 1995.

[8] See the discussion in Amate C.O.C., where he traces the origins of the Pan-Africanist Movement.

serves as one such example of the rise of civil society in the struggle for independence. A segment of Africans and "non-Africans" who shared the beliefs in freedom organised themselves to pursue unity and the restoration of the dignity of the African people. One can therefore say that there was a functioning civil society in Africa and in the third world which was able to forge a new political order leading to independence. This civil society was not confined to boundaries but was a community across nations.

The unfolding of events after independence suggest, however, a drifting away from the ideals of the struggle for freedom. Hence the consequent consolidation of power through repressive laws, the narrowing of political expression through single party systems with massive presidential powers all had the effect of denying room for the discourse or further development of civil society. How else can one explain the extravagant crowning of Emperor Bokassa in the poor country of Central African Republic; the construction of the prestigious cathedral at Yamoussoukro put up by President Houphouet-Boigny at a cost of about US$ 200 million when the country was experiencing serious socio-economic problems; the faltering of democracy in Zaire; and the cancellation of the election results in Nigeria with the subsequent arrest of the winning presidential candidate Abiola? Perhaps Bayarts[9] observation that "civil society exists only so far as there is self-consciousness of its existence and of its opposition to the state" may be relevant to certain areas of Africa.

In the oft referred to "lost decades" of Africa, there seems to have been a decline in the functioning of civil society such that its voice was either absent or unheard or muzzled. Several developments and in particular the unchecked rise of the state that promoted a culture of intolerance were particularly significant for the decline of civil society. Babu (African Association of Political Science (AAPS), 1992: vi) observes that:

> ... the Institutions of democracy did not have time to ground themselves in society. There was too much faith in the state taking up the mission of democratic social transformation without necessarily being subjected to democratic transformation itself ... non-democratic methods were invoked to deal with the people, and the struggle for freedom was thereby relegated to the background.

Observing the past three decades, the progressive trend towards repression under the guise of stability and unity is only too clear. The use of state machinery such as the police as repressive tools unleashed an era of fear and "persecution" such that moderating forces and by implication civil society became increasingly passive. One can recall the arrests of academics, journalists and even murder of bishops[10] who dared to write or speak of excesses or injustice. In time, however, the state has been able to penetrate the various platforms of civil society and thus dampen its impact. Hence when Anyang Nyongo (AAPS, 1992:vi) states that "if there is any single institution in civil society

---

[9] Bayart, J. F., *Civil Society in Africa*, quoted in Hutchful (1995).

[10] For example the murder of Bishop Luwum of Uganda during the terror reign of Idi Amin.

which has tried to champion the cause of freedom and justice in Africa it is the church", there is a counter statement by Hutchful (1995:73) that the higher clergy have in many instances identified with the state. And similarly when we assign an ethical disseminating role to the media as a branch of civil society, one can cite the use of the media as a propaganda instrument without any adherence to ethics. The case of Rwanda, where the Radio Milles Collines was used to disseminate messages of war and to incite and perpetuate violence stands as a reminder of the duplicity of what we calmly refer to as branches of civil society.

The implications of the foregoing for the role of civil society in conflict management are manifold. Firstly, that what is generally referred to as civil society in Africa may require a qualified definition depending on the issues at hand. Secondly, the impact of civil society in conflict management can be either positive or negative. Ideally, the strength of civil society will depend on its commitment to pursue, without favour, respect for human rights and thus promote the building of a just society. Thirdly, the relationship between civil society and the state as players on the socio-political and economic scene is not necessarily mutually exclusive. A proper assessment of their respective roles must take into account the specific environment in which they operate including such factors as the cultural and religious impact, the openness of the society and the degree of awareness. It is that environment that finally determines the "tools" to be used either for managing or fomenting conflict.

CONDITIONS FOR EFFECTIVE MANAGEMENT OF CONFLICT
BY CIVIL SOCIETY

According to Morgenthau (1985, 1948:526), there are three necessary conditions for domestic peace: overwhelming power, suprasectional loyalties and expectation of justice. These conditions are fulfilled when individuals are not inclined to war and in the event that they are, the existence of overwhelming force (read the state) makes this impossible. The second condition is fulfilled when loyalty to society as a whole supersedes that to any part of it. Finally society must meet individual expectations of both economic and social justice in fulfilment of the last condition. Morgenthau himself confesses that these are not sufficient conditions. They would probably need to be accompanied by rationality, social and economic advancement and other mitigating factors. Although these conditions are useful in analysing the peaceful co-existence of the state and society at large, they do not explain the conditions that enable civil society or what he refers to as social agency to intervene in favour of peace. The premise that neither state nor society is able to maintain peace on its own is nevertheless valid for our consideration of the role of civil society in conflict management.

It is to the conditions that enhance or constrain the civil society that we now turn to.[11] It has for example been stated that one can hardly speak of civil society in Southern Sudan. But there are certainly Southern Sudanese academics, lawyers, journalists, teachers and women associations who could constitute a civil society. This observation strengthens the view that there are conditions in which a civil society can be weakened or destroyed and some conflicts may well reflect that. This can be through laws or methods which curtail or prohibit its association, functioning or even existence. In the Sudanese conflict, civil society has either been silenced or displaced and functions more as an opposition force locally or abroad. Its role in managing the conflict consists mainly of getting and maintaining international focus and attention on the conflict, lobbying for political and social reforms, and formulating proposals for managing that conflict. Locally, the church, women's groups and relief and development agencies[12] have been involved in community-based peace and development initiatives so that hope and a better quality of life can be attained. Through such initiatives, the community can be educated on their role in promoting a solution to the conflict. The work of the Sudanese Women's Voice for Peace, although on a limited scale, is one such effort. Other groups such as the Sudan Working Group,[13] People for Peace in Africa and The Horn of Africa focal groups in Europe and North America are pivotal in keeping that conflict on the regional and international agenda. They have also been actively engaged in promoting dialogue and negotiation among the protagonists.

If civil society is to play the role of preventing a resort to violence, then it must develop tools for dealing with both the state and the society at large. Such tools include dialogue or effective communication between and among the various strata of society and the agents of the state. The promotion of such dialogue serves both a psychological and real need: it allows for the expression of issues of concern or tension or the letting out of what could amount to uncontrollable anger. This could prove critical to the management of a conflict.

The development and promotion of the welfare of the people must not be forgotten, otherwise their largely unmet needs will be cause enough for conflict. In a situation where the expectations vary so much, it seems necessary to have an understanding of societal or group needs in order to disseminate even a common notion of peace. Although we may argue that peace is not just an absence of war, there are segments of society or individuals for whom peace is just that! For civil society to develop effective tools of conflict management,

---

[11] See the discussion by Bilello (1996) op. cit. on the conditions that caused civil society to become silent and then to rise again.

[12] World Vision International through its programme for Sudan has been most recently involved in a successful food for work initiative in Yambio. This has strengthened the thinking that it is possible even during the conflict stage to engage in productive activities and not just relief and thus increase the options for a settlement of that conflict.

[13] This is an informal forum of groups working for the peace of Sudan established with the support of partners in Europe and operating under the umbrella of the All African Council of Churches.

peace must be comprehensively addressed[14] to deal with those elements that either create or are camouflaged in a false sense of security. The penetration of this barrier opens up the sources of fear or despondency, or even the needs or interests that are being sheltered. Even with the knowledge that a false sense of security cannot reign forever, it will find adherents both locally and also internationally. The diamonds of Sierra Leone and the minerals of Zaire kept the signs and symptoms of conflict camouflaged for a long time. The "collaborators" were not just the State but business people, prominent investors both local and foreign, and the "nouveaux riches" for whom peace meant their own welfare.

In the case of Zaire and a number of African countries, student movements with some support from their professors have been the ones that have dared to raise their voice. They have not always done this in a systematic and peaceful manner but have acted rather spontaneously and sometimes employing very unorthodox means. Although their actions have usually been violently quelled, they have demonstrated the demands of society. Universities in many parts of Africa are thus hated, disliked but nevertheless courted by the powers that be. Their control has been a prime objective for governments. The role of academia in managing conflict must thus have room in a discussion of this nature.[15] The strongest role for this group lies in their ability to analyse, disseminate and express conflict issues and trends. Just as the struggle for independence is part of the curriculum in many African countries, peace education may now be an equally if not more relevant aspect of the needs of our times.

Events in the Horn of Africa may serve to illustrate this point further. Kenya has been one of the more stable countries in that region. Nearly all her neighbours except Tanzania have suffered protracted civil war. Leaders have used this to discourage change arguing that this would be inimical to peace. Thus in 1991, when it became evident that the old guard of the single party system would be challenged, the message from those leaders to the general populace was that such a move would be an invitation to chaos, violence and civil war. The ethnic clashes that coincided with the ushering in of multi-partyism provided the perfect setting to proclaim the demon in the latter and promote despondency. Civil society was thus called upon to perform not just the psy-

---

[14] See the discussion in UNDP (1994) on the components of human security. These are economic, food, environmental, personal, community and political. The essential feature of this concept of human security is that it takes into account both the physical and psychological needs of people universally and even at the personal and community levels. The proposal of the African Leadership Forum (May 1991) to establish a permanent Conference on Security, Stability, Development and Co-operation in Africa (CSSDA) also recognised the economic, social and political dimensions of security and their linkages in Africa. See also the article by Laurie Nathan, 1992, "Towards a Conference on Security, Stability, Development and Co-operation in Africa" in *Africa Insight*, 22(3), pp. 212–217.

[15] See Odhiambo's comments in his article, "Economics of Conflict Among Marginalised Peoples of Eastern Africa" in Zartman and Deng op. cit. Odhiambo questions the role of the African educated elites in arms trafficking and calls for an examination of the "moral responsibilities of the African intelligentsia [in the] fuelling and fanning of regional conflict".

chological function of distinguishing the cause and effect in the matter of the ethnic clashes, but also to educate people on the political process that the country was undergoing. In the period immediately after the repeal of Section 2A (which conferred the single party status on Kenya), the number of publications with mass circulation rose dramatically as did the number of non-governmental organisations dealing with civic education and peace questions. To neutralise their impact, leaders invoked the suffering brought on by civil wars in neighbouring countries, telling Kenyans that the same fate could befall them. This posed a formidable challenge to the political reform process, particularly in the rural areas where alternative views were not so easily entertained or even heard. State control of the radio was another challenge. With an illiteracy rate of over 50 per cent, the radio constitutes the single most important source of news and contact with the outside world and is an important opinion shaper particularly for the rural population. To respond to these and other challenges, bodies such as the Law Society of Kenya, Kituo Cha Sheria (an organisation that offers legal advice as a community service), the National Council on the Status of Women, the National Council of Churches of Kenya and other civic groups became engaged in the education of voters, in pursuing the cause of the clash victims, and in making attempts to set an agenda for debate on important national issues such as constitutional reforms and equal opportunities for women among others. Their activities were instrumental in moderating the impact of the violence-ridden prophecies which any analyst will observe had the makings of a civil war. Quite clearly, however, the averting of the crisis was not just the work of civil society but was a joint effort with partners in the international community.

The introduction of political conditionalities emphasising values (e.g. accountability, good governance and transparency) common to a new international political order gave added impetus to civil society. Appearing first as a concern for socio-economic progress after a decade of declining output, the new demands easily found support within Africa. Their convergence came to symbolise the wave of democratisation. From an economic point of view, the "nightmare scenario" depicted by the World Bank (1889) was adequate ground to push for both economic and political reform. The statistics justified a new approach.[16] African countries constituted over 60 per cent of all low income countries (World Bank 1989) with six of them—Guinea, Ghana, Liberia, Nigeria, Sao Tome and Principe, Zambia—having slipped into this category in the last decade. The total debt of sub-Saharan Africa increased from approximately

---

[16] Where, Gideon S., 1981, "History, Public Morality and Nation Building. A survey of Africa since Independence", 17th Inaugural Lecture, University of Nairobi, Reprinted 1992. World Bank (1989): Chapter 1, discusses the economic performance of sub-Saharan Africa and concludes that a long term policy perspective that takes into account issues of governance is necessary. Diamond, in his article "Promoting Democracy in Africa", in Munene, Nyunya and Adar (1995:193–219,199) sees the World Bank publication as having been pivotal in "reorienting attention to the need for political accountability, public debate, press freedom, political participation, pluralism, decentralisation, consensus building ... to achieve real economic development".

US$ 6 billion in 1970 to about US$ 134 billion in 1988, thus drawing the total debt close to the gross national product (GNP). Noting that per capita incomes had declined so much that the combined decline of the 1970s and 1980s would negate the growth witnessed in the 1960s, the Bank concluded that for the first time in post world war history, "a whole region has suffered retrogression over a generation" (World Bank 1986:9). The UNDP (1994:212) put the annual GNP growth rate of sub-Saharan Africa at minus 1:1 in the period 1980-91. The adult literacy rate still stood at a high of 54 per cent in 1992 (UNDP:1995). The fact that Africa was both the source and home of over one-third of the worlds recognised refugees, hosting over 12 million displaced persons (Global Coalition for Africa:1993) compounded the situation further.

This economic scenario, which was presented for the first time as a political problem, even by international institutions that claim to shun politics, has perhaps provided the strongest impetus for civil society to become more vocal, finding a natural alliance in the democratisation process. It is therefore not surprising that the prominence of civil society in the social, economic and political processes and by implication in the management of conflict appears to be a recent phenomenon in Africa. The economic scenario remains a potential challenge to peace and therefore conflict management. Thus when Morgenthau states that the condition of expectations from society must be met in order to have peace, there are sufficient examples to support that. The civil unrest in Zambia, including strikes by the civil service in early 1996, is an expression of unfulfilled expectations, particularly on the economic front. Indeed, Chiluba's earlier lamentation was prophetic: "We are paying the sins of the past 27 years and there is no way that we can remedy or rectify the situation of 27 years of mismanagement in a year or two, we just have to continue to pay the price".[17] His sentiments are echoed by Konare of Mali: "People from all walks of life are expecting the state to meet their demands and to do so at once ... democracy can easily backslide ... we need economic results if we are to strengthen it." These statements show the challenges that expectations pose for conflict management. An avoidance of conflict requires support for economic development.

Mali and Zambia are of particular interest because they were among the successful transitions to multipartyism. Yet in Zambia, for example, it is civil society that has been vocal on the weaknesses of the new regime and this among other factors has almost popularised the old order. The change of guard in Benin back to the "former" dictator Kerekou is instructive. At the risk of appearing an apologist, some very serious questions must be posed here to civil society in terms of its responsibility in managing change and therefore conflict. Are there issues that civil society needs to play down in order to promote stability and peace? Can civil society define principles and be impartial on these and in particular the proper management of affairs, which is a precondition for

---

[17] *The Courier* No. 138, March–April 1993. Interview with President Konare of Mali pp. 2–4 and with President Chiluba of Zambia pp. 37–39.

peace? Civil society need not see itself as the proclaimed enemy of the government but must use its vast human resources not only vocally but productively. Hence branches of civil society involved in economically productive ventures, such as the promotion of small-scale enterprises and other income-generating activities or those engaged in providing health services or other basic needs, must be seen as playing a role in managing conflicts of expectations. In short, the economic and social empowerment of people is an equally important factor in managing conflicts.

The importance of the foregoing is to understand not only the conditions that have promoted the role of civil society but to emphasise the point that civil society's role in conflict management must be seen in the context or environment of the specific conflict, the understanding of the roots of that conflict, the formulation of options for peace and the ability to communicate these both locally and internationally. We must also understand that civil society, because of its varied composition and interests, does not always act in harmony.[18] However, due to the many sources of conflict, the developmental role of civil society becomes an integral aspect of conflict management. The foregoing allows us now to make some statements on the location and identification of civil society while bearing in mind its role as a conflict manager.

Against the democratisation process, we may concur that civil society has been located between the state and the "voiceless" ordinary citizen and has specifically comprised professional associations of lawyers, academics, trade unionists, journalists as well as women's groups, non-governmental organisations and religious groups, particularly the church. On the development front, civil society has consisted of local and international networks in the form of non-governmental organisations.

AN AGENDA FOR THE CIVIL SOCIETY IN CONFLICT MANAGEMENT

In the varying conflicts of Africa, civil society has been expected to play a role, yet it is only when civil society is given space that it can respond to issues. Without clear objectives which respond to the needs of society and to the maintenance of peace and justice, civil society cannot expect to receive the "moral mandate" upon which it acts. A central feature of a functioning civil society must remain the maintenance of a just and peaceful society. In situations of conflict, however, the impact of civil society is strengthened in its finding an echo in the international arena.

---

18 See for example ICVA (1995), the report of the symposium on the *Role of NGO Emergency Assistance in Promoting Peace and Reconciliation* on the occasion of The World Social Summit for Development. The report discusses the role of humanitarian agencies in aiding or abating conflicts.

Civil society, because of its composition, can play a role in preventive diplomacy through sensitising both politicians and ordinary citizens on issues that could flare up into conflict. The institutions of civil society most ably located for this are the media, non-governmental organisations, professional associations and the church due to their access to a wide spectrum of society. The role here would be to set an agenda for public debate on conflict issues, to inform both the local and international public and to influence policy-makers.

Since most wars in Africa are fought in the rural areas it is imperative that the presence of civil society be conspicuous there. In this respect, civil society has a duty to expose and seek response to the suffering of the civilians. Such conflicts need to be "rescued from obscurity and drawn into the [national and international] political mainstream and made the subject of peacemaking. Civil society, particularly that which is rural based (community groups, local and international NGOs, educators) needs to be vigilant and to draw attention to impending or existing issues of conflict. While drawing attention to the conflict, there is need also to propose means for a reduction of the conflict particularly at the community level.

Violation of human rights is a fundamental reason for conflicts in Africa. Yet almost half the African population is illiterate, unaware of its rights and vulnerable to manipulation. Illiteracy means that it is the spoken word or images and not the written word that constitute the channels of communication. In addition about 70 per cent of the African population resides in the largely underdeveloped rural areas, away from the centres of national activity and decision-making. It is reasonable to assume that a good part of Africa's population is vulnerable to manipulation for reasons of fear, want or egoistical desires for influence. The election process of Kenya's 1992 multi-party elections may bear us out. The use of the academia to write papers that distorted facts in favour of the ruling party and the buying of support by the then well-financed Youth For Kanu 92 are examples of this vulnerability. Civil society must be sensitive to the fundamental issues of this manipulation which in times of tension can become a source of conflict. Indeed, the ethics of civil society actions need to be brought into proper focus. In the meantime, matters like voter education and election monitoring for electoral processes, continuous civic education, the promotion of literacy programmes, the development of school curricula that address peace and conflict issues and the mobilisation of opinion leaders for the message of peace deserve attention. Civil society also needs to consider alternative but effective channels of communication, especially where the media is underdeveloped or not liberal. The concerns for rural development need to be articulated and supported to avoid the use of the rural population as a pawn in the conflict. Civil society links between the urban and rural areas need to be strengthened.

The building of partnerships among institutions or representatives of civil society at sub-regional, regional and international levels is essential for addressing conflicts comprehensively. The spill-over effects are, after all, felt beyond borders, for example in the form of refugees. In this respect, the results of the Arusha Conference of 1990 the "African Charter for Popular Participation in Development Transformation" and the African Leadership Forum are important bridge-building measures. Governmental organisations like the OAU should be encouraged to continue giving room to civil society in their deliberative process. The recent joint activities with a number of NGOs such as the International Peace Academy intended to deliberate on better ways of managing conflicts, are a move in the right direction.

One of civil society's greatest challenges is to work towards ending the cycle of violence that is now characteristic of conflicts in, say the Great Lakes region and participating judiciously in reconstruction. To do this, institutions for good governance need to be established or strengthened. Structures that are inherently conflictual need to be reviewed whether these be embedded in constitutions or in laws that promote discrimination and exclusion. Professional associations supported by the international community perhaps offer the best platforms for the reform of structures. The success of the role of civil society will depend on its ability to transcend ethnic, religious and "class" differences in the articulation and pursuit of common concerns.

Civil society also has a role in policy formulation and rethinking in order to influence the opinion of the public and ultimately that of the policy-makers and donors. Policies that address the concerns of both minorities and majorities need particular attention to reduce the sources of conflict. The cost of conflict and/or reconstruction is too high price to pay for neglect of any aspect of peace. The UN Budget for peace-keeping rose from US$ 30 million in 1987 to US$ 3.6 billion in 1994. It has been estimated that South Africa alone would require about US$ 10 billion for the creation of an economic base that will support post-apartheid democracy. Ways must be found to manage or end conflicts. It is time also to consider how the youth can be brought into the mainstream of conflict management. Perhaps the many talented actors and musicians of Africa who have a message for peace may here find a most honourable role. National civil society can play a useful role in this. In most of Africa, however, civil society will need to be strengthened and its concerns diversified beyond the political agenda. In defining a role for civil society, independence of opinion and action, confidence-building and a genuine concern for a peaceful and just society in Africa will be the central components. Indeed, the cross-roads for Africa provides both opportunities and challenges for civil society and the scope for action is vast. Rebuilding or strengthening the institutions of civil society, building national, regional or international coalitions and addressing conflict are issues that demand action. Civil society can and must rise up to the challenge!

In the final analysis, it must be stated that civil society is part of society and cannot be perceived as an isolated group. Hence, its own interests may blur or sharpen its vision for managing conflicts. On the whole, however, it is the assumption of civility that generates hope in its role. In concluding, it seems pertinent to offer some suggestions for strengthening civil society in Africa with the support of the international community. These include: a clear and unfaltering commitment to good governance; supporting political and legal reforms to make systems both inclusive and participatory; strengthening institutions of civil society such as the media through, for example, training and exchange programmes; support to universities and research institutions so that they can offer quality education and conduct serious and independent research even on issues such as conflict management; promotion of literacy programmes and civic education; empowerment of women and rural communities through development programmes in such areas as health, education, business and commerce.

# REFERENCES

African Academy of Sciences (AAS), 1993, *Arms and Daggers in the Heart of Africa: Studies on Internal Conflicts.* Nairobi: Academy Science Publishers.

Andreassen, B.A. et al., 1993, *A Bobbled Democracy: The Kenya General Elections 1992.* Bergen: Chr. Michelsen Institute.

Amate, C.O.C., 1986, *Inside the OAU: Pan-Africanism in Practice.* London: Macmillan.

African Association of Sciences (AAPS), 1992, *30 Years of Independence in Africa: The Lost Decades?* Nairobi: Academy of Science Publishers.

Anyang, Nyongo P., 1992, *The One Party State and its Apologists.* AAPS 1–7.

Babu, A.M., 1992, *The Struggle for Post-Uhuru Africa.* AAPS 9–24.

Bilello, S., 1996, "Mexico: The Rise of the Civil Society", in *Current History*, February, pp. 82–87.

Bloomfield, Lincoln P., 1996, "Civil Society Strengthens the Fabric of Peace", in *Christian Science Monitor,* 8 April, p. 19.

Bruchaus, E.M., 1994, "On the Way to the Civil Society: Non-Governmental Organisations in Africa", in *Development and Cooperation*, 1, pp. 18–20.

Clough, M., 1992, *Free at Last? US Policy toward Africa at the End of the Cold War.* New York: Council on Foreign Relations Press.

Deng, F.M. and W.I. Zartman (eds.), 1992, *Conflict Resolution in Africa.* Washington DC: The Brookings Institution.

Global Coalition for Africa, 1993, *African Social and Economic Trends: Annual Report.* Washington DC: The Global Coalition for Africa.

Johnston, D. and C. Sampson (eds.), 1994, *Religion, the Missing Dimension of Statecraft.* Oxford: Oxford University Press.

IPA/OAU Consultation, 1996, Conference Documents.

Kok Nyot, P., 1993, "The Ties that Will not Bind: Conflict and Racial Cleavage in Sudan", in *African Academy of Sciences,* op. cit.

Lund, M., 1994, *Preventive Diplomacy and American Foreign Policy: A Guide for the post-Cold War Era.* Washington DC: United States Institute for Peace.

Morgenthau, H., 1985 (1948), *Politics Among Nations: The Struggle for Power and Peace.* Alfred A. Knopf Inc.

Munene, M. et al., 1995, *The United States and Africa: From Independence to the End of the Cold War.* Nairobi: East African Educational Publishers.

Nathan, L., "Towards a Conference on Security, Stability, Development and Co-operation in Africa", in *Africa Insight,* op. cit.

Nyinguro, P.O., 1995, "The Impact of the Cold War on Regional Security: The Case of Africa", in M. Munene et al., op. cit.

Okullu, H., 1987, *Church and Politics in East Africa.* Nairobi: Uzima Press Ltd.

Otunnu, O., 1995, *The Peace and Security Agenda of the United Nations: From a Cross-road into the Next Century.* New York: International Peace Academy.

OCMCT/SOS, 1993, Torture: *Africa: A New Lease of Life towards Economic Policies for the Prevention of Serious Human Rights Violations in Kenya. A Symposium Report.*

Project Ploughshares, 1995, *Armed Conflicts Report 1995.* Waterloo (CAN): Institute of Peace and Conflict Studies.

Regehr, E., 1993, *War After the Cold War: Shaping Canadian Response.* Ploughshares Working Paper 93:3.

Simone, M.A., 1992, "Between the Lines: African Civil Societies and the Remaking of Urban Communities", in *Africa Insight*, 22(3), pp. 159–164.

State of the World Forum, 1995, *Annual Report.*

UNDP, 1992; 1993; 1994; 1995, *Human Development Report.*

Were, G., 1992, *History, Public Morality and Nation Building: A Survey of Africa since Independence.* 17th Inaugural Lecture, University of Nairobi, 1981.

# PART III

*Technical pieces...*

# Africa and the Superpower—An Agenda for Peace

*Herman J. Cohen*

I admit it. I am nostalgic for the period 1980–1993 when the United States was the leading peace-maker in Africa. The list of African internal conflicts which were the objectives of US intervention during that period reads like the ribbons on a military regimental banner: Namibia, Angola, Ethiopia, Mozambique, Liberia, South Africa, Sudan, Rwanda and Somalia. There were victories. There were defeats. And there were some ambiguous results. Whatever the outcomes, our work was characterized by activism and leadership. Looking back at those heady days, I am not surprised at my own nostalgia because the United States was using its power in pursuit of very constructive policies, and it was exciting for me as a career diplomat to be a part of it.

Are those days gone forever? Has the United States, in its new inward looking mode, become a disinterested bystander? If Africa is to bear the major responsibility for managing its own conflicts, which is certainly a worthy objective, is there a role for the United States? Is there a unique "value added" element that the sole remaining superpower can provide in an interdependent world?

The answers to these questions lie in an analysis of the changes that are taking place in Africa, especially in the nature of conflict, in the evolution of regional geopolitical doctrines, and in the quality of political transitions. On the American side, the key analysis concerns the African paradigm as perceived from Washington, now that the continent has become "unstrategic".

## AFRICA'S CHANGING ENVIRONMENT

### The nature of conflict

Africa's major protracted civil wars are essentially relics of the past. The violent conflicts in Angola, Mozambique and Ethiopia involved big money and big powers fighting surrogate wars. The apartheid regime in South Africa, which expired in 1994, was a substantial contributor to the arming of insurgents in Mozambique and Angola. The Soviet Union was the chief arms supplier to the governments of all three countries. The United States Government supported the UNITA insurgents in Angola, and private American and Portuguese funding assisted the RENAMO guerrillas in Mozambique. Private interests in the

Middle East and North America, and the Government of the Sudan, provided important support to insurgents in Ethiopia. The Cold War, the apartheid system, and the overflow of the Middle East crisis are no longer sources of aggravated conflict in Africa.[1]

Two of Africa's most destructive internal conflicts since 1989, Liberia and Rwanda, were conceived, fuelled and sustained from neighbouring territories, with the active connivance of neighbouring governments. There were no non-African players. Both conflicts generated massive refugee flows and saturated their respective sub-regions with arms. Both military actions were designed to oust "unsavoury" regimes in rapid surgical strikes, but the unforeseen results have been catastrophic in terms of human and economic losses. In the case of Liberia, the neighbours that helped fuel the war suffered destructive rebounds in the form of hundreds of thousands of refugees on their soil, increased criminality, and lost commerce. Although there is no guarantee that such "neighbour-generated" actions will not be repeated in the future, the unexpectedly disastrous consequences of the wars in Liberia and Rwanda make it unlikely.

That leaves the type of conflicts we were witnessing in Burundi and Rwanda at the beginning of 1996 as the most likely prototypes for the future. These conflicts are fuelled by deep feelings of insecurity, severe economic hardship aggravated by discriminatory ethnic politics, and blocked political transitions. In such environments, regional or ethnic groups form armed militia in defence of their interests against states or other power structures deemed to be predatory and/or life threatening.

Another environment conducive to violent conflict exists in some African countries where a process of democratization or political liberalization is already underway. When these transitional processes become corrupted by rigged elections and the monopolization of power by minorities, or when "winner-take-all" politics preclude inclusion, violence may be more likely to ensue than if there had been no liberalization in the first instance.

In view of the changing nature of conflict in Africa, Americans can correctly question the utility of an active conflict resolution policy on the part of the United States Government. Where are the correct entry points, and what are the appropriate assets that can be brought to bear in situations where the external element is virtually absent, and the internal element is so dominant? Is its traditionally generous humanitarian response to both natural and man-made catastrophes the only role left for the United States?

---

[1] There is one significant exception to this optimistic forecast. As of early 1996, the Horn of Africa was under the threat of a spreading internal conflict in the Sudan which had important implications for the stability of neighbouring Ethiopia, Eritrea, and Uganda. Middle East involvement was indicated because of alleged Iranian support to the Islamic fundamentalist government of the Sudan, and private Saudi financing of the Sudanese National Islamic Front, the ruling party.

## Africa's changing geopolitical doctrine

One of the reasons the United States dominated the African peace-making scene until 1993 was the vacuum created by the doctrine of non-interference in internal affairs followed by the Organization of African Unity in all cases of internal conflict. Since civil war is "internal" by definition, the OAU was prohibited from addressing such crises.

By 1992, it had become clear that internal conflict in Africa constituted a threat to peace and security to all countries in the immediate vicinity of a civil war. Refugee flows and cross-border arms proliferation are no minor matters. It became not only appropriate for the African collectivity to address these conflicts, but a necessary element of development policy. Beyond the destruction of lives and infrastructure, the creation of famine conditions, and the destabilization of entire sub-regions, civil war also destroys the economic bases of countries, including the creditworthiness without which investments will not be forthcoming.

At their annual OAU meeting in 1992, the African Heads of State reached consensus on the need for a continental mechanism through which internal conflict could be addressed. After much debate, they decided in 1993 to establish a Mechanism for Conflict Prevention, Management and Resolution within the OAU Secretariat. They decided that policy for the Mechanism would be determined by a rotating board of directors at the ministerial and ambassadorial levels known as the Central Organ. Policy would be implemented by the Secretary-General of the OAU with the assistance of the Secretariat staff assigned to the Mechanism.[2]

The OAU decisions effectively broke the doctrinal barrier of non-interference in internal affairs in the area of conflict management. In addition, an unspoken doctrinal change was adopted with respect to the treatment of armed internal opposition. The club of heads of state, many of whom were "life president" products of the one-party system, must have winced when they realized that "conflict prevention, resolution and management" implied the recognition of armed opposition as citizens of their respective countries, with legitimate grievances that needed addressing. Gone were the days when armed oppositionists were automatically characterized as "bandits", "criminals" or "agents of imperialism or apartheid." The fact that both the UNITA and RENAMO insurgency movements had achieved political legitimacy in Angola and Mozambique respectively by 1992, thanks in part to strenuous arm-twisting by American diplomats, had an important impact on the OAU change of doctrine.[3]

---

2 See OAU documents: *Report of the Secretary-General on Conflicts in Africa: Proposals for an OAU Mechanism for Conflict Prevention and Resolution*, Dakar, Senegal, June, 1992; *Interim Report of the Secretary -General on the Mechanism for Conflict Prevention, Management and Resolution*, Addis Ababa, Ethiopia, February, 1993.

3 During my own intensive involvement with negotiations in both Angola and Mozambique between 1987 and 1992, I was persuaded that the refusal of the MPLA and FRELIMO regimes re-

Finally, the establishment of the OAU "Mechanism marked the end of an old form of interference in internal affairs just as it was inaugurating a new one. The "dirty little secret" practice of one African government assisting with impunity the insurgents fighting a neighbouring government would no longer be feasible, as in the cases of Liberia and Rwanda. Henceforth, such problems would have to be brought into the light of day, as in the case of the Sudan's support for rebels in Eritrea, Ethiopia and Uganda during all of 1995 and continuing into 1996.

## The impact of political transition

The evolution of the nature of internal conflict, and the revisions of geopolitical doctrine in Africa, have taken place against the background of a significant experiment in political transition that began toward the latter half of the 1980s. In place of the doctrines of "one-party democracy" and "African socialism" that dominated African political discourse between 1965 and 1985, the doctrines of "multiparty democracy" and "market economics" have come to the fore since 1988. The fact that the Cold War came to an end during 1988–89 was not unrelated to Africa's change of ideological direction.

African governments and their leaders have approached the issue of political and economic liberalization with varying degrees of zeal and enthusiasm. What is clear throughout, however, is that the opening of African societies to greater popular participation in decision-making, to increased freedom of expression and movement, and to increased competition for power and resources has had a noticeable impact on the nature and extent of internal conflict.

In some cases, the rise of democracy has underpinned a decline in conflict. This has been most noteworthy in southern Africa. In other cases, democratization has been mishandled to the point where conflict, or the potential for conflict, has actually been increased. This has happened in such major resource-rich countries as Zaire, Cameroon and Nigeria. In still other countries, democratization has been managed more or less correctly, but the implications for the realignment of political and economic power have been so traumatic that fear and insecurity have tended to overwhelm confidence. Examples of this phenomenon are discernible in Rwanda, Burundi, Gabon and Chad.

Political transition in the form of political and economic liberalization has brought new problems to Africa while seeking ways to solve old ones. This phenomenon has had an impact on conflict, both positive and negative. Friends of Africa, in seeking to be helpful, must therefore take the various manifestations of political transition very seriously.[4]

---

spectively to acknowledge any political legitimacy for the two insurgencies, UNITA and RENAMO, prolonged both wars two to four years longer than necessary.

[4] Africa Leadership Forum and Global Coalition for Africa, *Study on Transition to Democracy in Africa*. Consists of book-length case studies of transition in nine African countries written by

## THE UNITED STATES' INVOLVEMENT IN AFRICAN CONFLICT MANAGEMENT

### America's internal debate

At an OAU workshop on conflict management in Addis Ababa in January 1996, an American expert employed by the UN High Commission for Refugees described his own country's outlook on developing world conflict as follows:

"The United States suffers from a lack of political will. It lacks the political will to intervene in third world conflicts, and it lacks the political will to stay out."

When one observes the debates in the US Congress about intervention in Bosnia, and when one watches the many discussion groups on American television, the dilemma summarized by the above quotation is apparent.

One of the most admired and respected personalities among retired American career diplomats is Lawrence Eagleburger, who was Secretary of State during the last eight months of the Bush Administration. In his frequent appearances on television and at public meetings, Eagleburger is at great pains to enunciate a position on the role of the United States in conflict management. On the one hand, he does not want to appear uncaring about suffering. On the other hand, he wants to make it clear that American capacity for dealing with other peoples' troubles is limited. He is the first to acknowledge that the United States military has certain important capabilities that other governments do not have in terms of logistics, transportation and organization. But he also has a realistic understanding about the internal competition for resources. At a conference on conflict prevention sponsored by the Council of Foreign Relations in New York in December, 1995, Eagleburger said, "if we intervene in Rwanda, doesn't that mean we also have to intervene in Abkazia, and in East Timor, and in Azerbaijan?"[5]

Another illustration of the US dilemma was in the government's reaction to the Somalia crisis in 1992–93. During the first eight months of 1992, the State Department and the White House were bombarded by messages, many from members of Congress, demanding that the United States do something to stop the starvation in Somalia. After 16 American soldiers were killed in Mogadishu in October 1993, there was an analogous outpouring of demands for a rapid departure from Somalia.

To its credit, the Clinton Administration has attempted to formulate a policy on conflict intervention that seeks to reconcile America's external schizophrenia. In a national security document identified as Presidential Decision Directive (PDD) 25, Clinton attempted to establish a line between intervention and

academic teams residing in the countries concerned. Financing was provided by the Governments of the USA, Sweden, the UK and Norway. The study was still unpublished as of March 1996, but a transnational analysis was completed in November 1995, and was available for distribution as of March 1996. The analysis paper is entitled *Study on Transition to Democracy in Africa: Policy Issues and Implications.*

[5] The author was a participant in the meeting.

non-intervention based on "vital interests." In addition to serving as a guideline for American decision making, the "vital interests" criterion was also to be applied to potential United Nations interventions in conflict. The only problem with the directive is that the definition of "vital interests" is left to be determined on a case by case basis.[6]

The dilemma of defining "vital interests" was illustrated in the debate over American participation in the NATO intervention in Bosnia which began in December 1995 in support of the Dayton peace agreements signed by the governments of Serbia, Croatia and Bosnia. The "vital interest" defined by Clinton was not so much the importance of bringing peace to the Balkans, but upholding the credibility of NATO. In other words, conflict resolution, no matter how desirable, cannot be subsumed by the term "vital interests" on its own. Direct American intervention to end conflict must always be justified by something else that falls into the "vital interest" category.

What does all of this mean for African conflict? It is unlikely that any African conflict will qualify for the "vital interest" category. That means American troops are not likely to be exposed to possible harm anywhere in Africa, and are not likely to be involved in peace-keeping operations in support of peace agreements.[7] On the other hand, it does not necessarily mean the United States will stand in the way of UN Security Council efforts to intervene in African conflicts, provided sufficient resources are available, which depends in turn on the settlement of American arrears to the UN peace operations account.[8] In the final analysis, the United Nations continues to be the most viable outlet for that side of the United States persona that "lacks the political will to stay out" of developing world conflict.[9]

In the area of diplomatic intervention, the fact that the Organization of African Unity, sub-regional organizations, and civil society institutions are making an effort to develop their own capacity for managing conflict, provides a good opportunity for the United States to make a contribution to the African peace agenda. Unlike the period 1981–1993, during which the United States had a high profile, and played a leadership role in addressing African conflict, the new American role, to be effective, should henceforth be low key and sup-

---

[6] Department of State, *The Clinton Administration's Policy on Reforming Multilateral Peace Operations*, Washington, DC: Bureau of International Organization Affairs, 1994.

[7] This policy does not preclude the use of American armed forces to rescue American citizens or property who may be caught up in Africa's internal conflicts. For example, an American amphibious force with 1,500 combat troops was deployed in the Atlantic Ocean near Liberia in 1990 in order to facilitate the departure of 5,000 American citizens. The mission of this force excluded any intervention to stop the fighting near the capital city of Monrovia, less than 25 miles away.

[8] Inter Press Service International News: *UN Fights to Save its Peace-keeping Department*. Tuesday, December 19, 1995: IT85. Article by Thalif Deen.

[9] This is best illustrated in the case of the Burundi conflict which was the subject of considerable hand wringing in Washington during the period January–March 1996. Despite the restrictions of PDD-25, the Americans were the strongest supporters of UN Secretary-General Boutros-Ghali's proposal to deploy 25,000 troops in a neighbouring country as a measure to prevent a possible genocide.

portive of Africa's own programmes. A low key, low profile approach on the part of the United States is the only one that makes sense from both the African and American political points of view.

## Building African capacity

Quietly, and with a minimum of self-congratulation, the United States Government has been increasingly supportive of the various conflict management programmes begun by Africans themselves. As early as 1991, for example, the United States provided supplies and materiel to completely equip 1,500 Senegalese troops for peace-keeping duties in Liberia. In the same conflict, the American contribution to overall peace-keeping operations conducted by the Economic Community of West African States between 1990 and 1996 has been in excess of $50 million. Of additional significance is the fact that US–African cooperation in the Liberian conflict has been carried out without any reference to the United Nations.

Since the establishment of the OAU Mechanism for Conflict Prevention, Management and Resolution in 1993, the United States has been the leading donor to this new operational unit. During 1994 and 1995, the United States provided assistance valued at $ 5 million for the purchase of communications gear, computers, transportation and consultant services.[10] The objective of this ongoing American assistance programme as of 1996 was twofold: (1) support implementation of the OAU decision to install and operate a command and control system for information gathering and the conduct of peace operations out of its headquarters in Addis Ababa; and (2) support the establishment of a 100-person OAU military observer force that could be deployed to carry out peace monitoring duties on short notice. While modest in scope, the fulfilment of these two objectives would demonstrate seriousness of purpose on the part of the OAU, which could lead eventually to more ambitious programmes such as the establishment of a rapid reaction peace-keeping force of up to 1,000 soldiers.

Although it is a leader in the field of capacity building for peace operations in Africa, the United States is not alone in providing cooperation in this field. The French and the British Governments, which have the most experience in providing assistance to African military establishments, are also very active. The two former colonial powers are concentrating mainly on the development of doctrine and capacity for peace-keeping operations. As modest beginnings, the French are supporting a West African census of available military units for training and service in a rapid reaction force, and the British are supporting the development of peace operations training curriculums for African military academies. These activities are in addition to bilateral military cooperation support

---

[10] There were additional US funds available for support to the OAU Mechanism during 1994–95 which had to be utilized elsewhere in Africa because of the OAU's inability to absorb the additional money in a timely manner.

provided to African countries in the form of training and technical assistance. There are also interesting activities taking place at various sub-regional levels. In 1996, for example, the Norwegian Government began financial training for peace-keeping in Southern Africa in cooperation with the South African Institute of Defence Policy.[11]

### Support for negotiations

In recent years, the United States has established a pattern of indirect support to African peace negotiations which merits further study and possible institutionalization. Several observers, including Professor Donald Rothchild of the University of California (Davis), consider this to be both effective and highly relevant as we look to the future of conflict management in Africa.[12]

The Mozambique peace negotiations and implementation process from 1987 to 1994 enjoyed official US participation only in its later stages, mostly with respect to implementation of the October 1992 Rome accords. The official mediators were the St. Egidio Catholic lay order based in Rome, and later the Government of Italy. Throughout this period, however, the United States provided invaluable indirect support. Presidents Reagan and Bush both exercised considerable influence on Mozambique's President Chissano in the course of negotiations. After negotiations started, the State Department's Bureau of African Affairs utilized the American Embassy to the Vatican as a base of technical support for juridical, military, and political negotiators on both sides. Talent and expertise from the entire American national security apparatus was called upon at various times. When negotiations reached temporary stalemate, as they did from time to time, the US launched high level interventions with the different players as well as with Mozambique's neighbours. The American Assistant Secretary of State, for example, held a number of discreet meetings in Malawi with RENAMO leader Alphonso Dhlakama in an effort to break deadlocks. A number of high level missions were also undertaken to Kenya under the cover of US–Kenyan bilateral relations, with the main purpose to enlist the help of President Daniel Arap Moi, who had considerable influence with the RENAMO leadership.[13]

The United States maintained a similar posture in the second Angola negotiation between 1992 and 1994 leading to the Lusaka accords. A retired diplomat, Ambassador Paul Hare, was assigned to assist the lead negotiator, UN Special Representative Blondin Beye, in a secondary role. The US contri-

---

[11] Cohen, Herman J. *Conflict Management in Africa*, CSIS Africa Notes 181 of February, 1996. Published by the Center for Strategic and International Studies, Washington, DC.

[12] David R. Smock and Chester A. Crocker (eds.), *African Conflict Resolution: The US Role in Peacemaking*. United States Institute of Peace, Washington, DC 1995. Chapter 4 by Donald Rothchild, *The US Role in Managing African Conflicts: Lessons from the Past*, pp. 39–56.

[13] Hume, Cameron, *Ending Mozambique's War*, United States Institute of Peace, Washington, DC 1994.

butions to the Arusha accords for Rwanda and the Accra accords for Liberia were also indirect and supportive of African mediators. This mode of indirect intervention carries the advantage of making available extensive American expertise and widespread information networks, while keeping the lead role in African hands.

## Support for post-conflict reconstruction

For African countries coming out of civil war, support for demobilization and reconstruction is essential to prevent a return to civil war. United States assistance programmes in those countries have quite correctly taken this requirement into account. As of the beginning of 1996, American support to demobilization programs was ongoing in Ethiopia, Angola, Niger, Sierra Leone, Eritrea, Uganda and Mozambique. Similar assistance was planned for implementation in Liberia as soon as a real cease-fire can be achieved.

The elimination of anti-personnel and anti-vehicle mines on roads and agricultural areas is essential to the revival of rural economic activity. The US assistance programmes in Angola, Rwanda, and Mozambique all have significant demining components.

The reintegration of former combatants is important to reduce the prospects for renewed warfare. Such reintegration programmes are sometimes linked to the rehabilitation of war damaged infrastructure, thereby hastening a return to normal peacetime conditions. Reintegration/rehabilitation programmes receiving support from the US include Angola, Eritrea, Mozambique and Ethiopia.[14]

## Support for democratization

Since 1990, the United States has been increasingly supportive of political liberalization. That support has taken a number of forms. The largest has been financial and technical support for democratic elections. In addition, American assistance programmes have contributed to improved governance, especially in the areas of legal and judicial reform, and educational support to the growth of a free press. The Americans have also assisted the strengthening of civil society organizations, especially among African women. Although not directly related to conflict resolution, support for democratization and good governance helps create the type of environment in which normal political conflict and competition can be resolved without resort to violence. Good governance is effectively the most important element of conflict prevention.

Not everyone is convinced that the United States is either sincere or effective in its support for democratization in Africa. On the one hand, there is a growing

---

[14] United States Agency for International Development. *USAID Activities Inventory* in the areas of conflict resolution, preventive diplomacy, early warning systems, and relief to development activities. Unpublished internal document prepared within the Policy and Program Coordination Bureau (PPC) by Kathleen Michels and Heather McHugh, February, 1996, Washington, DC.

concern that the United States is insensitive to Africa's own concerns and practices, and seeks only to make lists of successful "free and fair" elections. In addition, the US is considered to be inconsistent, denouncing the cancellation of a democratic election that favoured the islamic party in Algeria, while negotiating with President Mobutu in Zaire who is accused by many of doing everything possible to subvert the democratic process in that country.[15]

On the other hand, the American fascination with democratization as the motor force of post-Cold War doctrine appears to be alive and well at the beginning of 1996 only in Africa. In other regions, "not every democrat is being portrayed as an ally, and not every ally as a democrat." Trade, arms proliferation and drugs have become more important issues in most regions. Moreover, "fake democracies" with no depth in "civic virtue" can be causes of violence and conflict. Some policy makers feel, therefore, that democracy is not as important as stability. In Africa however, where the United States has no significant economic or national security issues, democracy continues to be a top priority, for better or for worse.[16]

The fact that "democracy" is the main game in town in Africa for the Americans suggests that the United States will probably continue to be available for support to Africa's own conflict management efforts.


BEYOND CAPACITY BUILDING—RECOMMENDATIONS TO THE AMERICAN GOVERNMENT

**Favourable policy environment**

Support for conflict management and resolution in Africa continued to be an official policy of the Clinton Administration as of the beginning of 1996. In a statement before the House of Representatives Foreign Affairs Committee in June 1994, the American Assistant Secretary of State for Africa, Ambassador George E. Moose, said: "Conflict resolution in Africa is a central issue for those of us involved in African policy, and one that warrants ongoing attention".[17] The Clinton policy has the support of the United States Congress, articulated in the Africa Conflict Resolution Act of 1994 which calls for assistance to capacity building in Africa. Equally important, the legislation authorizes the expenditure of foreign assistance funds to implement the policy.[18]

The Clinton Administration's emphasis has been on capacity building which is the main intent of the Congressional mandate. An interagency plan to im-

---

[15] Zartman, I. William. *Guidelines for Preserving Peace* in *African Conflict Resolution*, United States Institute of Peace, Washington, DC, 1995: p. 102.

[16] Miller, Judith. *America's Burden: At Hour of Triumph, Democracy Recedes As the Global Ideal:* The New York Times, February 18, 1996. Sec. 4, p. 1.

[17] Moose, George E. Assistant Secretary of State for African Affairs: Testimony before the House Foreign Affairs Africa Subcommittee, June 8, 1994. Transcript available in *Hearing, on Conflict Resolution in Africa on H.R. 4541*. Washington, G.P.O. 1995.

[18] United States Congress. Public Law 103–381, 1994: *Africa Conflict Resolution Act*. Washington, DC.

plement the legislation was circulated within the United States Government in April 1995. The paper included a variety of activities that were already ongoing at the time the legislation was enacted. For example, the Defence Department (DOD) provided twenty trucks to the Ghanaian Army for use in the West African peace-keeping operation in Liberia. The United States Information Agency (USIA) completed a project in South Africa entitled "The Media and Conflict Resolution." The Arms Control and Disarmament Agency (ACDA) proposed to provide technical assistance to the Southern Africa region for "arms control, confidence and security building measures." The Agency for International Development (USAID) provided funds to NGOs in six African countries for "the psycho-social needs of children affected by war." For fiscal year 1995, the Defence and State Departments programmed $ 33 million in support of African "demobilization and reintegration efforts" which included demining. These are just examples from a much longer list of related activities.[19]

What is important about the Clinton Administration's response to the Congressional mandate to support conflict resolution in Africa is not the various activities that have been undertaken, but the creative methods utilized to target scarce funds from a variety of sources and agencies. It is clear that the national security agencies have been instructed to make a real coordinated effort in Africa, and the Republican majority that took control of the Congress in early 1996 has done nothing to reverse or even modify the policies established by their Democratic predecessors.

### African military reform

*Democratic Transition Must Include the Military:* While violent conflict remains the greatest impediment to African development, African military establishments are among the major perpetrators of violence, and are among the least sympathetic to political liberalization. There are important exceptions to this generalization, of course. The armies of Senegal, Mali, Kenya, Malawi, Tanzania, Botswana, and Zimbabwe have established good reputations for apolitical professionalism and support for civilian control. But events in Burundi, Nigeria, the Gambia, Niger, Zaire, Chad and the Sudan since 1992 indicate that the days of the military coup, military dictatorship, military repression and minority ethnic control over the military are still far from over in Africa. The need for reform of African military establishments would appear to be an essential element of the overall peace agenda.[20]

---

[19] *Africa Conflict Resolution Act Interagency Plan:* Agency for International Development, Department of State, Department of Defense, US. Information Agency, Arms Control and Disarmament Agency. April 19, 1995. Washington, DC. Available from Department of State, Bureau of Public Affairs.

[20] Overseas Development Council, 1875 Connecticut Avenue, NW., (Suite 1012), Washington, DC 20009. *Policy Focus*, 1993 No. 6: *Development Aid for Military Reform: A Pathway to Peace*. In addition to a convincing analysis of the importance of military reform to civil peace, the paper criticizes the

*Past US–African Military Cooperation:* The United States has nibbled at the edges of military reform since the 1970s. Perhaps use of the term "military reform" is an exaggeration as far as American military cooperation programmes in Africa are concerned. A more appropriate characterization might be "Training for Nation Building and Development." For example, in 1978 the American ambassadors in northwest Africa met to discuss regional issues.[21] Among other problems, they determined that protection for coastal fisheries was a high priority subject.

Foreign fishing fleets were obtaining licenses to fish in coastal waters, but were engaging in all sorts of unlawful and dishonest practices. These included fleets that had licenses to fish in Mauritanian waters, but were fishing undetected in Senegalese waters where they were denied licenses. In addition, fleets were giving false declarations of their catches in order to cheat on their contractual obligations to share profits with the African governments. The Africans lacked appropriate enforcement capabilities.

As the result of a collective recommendation from the US ambassadors, the "West African Coastal Security Program" was established. This project utilized military cooperation funds to provide materiel and training to African naval and air force units for the purpose of enforcing laws and contracts covering their ocean economic zones.

Similar military cooperation programmes were inaugurated in the areas of military health, the protection of national parks and wildlife, and the use of military engineering equipment for rural road construction and maintenance. These programmes were given names such as "civic action" and "biodiversity" in order to make clear to the budget overseers in the Congress the "nation building" aspects of the activities.[22]

For many years, the US Defence Department has conducted a world-wide programme entitled "International Military Education and Training" (IMET). This programme brings foreign military personnel to the United States for specialized training. This training takes place in the same classrooms as American military personnel. Americans and foreign military personnel train and work side by side. The purpose is to impart relevant and useful skills, and to forge bonds between the American military and their foreign counterparts. IMET training has been made available to approximately 250 sub-Saharan African military personnel per year.[23]

---

United States for lagging behind other industrialized countries in devising an overall policy in the area of military reform.

[21] The author was then US Ambassador to the Republics of Senegal and the Gambia (1977–1980).

[22] Details about these activities are available in the annual reports of the Office of the Deputy Assistant Secretary of Defense, International Security Affairs, Middle East and African Affairs. Department of Defense, Washington, DC.

[23] Some of Africa's top military and governmental leaders are graduates of the IMET program. For example, Rwandan Vice President Paul Kagame (as of early 1996) was a Ugandan Army IMET student at Fort Leavenworth, Kansas in 1990 when the Rwanda Patriotic Front invaded Rwanda

*An activist approach outside of Africa:* During the period 1970–1990, the United States military successfully utilized education and technical assistance programmes in Latin America to help the democratization process in the western hemisphere. American programmes were utilized to assist with military downsizing, improvements in defence resources management, and education for civil-military relations. In 1970, there were very few democracies in Latin America. By 1990, most of the hemisphere was democratic. The US defence establishment played an important supporting role in that transition.

Since the end of the Cold War, the American defence establishment has expanded the training offered under IMET to reflect the changing needs of military cooperation. In 1994, for example, the Congress appropriated $ 665,000 in additional funds to create training courses in such subjects as effective military justice systems, codes of conduct, and the protection of human rights. In this context a course entitled "Civil Military Strategy for Internal Development" was established for Latin American military invitees.[24]

With Latin American military establishments beginning to "graduate" from dependence on the United States for democracy training, the American Government has turned mainly to the CIS states of the former Soviet Union and the former communist bloc countries. Major efforts have been underway in those countries since 1994 to assist their military establishments to take part in the process of democratic transition. The US Agency for International Development has provided much of the funding for this effort. The armies of Bulgaria and Croatia, for example, received support for their reorganizations from retired American military officers funded by USAID. On their side, the American military have recycled their former Russian language training center at Garmisch, Germany into a "democracy training center" for CIS and Eastern European military personnel.

*Why not a NATO role?:* In its zeal for African capacity building in conflict management described earlier in this paper, the United States has effectively recognized the central importance of "civil security" in African development. In its work in Latin America and the CIS states on the democratization of military forces, the United States has effectively recognized the importance of military reform in the process of democratic transition. It is also changing the nature of the military's role which has been done effectively in Latin America. How can all of this good experience and constructive outlook be invoked for the benefit of Africa, which has undertaken very arduous simultaneous processes of economic and political reform?

Although an important player, the United States has never been the leader of development cooperation in Africa. As of early 1996, the outlook for American future leadership in Africa was even less bright because of severe budgetary constraints and decreasing support for foreign development co-

---

from Uganda. Kagame interrupted his studies to return to Uganda and immediately went to the front lines in Rwanda.

[24] Department of Defense reports cited in note 21.

operation. In this author's opinion, the United States could make a significant contribution to African military reform in the context of a NATO programme.

The three most important military powers in NATO, the United States, France and the United Kingdom, are also the three countries with the most experience with military cooperation programmes in Africa. The United States European Command (EUCOM), which is part of the NATO military system, holds bureaucratic responsibility for almost all US military activities in Africa.[25] It would appear natural, therefore, for all NATO countries with military cooperation programmes in Africa to work under a NATO umbrella, thereby achieving economies of scale, appropriate coordination, and good opportunities for funding. The NATO theatre of operations has the schools, the equipment, and the personnel to work with African counterparts on military transformation as part of the process of democratic transition.[26] In their own debate on African military reform, the French Government has expressed an interest in folding European military cooperation with Africa into the Western European Union (WEU). This proposal would appear to have merit, except for the fact that as of early 1996 the WEU had not yet become operational in any military area. In addition, the WEU does not include the United States.[27]

### Whither political transition?

In the overall debate about political transition in Africa, there appears to be one conclusion upon which there is unanimity of view. A free and fair election does not necessarily bring about a democracy. The purists among theoreticians would argue that "democratization" is a never ending process that constantly reinvents itself even in the most advanced democracies. By contrast, some Africanists argue that free and fair elections are important, but in Africa much more is needed by way of cultural evolution before democracy can become relevant to Africans themselves,[28] All who study political transition in Africa divide into the "cup is half full" vs. the "cup is half empty" camps. There are

---

[25] Because of its Middle East responsibilities, the US Central Command (CENTCOM) based in Tampa, Florida, controls military cooperation programmes in Ethiopia, Eritrea, Somalia, Sudan, Kenya, and Djibouti.

[26] Smock and Crocker (eds.), *African Conflict Resolution*, op. cit., Chapter 6, pp. 77–94 by Cohen, Herman J., *African Capabilities for Managing Conflict: the Role of the United States*.

[27] In February, 1992, the Deputy Commander of the United States European Command, General James Jamerson, visited several African countries. In Angola, he told the press that the US "may soon begin to help Angola train soldiers in a future integrated army which would include UNITA guerrillas". Reuters despatch from Luanda, Angola, 6:35 a.m. GMT, February 23, 1996. In a NATO context, such activities would be automatically coordinated with the Portuguese, French, and British who are also involved with military reform in Angola.

[28] Bratton, Michael, "Are Competitive Elections Enough?", in *Africa Demos*, Volume III, Number 4, March, 1995. Bulletin of the African Governance Program of the Carter Center: One Copenhill, Atlanta, Georgia, 30307, USA.

also those who argue that the idea of political transition is meaningless. What is important is to fix what is wrong today.[29]

Political transition is important because if democratization does not constantly improve, expand and adapt it will inevitably regress. When President Clinton was campaigning for election in 1992, he had a sign in his headquarters that read "It's the economy, stupid", thereby reminding his supporters of the key issue of the election. There should be a similar banner in the Africa Bureau of the Department of State in Washington which would say, "It's the transition, stupid." It's not the holding of free and fair elections that is so important, but the movement toward a society that is more participatory, more equitable, and more tolerant under a government that is more helpful, more transparent and more accountable.

What does political transition have to do with an American agenda for peace in Africa? After five years of intensive involvement in African democracy programmes since 1991, the United States needs to take stock and determine whether or not a change of course would be appropriate. Between 1990 and 1996, the bulk of American support for democratization in Africa has gone into elections. For example, the United States allocated ten million dollars to support the Ghanaian elections scheduled for 1997. Considering the total US assistance budget for Africa, this is a massive amount of money. Since elections doe not always bring about real democracy, and can sometimes be destabilizing, should not the United States change its priorities in Africa?

This author believes that the highest US Government priority should be assigned to urgent improvements in governance which can serve to minimize the prospects for violent conflict. The elements of governance which are important include an equitable distribution of resources, especially the earnings from oil and other extracted minerals, the assurance of basic government services in education, sanitation, health and transportation, the assurance of personal property rights, the maximum feasible decentralization of power, and tolerance for opposing points of view. The achievement of these elements of good governance require resources, education, and a strong civil society as a counterweight to government. In general, therefore, scarce US resources should be redirected from massive support to elections to effective support for better governance, and the development of institutions that underpin it.[30]

THE STRUCTURE OF A US–AFRICAN COOPERATIVE RELATIONSHIP FOR PEACE

**African commitments**

1. Bring to operational status as soon as possible the OAU capacity to mount and control peace operations from its headquarters in Addis Ababa.

---

[29] Sklar, Richard L. *African Politics: The Next Generation,* in *Africa Demos,* op. cit., pp. 26–28.

[30] Cohen, Herman J., *Good Governance, Democracy and 'Citizen Expectations' in Africa,* in *Africa Demos* op.cit., pp. 6.

2. Designate a minimum of five African country "ready" battalions that could be called upon for peace operations by the OAU Secretary-General. The designated units would have similar training and compatible equipment.

3. Encourage the growth of an African early warning and mediating network within African civil society in every country.

4. Adopt a policy of zero tolerance for the reversal of democracy anywhere in Africa. Military coups to overthrow democratic regimes should be universally condemned by the Organization of African Unity.

5. Encourage good governance within all regimes regardless of how far they have advanced on the road of political transition.

## United States commitments

1. Continue and expand support to African capacity building for conflict management.

2. Develop, in conjunction with NATO and the OAU, a well funded programme of support to military reform and civil-military relations in Africa similar to those already undertaken in Latin America and the CIS states.

3. Expand support for improved governance, even if it requires a reduction of support to elections.

4. Eliminate financial arrears to the United Nations, and support UN collaborative programmes to share the conflict management burden with Africa.

# Mediating Africa's Civil Conflicts
# —A User's Guide

*Timothy D. Sisk*

Despite a common perception that in the post-Cold War era Africa's civil wars are especially intractable and not susceptible to international efforts to end them, the record reveals a more mixed and complex picture. Some severe, violent conflicts have been effectively brought to an end—Mozambique, Angola, Uganda, South Africa, Namibia, and Ethiopia, for example. Others, however, continue to take a high toll in human suffering and environmental degradation—Somalia, Liberia, and Sudan stand out in this category. Yet other experiences are more ambiguous. Rwanda is currently relatively calm but still suffers from the shock of the April 1994 genocide and mass violence could easily re-emerge; Burundi similarly experiences a cyclical pattern of civil strife and teeters on the edge of a crisis of similar proportions to Rwanda's. Nigeria and Zaire, two of Africa's largest and most important states, seem poised on a slippery slope, ready to slide into civil war or anarchy once the unstable status quo is altered.

In past, current, and prospective civil wars in Africa, mediators were or are actively involved in conflict resolution, management, or prevention. African conflicts do not want for mediation efforts, in which an external party (or parties) seeks to guide the disputants to a negotiated settlement through an extended peace process. Whether the role of primary mediator is played by a regional African leader or group of eminent persons, a sub-regional organization, the Organization of African Unity (OAU), the United Nations (UN), or a single state or group of donor states, these mediators work to end civil wars in Africa by encouraging and structuring talks and by structuring incentives and disincentives—or wielding carrots and sticks—to get the parties to exchange armed conflict with bargaining and ballots. More often than not, all of these types of mediators are engaged simultaneously. In some conflicts in Africa, external parties have used the most extreme measures of intervention, such as the

The author gratefully acknowledges the Norwegian Nobel Institute's support of the background work on which this chapter is based; research on comparative peace processes, resulting in the "phases approach" outlined in this chapter, was conducted while the author was a fellow at the Institute in 1995. The author is also grateful to the editors for their thoughtful comments on an earlier version of this chapter.

US-led multilateral military invasion of Somalia in late 1992 (Operation Restore Hope) or the French intervention in Rwanda in 1994 (Operation Turquoise), to bring a civil war to an end. Moreover, even when a conflict ends in military victory, such as the Tigrean and Eritrean rebel forces' victory over Mengistu Haile Mariam's Ethiopia in 1991, last-minute external mediation helped avert a bloody showdown over the capital, Addis Ababa.

Some efforts to end civil wars in Africa through negotiation and mediation have clearly been successful, if success is defined as ending the violence and getting parties beyond initial elections and into a nascent system of democracy. Other efforts have failed to get the parties to agreement, while still others have failed to get negotiated settlements implemented without a return to violence. Why do some mediation efforts succeed and why do others fail? How can mediation efforts be improved? This chapter seeks to shed light on these questions by probing the dynamics of civil wars in Africa and analyzing the phases of conflict de-escalation that produces viable negotiated settlements. Specific references are made to current or just-ended civil wars in Angola, Burundi, Liberia, Mozambique, Rwanda, Somalia, and South Africa. The phases approach to peace processes and an analysis of the mediator's role can serve prescriptive, as well as analytical, ends. Thus, the analysis presented here can serve as a user's guide for would-be mediators as they seek to shepherd a peace process to fruition.

THE INHERENT PROBLEMS OF ENDING CIVIL WARS

Whether any peace process succeeds or fails clearly lies beyond the capabilities of the mediator; instead, success is ultimately contingent on the willingness of the parties to live together nonviolently. For many reasons, some armed factions don't want to negotiate an end to civil war; they want to keep fighting either because they think they can eventually win, will do better in negotiations by fighting longer, or have to much to lose in a negotiated settlement. Thus, it is critically important for mediators to better understand the dynamics that keep civil wars going and those through which they end.

The perception that Africa's civil wars are somehow different and more intractable than those in other world regions is not borne out by experience. Indeed, current civil wars in Africa display many of the same characteristics of civil wars more generally. One of the most important consequences of the Cold War's end is the resurgent focus on the difficulties of internal conflicts (violence within states), as opposed to international conflicts (violence between states). Civil wars in Central America, Eastern Europe and particularly the former Yugoslavia, the former Soviet Union, and in South Asia have been no less bloody or intractable than those in Africa.

Although Africa is increasingly marginalized in global politics, the problems of Africa's internal conflicts remain the subject of intense mediation efforts precisely because no conflict in the contemporary world is truly "internal." These conflicts and their consequences have become internationalized, both analytically and empirically.[1] During the Cold War, internal conflicts in Africa were often seen as contests between the superpowers' proxies, despite the fact that the actual military forces of the Soviet Union and the United States never met directly on the battlefield.[2] Genocide, "ethnic cleansing," mass starvation, and massive refugee flows have kept the management of internal conflicts in Africa on the international agenda, even as an assertive doctrine of humanitarian intervention has quickly faded in the messy local complexities of conflicts such as Somalia.

### Characteristics of civil wars in Africa

Whether in Africa or elsewhere, civil wars pose special problems for mediation not only because of the doctrines of sovereignty and of non-interference in internal affairs enshrined in Article 1(7) of the United Nations Charter. Scholars and policy-makers alike have long appreciated that such conflicts are less amenable to conflict management than international ones.[3] Internal wars are more difficult to resolve because of the intensity of violence that they entail and because when the fighting is over, the combatants cannot withdraw into their own self-contained states but, barring partition, must go on living together.[4] Civil wars are not just encounters between opposing militaries; they are what international conflict analysts term "protracted social conflicts" in which communities and/or political organizations that share a common state are pitted against each other.

The fact that contemporary Africa's civil wars are invariably infused with ethnicity argues that the common elements these type of conflicts deserve special consideration.[5] Only Somalia, a sub-ethnic conflict, and Mozambique, an ambiguous case, are not generally considered by analysts of civil wars in Africa as being linked in some way to ethnicity. Analysts increasingly agree that the problem of civil wars in Africa and elsewhere is not the persistent and

---

[1] The linkages between internal conflict and international conflict have been appreciated by some analysts for many years. For an earlier treatment of the theme, see Rosenau (1964).

[2] Indeed, the danger of quick escalation to an all-out nuclear exchange worked against such direct engagement.

[3] Roy Licklider summarizes the scholarly consensus when he observes that internal conflicts are inherently more difficult to resolve than international encounters, because after the war the combatants "must live side by side and work together in a common government to make the country work ... How do groups of people who have been killing one another with considerable enthusiasm and success come together to form a common government?" (1993:3).

[4] On the question of partition versus sharing as outcomes to conflicts, see Sisk (1996). The subject of outcome options in internal conflicts is also briefly considered in Part III below, "Substantive Formal Negotiation."

[5] For an overview of this literature by the author, see Sisk, (1996). Some of the best recent work done in this genre is Brown (1993, 1996), Gurr (1993), Esman (1994). Horowitz's seminal work *Ethnic Groups in Conflict* (1985) remains the best available scholarship on the essential causes and manifestations of ethnic conflict.

deep and abiding enmities among peoples, but the problem of political leaders "playing the ethnic card." Civil wars in Africa are clearly perpetuated, if not begun, but such ethnic entrepreneurs. A 1995 Human Rights Watch report, Playing the Communal Card: Communal Violence and Human Rights, argues that "time after time, [a] proximate cause of violence is governmental exploitation of communal differences ... The 'communal card' is frequently played, for example, when a government is losing popularity or legitimacy, and finds it convenient to wrap itself in the cloak of ethnic, racial, or religious rhetoric" (1995:viii). Certainly, fanning the flames of ethnic strife is not only perpetrated by governments in Africa, as the report highlights, but by challengers as well. There is an ongoing debate, for example, as to whether the conflict in Liberia is fuelled by ethnic enmities or by "predatory warlordism."[6]

A second common element is that civil wars are usually a competition among ethnic groups for ownership of the state. The expropriation of the symbols, power, and resources of the state to the exclusion of significant components of the population in multiethnic societies is a strong indicator of the likelihood of violence, in which group membership for some is an entitlement system of state-sanctioned status and wealth to the exclusion of others. Patterned inequality and discrimination, usually reinforced by public policy, is argued by some analysts to be the greatest predictor of intergroup violence (Gurr, 1993). Whether in Sudan, Rwanda, Burundi or apartheid South Africa, one identity group's attempt to exclusively own the state seems to inexorably lead to violence.

In addition to competition for control of the state (through revolution or rebellion), many civil wars in Africa also have a distinct territorial dimension. For this reason, conflicts with a strong territorial dimension are more likely to lead to the vexing problems of secession, irredentism, or ethnic cleansing. Contests over the extent of territorial autonomy like the relationship of southern Sudan to the North, or the division of powers between the central government of South Africa and the province of KwaZulu Natal—are often a justification of violence.

Increasingly, analysts of civil war in Africa are focusing on the "transnational" linkages of inter-group relations. The spillover of refugees across borders is but one element of the transnational characteristics of civil wars. Indeed, there is a burgeoning literature on the "internationalization" of conflict and the cross-border ties through which many combatant groups derive critical moral and material support. In many instances—exemplified by the interdependent nature of conflict in Rwanda and Burundi—civil wars are fuelled and complicated by strong ties that transcend state borders. Whether a conflict like Sudan, where the internal conflict is embedded in larger regional tensions, or like Angola, where the cross-border trade in diamonds kept the war machines humming, or like Mozambique, where cross-border assistance to insurgents

---

[6] See Cindy Shiner, "Liberian Warfare: Surreal and Deadly," *Washington Post*, 14 May 1996.

kept the conflict at a fever pitch, regional dynamics are part and parcel of civil wars and any successful mediation attempt needs to address them.

Thus, three general characteristics of contemporary civil wars in Africa can help identify why they are so difficult to resolve and why mediation efforts are so inherently difficult.

—*The issues at stake.* Ethnic or religious group identities are often contested, implying that the underlying disputes include both tangible concerns such as territory and access to economic resources and intangible issues such as language, group rights, patterned discrimination, and minority or majority domination. For example, civil war in Burundi won't be ended or averted until patterned discrimination is eradicated.

—*The players involved.* Conflicts are often multipolar, with splintering and factionalism among the parties a prevalent phenomenon; state and non-state combatants such as movements, paramilitary militias, and even criminal enterprises are involved, as are organized military forces and irregular armed militias. Often the parties involved are disparate, incohesive, and incoherent, without a clear or coherent organizational structure, a single, well-integrated leadership, or a clear public mandate for action. The factionalized situation in Liberia reflects this characteristic well.

—*Linkages across frontiers.* Although the conflicts are internal, there are cross-border linkages among groups and organizations that enhance capabilities for armed conflict and diffuse or obfuscate the arenas of conflict. The behaviour of Ethiopia and Sudan in backing insurgents against each other exemplifies how regional dynamics play into civil wars.

These complexities of internal conflicts in Africa contain important implications for international mediation. Research into war termination in civil wars confirms they are on average more extended than international wars and that the depth of enmities mitigates the prospects for negotiated settlements. Zartman (1993:20) sums up the consensus of war termination analysts when he writes that "internal conflicts seem to have the ability to continue for decades and arrive neither at victorious resolution for one side nor at satisfactory reconciliation for both." In other words, civil wars are widely understood as doggedly intractable and prone to recurrence. Moreover, civil wars once thought ended through negotiation, such as Sudan's 1972 peace agreement, can re-erupt in subsequent years. In civil wars, the levers of influence available to mediators are reduced by their inherent complexity.

## International intervention and negotiated settlements in Africa

Despite their inherent immunity from mediation attempts, most civil wars in Africa have been the subject of some form of international intervention. Such interventions tend to level the playing field for belligerents and reinforce the likelihood that when a civil war does end (as they all inevitably do), it will do so through a negotiated settlement produced with some degree of mediation. International intervention in internal wars may be benign, seeking a negotiated settlement through mediation and peace-keeping, or malevolent, for example aiding combatants with arms and safe havens. Whatever the purpose of international intervention, it tends to "level" the playing field for belligerents because even when military victory on the ground occurs, negotiation with the vanquished is a necessary fact of life.

For example, despite the routing of Hutu extremists by the Tutsi-led Rwandan Patriotic Front following the genocide in 1994, most observers in the inter-national community agree that the vanquished refugees (among them perpetrators of violence) must be accommodated if peace is to come to Rwanda. Prosecution in Rwanda is limited to individuals participating in the genocide, not to the entire Hutu ethnic group. Despite military victory, negotiation cannot be avoided when the international community intervenes to prevent the permanent expulsion or elimination of opponents. International insistence that Rwanda's refugees return, along with self-interested prodding by host countries such as Zaire and Tanzania, assure that Rwanda's problems of coexistence have not been solved by the Rwanda Patriotic Front's military victory over the Hutu militias that waged genocide.

International mediation in Africa's civil wars is no longer a matter of if, but rather of when, how, and to what end. Despite international mediation, the means by which Africa's civil wars arise and are perpetuated, and whether they are ultimately tractable or intractable at a specific moment, depends much more on the perceptions of the parties to a conflict themselves than intervention by the international community. One of the lessons of mediation in Africa is that progress toward peace can be enhanced by the international community by affecting the parties' perceptions of the costs of conflict and the benefits of peaceful settlement, but peace cannot be imposed on disputants. Efforts to impose "nation-building" in Somalia in the wake of international humanitarian intervention are seen in retrospect as a dismal failure.

One lesson of intervention in Somalia, widely appreciated by many conflict analysts and policy-makers alike, is that the key to unlocking a better understanding of internal conflicts is to better understand the essentially internal or domestic relationships among parties to a civil war, especially the critical decisions and strategic choices that lead them to either choose the path of violent escalation, to maintain a stalemate, or to choose a negotiated settlement. The critical question facing international mediators in Africa is understanding the nature of a given civil war, and particularly assessing whether it is possible for the conflict to come to an end through a negotiated settlement.

MEDIATING THE DE-ESCALATION OF CIVIL WARS: A PHASES APPROACH

A negotiated settlement to a civil war, such as those that have occurred to stop the fighting in Namibia, Mozambique, South Africa, and Angola, are but one step in a protracted process of bringing war to an end. In Africa, perhaps more than any other region, the lesson that a settlement does not mean that peace will reign has been learned time and again. Despite a negotiated settlement in Angola in May 1991 (the Bicesse Accords),[7] fighting re-emerged at a critical moment in the peace process—when elections were held that left the insurgent group UNITA's presidential contender a loser; rather than accept a defeat in elections that they would not have suffered on the battlefield, UNITA's generals preferred to keep fighting. So too, in Rwanda, a reasonably sound peace settlement was reached in 1993 (the Arusha Accords) before the April 1994 spasm of genocidal violence. International mediators of civil wars in Africa have learned that clinching an agreement to end violence is only one step in a broader process of conflict de-escalation.

Efforts to mediate civil wars in Africa can be usefully understood by employing a phases approach to conflict de-escalation. Barring complete victory or defeat, mediation efforts in contemporary internal conflicts entail the de-escalation of violence through a series of phases or stages of bargaining or negotiation, which can be overlapping and mutually reinforcing. As noted above, the phases approach may equally serve a prescriptive purpose in situations where a peace process is perceived as possible by conflict resolvers, but not yet begun. The phases approach can also help specify under what conditions mediators help the parties progress from one step to the next, or fail to do so by sustaining a stalemate or by terminating talks.

## Phase I: Causes, triggers, escalation, and commitment

An important distinction is between the background conditions of civil wars in Africa, that is, the "causes" of the dispute, and escalatory dynamics, the progression of moves and counter-moves that have led parties away from co-operation and toward violence. For example the background condition for civil strife in apartheid South Africa was the inequality and racism of apartheid, but the escalatory pattern was one of increasing revolt and repression—an escalation spiral (Sisk, 1995:65). In Angola, external parties played a much more extensive role in the origins of the conflict—the scramble for power following an ill-conceived Portuguese decolonization process—and its perpetuation by the superpowers, Cuba and South Africa during the Cold War. Richard Goldstone, the international special prosecutor investigating genocide in the former Yugoslavia and Rwanda and who conducted inquiries into political violence in his native South Africa, finds that patterns of social discrimination set the stage for

---

[7] For further on the Bicesse agreement, see Ohlson and Stedman (1994:107–110).

mass violence, allowing normally peaceful and tolerant people to forego social norms against violence and to lash out against their fellow countrymen.

A useful conceptual method for identifying the outbreak of civil wars is to focus on a specific event or series of events that trigger the outbreak of violence. For example, the fall of Somali strongman Siad Barre in January 1991 created a power vacuum in which several aspiring presidential contenders, each with an identifiable sub-ethnic clan affiliation, sought to seize power. Conflict triggers can include provocative acts by political leaders, failed elections, abrupt changes in the regional security environment, or violent upsurges such as riots or spontaneous uprisings. They can also be externally induced. Mozambique's civil war was sparked by then-apartheid South Africa's intelligence services helping to create the guerrilla force RENAMO to undermine the regime in Maputo, which was sympathetic to the cause of liberation in South Africa. Liberia's civil war began with armed, cross-border incursions from Côte d'Ivoire by Charles Taylor's faction on Christmas Eve in 1989.

Once widespread violence is anticipated or low-level violence breaks out, the time is ideally ripe for mediating parties to launch preventive efforts. Often, however, the situation does not appear dire enough, or the expectation of impending civil war is uncertain, and so the international community fails to act more consistently to prevent conflict triggers from igniting civil war. The failure of international efforts to deter Somalia's slide into anarchy is well described in former UN special envoy Mohamed Sahnoun's treatise, aptly titled *Somalia: The Missed Opportunities* (Sahnoun, 1994). A related problem for would be mediators, of course, is assessing when the time is truly ripe for early intervention. Is Zaire headed for a catastrophe in the post-Mobutu period, as many analysts suggest? Or is the long-predicted implosion of Zaire into civil war simply never going to happen?

Civil wars are commonly contests between regimes and their challengers, either over the purposes of rebellion and revolution (as in Somalia) or for secession (as in Eritrea). Although this dichotomy describes a wide variety of conflicts, there are several contemporary civil wars in Africa where the state has completely collapsed, leaving a more anarchic situation in which a myriad of splinter groups vie for power in a free-for-all (for example in Liberia and Somalia)—there is no government to oppose.[8] Increasingly, armed militia groups with incohesive structures and lines-of-command foment civil war in Africa. That is, rarely is the conflict a simple face-off between a cohesive insurgency and an incumbent regime, like in Angola. More often, like in Liberia, Somalia, or Sudan, the regime-versus-challenger paradigm does not reflect the exceptional complexity of the conflict. The somewhat murky nature

---

[8] Scholarly studies of civil wars in Africa highlight not only the role of political leaders who articulate grievances and organize and lead conflict organizations and the masses that support them, but particularly the influence of mid-level mobilized elites (for example, a local party functionary or provincial police or guerrilla commander) as critical players in the emergence and sustainment of violence. See Stedman (1996).

of Africa's civil wars, and indeed such wars in general, is one of the reasons why they are especially difficult to settle and why efforts at preventive diplomacy in situations like Burundi are so difficult to conduct.

An important point is that once initial violence becomes civil war, the violence itself generates new incentives for its perpetuation. Both psychological and strategic reasons account for the self-perpetuating nature of civil wars. Psychologically, studies have shown that participants in violence become committed to it as a way of life—the "culture of violence". This term is routinely used in reference to contemporary Burundi. Strategically, governments have an incentive to show firmness, resolve, and staying power in the face of resistance and challengers have an interest in demonstrating their power to cause further instability, and for stating demands that, if granted, demonstrate that the turn to violence was warranted.

A seemingly perpetual stalemate of this nature is apparent today in Sudan. That is, following an initial catalyst (the imposition of Islamic *Shari'a* law on non-Islamic peoples of the South by the ailing regime of former President Gafaar Nimeiri in 1983), parties become committed to war, and as violence intensifies so too does the commitment. Thus the turn to violence and its escalation creates "social traps," or cycles of violence from which the parties find it difficult, if not impossible, to escape. In many cases, like in Sudan, faction leaders handsomely profit from war and so the incentives for starting one, and keeping it going, are powerfully strong. Once parties become deeply committed to violence, the tasks of mediation become increasingly difficult.

Current efforts to mediate the Sudanese conflict through the East African sub-regional organization IGAD (Inter-governmental Authority on Development) are stymied for many reasons,[9] but clearly one of them is the fact that the parties are so deeply committed to armed conflict—particularly the northern Islamist regime of Gen. Omar Hassan Bashir—that any indication of flexibility in negotiations threatens its very reason to exist. Prosecuting the war has become, as a result of so many years of war rhetoric and materiel investment, a prerequisite for the survival of the regime.

### Phase II: The mutually hurting stalemate

When governments are unable to defeat challengers, and challengers are unable to decisively topple governments, over time a mutually hurting stalemate can develop. No side can ultimately prevail through force, and no side can force the opponent to capitulate. When negotiated settlements have been reached in Africa's recent civil wars, such as Angola, Mozambique, and South Africa, they

---

[9] See the United States Institute of Peace *Special Report*, "Sudan: Ending the War, Moving Talks Forward," June 1994, for an analysis of the problems of the IGAD process.

have been based on the parties' common realization that such a stalemate existed.[10]

The arrival at a "mutually hurting" stalemate suggests that parties have reached the point where further escalation is self-defeating, and indeed further pursuit of the conflict imposes greater costs than benefits. The condition to turn a stalemate into a pathway for a negotiated settlement is a demanding one: the parties must share a common perception of a rough balance of power between (or among) them; and they must not expect that situation to change appreciably in the future. Zartman writes that a mutually hurting stalemate must be perceived by parties in a conflict "not as a momentary pause, but a flat terrain stretching out into the future, providing no later possibilities for decisive escalation" (Zartman, 1989:352). Meeting this condition in complex conflicts such as Liberia, Burundi, or Somalia is exceedingly difficult because of the ever-changing political fortunes of factions; something akin to the alignment of the stars would be necessary to get all the parties to view the conflict as unwinnable through violence.

In conflicts where more cohesive regimes and challengers face off, however, the mutually hurting stalemate can be an impetus to talks. Only after many rounds of violence in Angola, including a failed settlement, did the parties ultimately agree—through the Lusaka Protocols of 1994—that neither the incumbent MPLA government nor the UNITA rebel movement could prevail militarily. Similarly, it was the mutual recognition by the South African government and the African National Congress in about 1989 that a mutually hurting stalemate existed that opened a pathway toward mutually beneficial talks (Sisk, 1995:74). The government could not defeat the ANC and win control of the townships, but neither could the ANC effectively defeat the largest and best-equipped military force in Africa.

**Phase III: Pre-negotiation and the ripe moment**

The mutually hurting stalemate is a necessary structural condition for the onset of a negotiation process in internal conflicts, but it is certainly not a sufficient one. In civil wars, a mutually hurting stalemate may "objectively" exist with doggedly persistent violence. How much does a mutually hurting stalemate have to hurt to turn intransigence into opportunities for accommodation? The answer to this question is often phrased in terms of ripeness. Indeed, in scholarship and practitioner parlance, the term ripeness is employed to describe the conditions when a stalemate can be turned into an avenue for negotiation. Experiences with Africa's civil wars confirms that the notion of ripeness has value for identifying opportunities for external mediation.[11]

---

[10] Stedman (1989) illustrates in an extensive analysis a similar conclusion about the conditions that led to the end of the Rhodesian civil war that led to the creation of an independent Zimbabwe.

[11] The ripeness concept, much debated in the conflict management and negotiation literature, is defined as the moment when the perceptions of all parties converge on the belief that negotiation,

The turning point from stalemate to ripeness begins with the emergence of a small core of moderates across conflict lines willing to engage in meaningful and potentially binding discussions about the onset of formal negotiations—or "talks about talks." Pre-negotiation precedes formal negotiation among the parties precisely because it is exploratory talk: "feeling out" the position of the other side, assessing whether the other party is willing to engage in concession-making and reciprocity, and determining its ability to deliver at the bargaining table. Because it is exploratory, pre-negotiation is often held in secret, and often includes important but unofficial opinion-leaders in conflict settings who are close to, but not official representatives of, government or other parties in conflict—"track two" diplomacy.[12]

For those civil wars that have been solved through negotiation in Africa, each involved a significant degree of pre-negotiation. In South Africa, for instance, extensive contacts between the white-minority government and the exiled and internally imprisoned African National Congress began nearly seven years prior to the first face-to-face, formal negotiations (Sisk, 1995:75–85). Many rounds of informal, non-official talks were held among leading opinion-makers from both sides of the conflict. It is widely appreciated that a significant leadership change can induce ripeness, as new leaders fail to carry all of the "sunk costs" or depth of commitment of their predecessors. Former South African president De Klerk did not carry the baggage of his predecessor, P.W. Botha, and was thus in a better position to agree to direct talks. A second conflict condition that ripens a conflict is when the previously disadvantaged party is ascendant and the more advantaged party is descendent.

External mediators are critical in turning damaging stalemates into ripe moments.[13] While some mediators, particularly international organizations such as the UN or OAU, are permanently "on call" to mediate civil wars in Africa, other mediators (such as states) must carefully time their entry and actions to help ripen a conflict. The *Sant' Egidio* community's effort to mediate Mozambique's civil war was successful in part due to the organization's keen sense of when RENAMO and the FRELIMO government were ready to seriously discuss a negotiated settlement (Hume, 1994). Most importantly, they provided a venue in Rome in which the parties could negotiate in consultation

---

reciprocal compromise (requitement), and the arrival at a mutually beneficial settlement will yield greater dividends than continued conflict. For application of this in Africa, see Zartman, 1985.

[12] See Ronald Fisher, "Pre-negotiation Problem-Solving Discussions: Enhancing the Potential for Successful Negotiation" in Stein (1989).

[13] Mediators are critical in each of the seven functions that characterize the pre-negotiation phase: helping keep risks low by keeping talks informal and exploratory; helping parties analyze the relative costs and benefits of agreement to negotiated versus the *status quo*; establishing a pattern of reciprocity and trust among the parties that conciliatory moves will be not be exploited for unilateral gain; helping parties build an internal support base for conciliation by offering support and, potentially, tangible side-payments; setting the agenda for talks and determining the parameters of the range of possible outcomes; identifying the participants at formal talks, not only those to be included but the equally important task of excluding certain players; and building bridges or coalitions across conflict divides (Stein 1989).

with the UN, OAU, and major players in the conflict such as the US, Portugal, and South Africa. The Catholic lay society—arguably an unlikely mediator to successfully settle a civil war—was able to turn initial, tentative pre-negotiations into a meaningful process that led to a successfully implemented negotiated settlement.

Although in most situations it is difficult to pinpoint precisely when the conflict is ripe for resolution, there is wide agreement that progress is being made when, as the outcome of pre-negotiation talks, the parties agree on a public commitment to negotiate in good faith, and, more often than not, a declaration of cease-fire. These agreements, which are usually explicit but not invariably so, form the basic framework to guide the ensuing negotiations. Without them, parties use mediators' efforts to promote pre-negotiation as a tactical diversion from their true aims of prosecuting the war; given their tentative but consistent participation in current "track two" diplomacy initiatives, Sudan's northern regime and southern rebel movements seem to be doing just that.

### Phase IV: Preliminary, formal negotiation

The movement from pre-negotiation to open, formal negotiation is signalled by the parties' "going public" with their intent to replace fighting with talking. The announcement to the public that a party is negotiating with a bitter adversary is a major turning point in the de-escalation process. The preliminary formal negotiation phase is also marked by the changing dynamics of coalition-making. Erstwhile enemies on the battlefield find themselves in an implicit coalition defending the choice for negotiation, re-orienting their rhetoric toward moderation and compromise, and articulating the benefits of negotiation and the costs of continued violent conflict. At the same time, however, they remain adversaries in the negotiation, with widely divergent aims and hopes for the ensuing talks. Importantly, the relationships among parties at the table are marked by both cooperation (as partners in talks) and competition. As the parties gather around the negotiating table, they continue talking while fighting.

Political leaders who enter negotiations generally expect that they have a sufficiently cohesive coalition to support the onset of talks and that they can sustain that support throughout the negotiation process—they hope to "carry" their constituencies with them, and even to potentially benefit politically by bringing the conflict to an end. On the other hand, political leaders may not enjoy sufficient deference from within their own organizations or within their own constituencies; entering into negotiations with erstwhile adversaries may lead to deep fissures and enhance factionalism within parties and within supportive segments of society. Especially acute is the problem of "rogue" elements which may not see the need for accommodation that political leaders do. It should be kept in mind that only a small faction of the Hutu extremists who opposed a peace settlement in Rwanda—particularly the cliquish Committee for the Defence of the Revolution—were responsible for planning and fomenting the genocide of April 1994 (Jones, 1996).

Cease-fires, when they hold, are signals that the parties have solved the essential dilemma of the pre-negotiation phase: one side or sides may demand an agreement on a conflict's outcome prior to a cease-fire, whereas other parties demand a cessation of violence before talking about outcomes. The agreement on broad principles and general negotiating procedures, rather than specific settlements, is the common answer to such a dilemma. Moreover, it is at this stage of the de-escalation process where disputants begin to link issues, entering in earnest the problem-solving mode and signalling that they understand and are willing to accommodate the other side's interests. It was only after broad agreement was reached that South Africa would strive toward a unified, non-racial democracy that the ANC agreed to terminate its armed struggle in 1990.

There is good reason not be sanguine about cease-fires. The problem of tactical cease-fires is well-known, with many an example of cease-fires that do not hold. Liberia has experienced more than its share of failed cease-fires, for example. In civil wars, a critical question is whether being at the table is a tactical move by parties—subduing the opponent through other means—or a genuine search for a mutually beneficial solution. The test is whether the parties progress and reach preliminary agreements on the cessation of violence, or whether the negotiation process fails to progress to the next phase. Progress beyond a simple cease-fire is the key barometer of a potentially viable peace process.

The preliminary formal negotiation phase, which deals with detailed and often technical security issues,[14] is a phase in which the parties further establish confidence (or trust) as well as test the general viability of the underlying principles agreed to during the pre-negotiation phase. The preliminary negotiation phase also establishes the pattern of concession-making, which in a successful negotiation will be characterized by reciprocal moves and more-or-less equal commitment to taking steps that move the process forward. Disputants trade away some of their bargaining chips while reserving some for later rounds of talks. In sum, a difficult but successful tussle over security issues in a negotiation process helps set the stage for subsequent good-faith bargaining when it comes to tackling the equally and perhaps more difficult, substantive issues that lie at the heart of the dispute.

---

[14] During preliminary formal negotiation, the parties focus on security issue such as the implementation of the procedures of cease-fire, release of political prisoners or hostages, demobilization or redeployment of troops, the implementation of security guarantees (such as the deployment of external observers/monitors and often United Nations peacekeeping troops), measures for police and security force reform, etc.

**Phase V: Substantive formal negotiation**

As the talks move from security issues to substantive issues, such as the division of territory or the nature, form, and structure of the state, it is a signal that parties have entered the phase of negotiation in which the actual terms of a settlement are being thrashed out. Parties in internal conflicts face essentially two choices for the settlement of underlying disputes: "separation," that is political divorce or secession, and power sharing, or creating the structures for living together (Sisk, 1996). The purpose of a substantive settlement is to reconstitute "normal" politics in a society and to create new, mutually beneficial rules of the political game: procedures through which to arbitrate their differences peacefully in parliament rather than violently on the street.

Importantly, settlements do not end conflicts, they are simply agreements to continue bargaining under consensually defined rules of interaction. Not surprisingly, settlements in internal conflicts often take the form of new constitutions or significant packages of amendments to existing constitutions. Settlements are attractive for all parties when they contain the likelihood of greater benefits for parties than they would achieve by abrogating negotiations and returning to the battlefield. Successful settlements are a formula of positive sum gain for all parties.

Although the foregoing discussion suggests that it is primarily the interests and power of the disputants that frame the terms of a settlement in an internal conflict, international mediators and others external to the conflict seek to influence (on the basis of either principle or interests) not only the process of internal conflict resolution, but also the outcome. By insisting on the territorial integrity of a state, for example in Sudan, external mediators help shape the outcome to the conflict.

With the exception of Mozambique, most civil wars in Africa have ended through agreements on some form of power sharing, even if such arrangements are only transitional. Recent settlements in Liberia, South Africa, Angola, and even failed pacts such as Rwanda's Arusha Accords or Burundi's Convention of Government, have all been based on the creation of governing structures in which all parties are represented. The advantages and disadvantages of power sharing cannot be adequately dealt with in this chapter, but suffice it to say that the absence of power-sharing often means that a settlement will not be possible. International mediators have much to learn about the consequences of promoting power sharing as an outcome to civil wars. Most important, of course, is the question How inclusive should they be? Should all the faction leaders in Liberia's conflict be included in the Council of State, and if not, who should be excluded and with what consequences? Should former perpetrators, or at least supporters of, brutal repression and even genocide or ethnic cleansing (as in the cases of Rwanda and Burundi, for example), be given a place in a national unity government? These are vexing questions for which there are no easy answers for external mediators.

## Phase VI: Implementation

Clearly, as the failure of several recent settlements in Africa demonstrate—particularly the ill-fated 1993 Arusha Accord for Rwanda—reaching an agreement, however inclusive it may be, is not the end of the process. Violence can erupt with a vengeance even after moderates have agreed to a comprehensive settlement. The implementation phase of peace processes can be just as volatile and just as violence-ridden, as earlier phases of the process. Because the terminal point in ending a violent civil war is fresh elections to reconstitute legitimate government—often at the insistence of international mediators—the implementation phase is rife with uncertainty and insecurity on the part of the erstwhile combatants.

Much of the ink that has been spilled on internal conflicts in the post-Cold War era deals with the complexities of the implementation of peace agreements and the ingredients for "successful" international intervention at the implementation stage (e.g., Namibia, El Salvador, Nicaragua, Cambodia, Mozambique, South Africa, and Haiti) and failure (Rwanda, Angola in 1992).[15] Issues such as demobilization, removal of foreign troops, de-mining, resettlement of refugees and displaced persons, economic reconstruction and development, and new elections are but a few of the myriad aspects of peace accord implementation. In many ways, these are critically important aspects of a mediation effort.

Nearly all settlements in contemporary internal conflicts envisage elections as the turning point that unambiguously signals the advent of the post-conflict era. Elections serve many purposes, but clearly one of them is to legitimize the terms of the accord through popular participation. Increasingly, the international community becomes engaged in elections in internal conflict situations, such that the mediator, or international organizations such as the United Nations, become participants in guaranteeing the terms of the accord. All efforts to end Africa's civil wars have envisaged elections as the terminal point of the mediation process.

The perceived free and fair nature of elections is a final turning point that must be crossed. Elections can be triggers for conflict, as mentioned above, even with the acceptance of a comprehensive peace agreement. Angola's failed 1992 election, in which the loser of the election's first round of balloting (Jonas Savimbi's UNITA party) returned to the battlefield rather than accept the inevitable loss at the polls, stands as a constant reminder from contemporary experience of the critical importance of implementation. In this case, the United Nations peace-keeping force was wholly inadequate for the task, and the UN overseers of the peace process implicitly allowed the parties to contest the election before security agreements—particularly the demobilization and containment of the government and UNITA militaries—had been completed.

---

[15] On implementation of peace accords in Africa, see Rothchild (1994), and Stedman (1995, 1996).

Settlements in civil wars contain inherent problems of enforceability and compliance. When the election is over and the UN peace-keepers leave, there is no external party to further guarantee the accord. The transformation of a regime and the inculcation of new values of compromise and coexistence after a bitter and often protracted war are difficult and long-term tasks. Civil wars leave economic and environmental catastrophes in their wake, legacies of enmity that require years and even decades of purposeful socio-economic development to address. Clearly one of the most important failings of mediation in Africa's civil wars has been the short attention span that the international community has given to effecting long-term reconciliation and reconstruction. Moreover, the injustices of the past—another inherent feature of civil wars—must be addressed if social healing and reconciliation is to occur. The more recent focus on transitional justice in post-conflict situations such as South Africa, Rwanda, and Ethiopia, for example, signals that awareness is growing that civil wars leave a myriad of legacies that must be addressed before a sense of social normalcy can be nurtured.

CONCLUSIONS: IMPROVING MEDIATION STRATEGIES

Sustaining mediation through the implementation phase and extending international engagement for peace-building into the indefinite future is but one of the recent lessons learned for improving mediator strategies to end Africa's civil wars. If, hypothetically, the international community had the chance again to implement the 1993 Arusha Accords in Rwanda, it would not be likely to make do with such a weak UN peace-keeping force and such a slow response time as when the process went off the rails in early 1994. It would have done much more to prevent genocide. Today's effort to implement peace in Angola, which includes the largest existing UN peace-keeping operation and sustained attention by a coalition of mediators including the UN, the US, Portugal, and regional leaders such as Zimbabwe and South Africa, reflects lessons learned from the failures of peace implementation in that country in 1992 and the failings in Rwanda.[16]

In many ways, the success of Mozambique's peace implementation phase was also based on a realistic assessment of the earlier failures in Angola, particularly the lesson that demobilization must occur prior to elections and that mediation efforts must be sustained right up until the time of the election to prevent the party that expects to lose (in the Mozambique case, the guerrilla movement RENAMO) from disputing the election results, or "spoiling" the process. It was only through sustained mediation in South Africa, particularly the efforts of Kenyan Professor Washington Okumu, that widespread violence was avoided during South Africa's celebrated April 1994 election that ended

---

[16] On the implementation of the November 1994 Lusaka Protocols, the most recent agreement to end Angola's civil war, see Prendergast and Smock (1996).

apartheid; working quietly and behind the scenes, Okumu was able to prevail on recalcitrant Inkatha Freedom Party leader Mangosuthu Buthelezi at the very latest of moments to contest the election and agree to serve in the transitional government of national unity.[17] Other, higher profile leaders had worked publicly and privately to encourage Inkatha's participation, but to no avail. It would seem that the international community had learned the lesson of sustained engagement, although the recent re-emergence of violence in Liberia—due in part to inattention by international mediators to the disarmament process and an insufficient UN peace implementation force, UNAMIL—questions how deep the learning has been.

Current and future efforts to mediate Africa's civil wars, particularly those in Burundi, Liberia, and Sudan, reveal other important trends and lessons as well. Efforts to mediate such conflicts today, whether the mediator be a group of eminent persons, a sub-regional organization, the OAU, the UN, or the diplomacy of key states such as the US or France, all occur in an environment of declining resources. Disengagement from international efforts to manage conflicts in Africa is a by-product of the post-Cold War era. Such disengagement is a function of donor fatigue, declining resources for peace-keeping and UN diplomacy, other commitments of key powers such as those in Bosnia and the Middle East, and recognition that some civil wars (such as Sudan's) are seemingly intractable in the short-run.

The disengagement environment, coupled with lessons learned from previous experience, has led to several new approaches for international mediation efforts. These new approaches are based on a realization of the special complexities of civil wars as outlined above, as well as a keen appreciation that successful mediation efforts need to be persistent and sustained throughout all phases of the de-escalation process. The new approaches are also grounded in the realization that Africa's place in the international system has fundamentally changed in the post-Cold War world—it is becoming increasingly marginalized (Keller and Rothchild, 1996).

One of the most important lessons learned about the mediation of civil wars in Africa is that not only must mediation efforts be better sustained, they must be better coordinated. Rarely is a single mediator, as in a single person or even state, the sole conciliation-seeker. Today, it is more accurate to think in terms of coalitions of mediators working together (or sometimes, at cross-purposes) to bring a civil war to an end. For example, in Liberia the UN, OAU, ECOWAS and its military force ECOMOG (particularly Nigeria and Ghana), and individual states are all engaged in efforts to quell the fighting. Better coordination of mediation strategies through all phases of the escalation and de-escalation of civil wars is an urgent task for improving the likelihood of bringing such wars

---

[17] Interestingly, one provision of the agreement through which the IFP agreed to participate in the election was the promise by the ANC of future, post-election international mediation on outstanding constitutional issues. This mediation has not occurred (the ANC has yet to agree to it), and remains a significant bone of contention between these two parties.

to an end (Smock, 1993:18). In a similar manner, better coordination needs to occur between those who mediate agreements and those charged with implementing them; one of the criticisms of peace implementation in Rwanda was the lack of continuity between the mediators (the OAU and Tanzania) and the implementation force (the UN peace-keeping force UNAMIR).

Efficient coordination of mediator strategies, such as the *Sant' Egidio*-led process for Mozambique, can prove decisive in bringing a war to an end when the underlying will of the parties is to settle. Failure to efficiently coordinate strategies can create conditions under which parties can play one mediator off against another, or use a parallel mediation process to divert attention away from another. For example, the Sudanese government's efforts to enlist private mediators or other channels of communication to the South is a ploy to divert attention away from where the real prospects for peace lie, the IGAD initiative. Similarly, mediation efforts are bolstered when members of the coalition harmonize their use of carrots and sticks to get parties to settle and to implement agreements. In Angola, UNITA's decision to finally agree, and abide by, a negotiated settlement was the result of carefully coordinated diplomacy on the part of regional leaders such as South Africa's Nelson Mandela and Zimbabwe's Robert Mugabe as well as the pressures of sanctions imposed by the insurgent's erstwhile Cold War patron, the United States.

Other conclusions on improving mediator strategies are also related to the analysis of the dynamics of civil wars and to the phases approach to peace processes. One lesson is that regional strategies to address complex internal conflicts may offer avenues toward the resolution of essentially internal civil wars (e.g., the regional approach to Namibian independence, which eventually paved the way for negotiated settlements in Mozambique and South Africa). Similarly, the current efforts of former Tanzanian President Julius Nyerere and former US President Jimmy Carter to mediate the conflicts in Rwanda and Burundi by adopting a broader "Great Lakes" initiative for Central Africa reflects the need to deal with civil wars in terms of the overall environments in which they occur.

A related lesson is the critical task of blending private and official mediation. The Nyerere/Carter initiative is occurring with the explicit blessing of the UN and the OAU, and is being supported diplomatically and financially by governments outside the continent (including the US and other donor states). This private initiative, and particularly the efforts to stave off impending civil war in Burundi, are aided by the seemingly tireless efforts of many private nongovernmental organizations (NGOs), who have been routinely coordinating their preventive diplomacy efforts with the UN Secretary General's Special Representative in Bujumbura and the OAU's human rights observer mission deployed in that country. Eventually, the private mediation initiative is to be handed over to the OAU.

Innovations such as these, along with the track record of successful mediation to end civil wars in Africa, should go a long way toward ameliorating the despair borne of bitter experiences with mediation such as those in Rwanda and Somalia. With a keener recognition of the inherent complexities of mediating civil wars; an awareness of the shortcomings of military intervention; a better appreciation of the multitude of steps and tasks in bringing civil wars to an end; and with improved efforts to focus external leverage on the parties to reach and abide by negotiated settlements, Africa's civil wars can be prevented from occurring or managed when they do occur. Although deriving better mediation strategies for ending Africa's civil wars won't end those wars that the parties are unwilling to end, more effective mediation can make the difference when peace is possible, but remains elusive.

## REFERENCES

Brown, Michael (ed.), 1993, *Ethnic Conflict and International Security*. Princeton, NJ: Princeton University Press.

Esman, Milton J., 1994, *Ethnic Politics*. Ithaca, NY: Cornell University Press.

Gurr, Ted Robert, 1993, *Minorities at Risk: A Global View of Ethnopolitical Conflicts*. Washington, DC: United States Institute of Peace Press.

Horowitz, Donald, 1985, *Ethnic Groups in Conflict*. Los Angeles: University of California Press.

Hume, Cameron, 1994, *Ending Mozambique's War: The Role of Mediation and Good Offices*. Washington, DC: United States Institute of Peace Press.

Keller, Edmond J. and Donald Rothchild (eds.), 1996, *Africa in the New International Order: Rethinking State Sovereignty and Regional Security*. Boulder, Colorado: Lynne Rienner Press.

Jones, Bruce, 1996, "Sound and Fury: The Failure of Mediation and Intervention in Rwanda." Paper presented at the conference on "Military Intervention in Civil Wars", Institute of War and Peace Studies, Columbia University, May 1996.

Licklider, Roy (ed.), 1993, *When the Fighting Stops: How Civil Wars End*. New York: New York University Press.

Ohlson, Thomas and Stephen John Stedman with Robert Davies, 1994, *The New is Not Yet Born: Conflict Resolution in Southern Africa*. Washington, DC: The Brookings Institute.

Prendergast, John and David R. Smock, 1996, *Angola's Elusive Peace*. CSIS Africa Notes, No. 182. Washington, DC: Center for Strategic and International Studies.

Rosenau, James N., 1964, "Internal War as an International Event", in James N. Rosenau (ed.), *International Aspects of Civil Strife*. Princeton: Princeton University Press.

Rothchild, Donald, 1994, "Implementing Peace Accords in Africa." Paper presented at the 1994 African Studies Association Annual Meeting, Toronto.

Sahnoun, Mohamed, 1994, *Somalia: The Missed Opportunities*. Washington, DC: United States Institute of Peace Press.

Sisk, Timothy D., 1996, *Power Sharing and International Mediation in Ethnic Conflicts*. Washington, DC: United States Institute of Peace and the Carnegie Commission on Preventing Deadly Conflict.

Sisk, Timothy D., 1995, *Democratization in South Africa: The Elusive Social Contract*. Princeton, NJ: Princeton University Press.

Smock, David R. (ed.), 1993, *Making War and Waging Peace: Foreign Intervention in Africa*. Washington, DC: United States Institute of Peace Press.

Stedman, Stephen John, 1996, "Negotiation and Mediation in Internal Conflicts" and "Conflict and Conciliation in Sub-Saharan Africa," in Michael E. Brown (ed.), *The International Dimensions of Internal Conflicts*. Cambridge, Massachusetts: MIT Press.

Stedman, Stephen John, 1995, "United Nations Intervention in Civil Wars: Imperatives of Choice and Strategy", in Donald C. Daniel and Bradd C. Hayes (eds.), *Beyond Traditional Peace-keeping*. London: MacMillan.

Stedman, Stephen John, 1991, *Peacemaking in Civil War: International Mediation in Zimbabwe, 1974–1980*. Boulder: Lynne Rienner.

Stein, Janice Gross, 1989, "Getting to the Table: The Triggers, Stages, Functions and Consequences of Pre-negotiation", in Janice Gross Stein (ed.), *Getting to the Table: The Processes of International Pre-negotiation*. Baltimore: The Johns Hopkins University Press.

Zartman, I. William, 1993, "The Unfinished Agenda: Negotiating Internal Conflicts", in Roy Licklider (ed.), *Stopping the Killing: How Civil Wars End*. New York: New York University Press.

Zartman, I. William, 1989, "Pre-negotiation: Phases and Functions", in Janice Gross Stein (ed.), *Getting to the Table: The Processes of International Pre-negotiation*. Baltimore: The Johns Hopkins University Press.

Zartman, I. William, 1985, *Ripe for Resolution: Conflict and Intervention in Africa*. New York: Oxford University Press.

# From Mogadishu to Kinshasa
# —Concluding Remarks

*Gunnar M. Sørbø*

## INTRODUCTION

The main purpose of the Bergen Workshop was to identify lessons learnt from recent conflict management experiences in Africa and to develop recommendations for a more consistent, coherent and effective international response. We were particularly concerned with exploring possibilities for developing a regional (i.e. African) capacity to prevent, contain and resolve armed conflicts, relying principally on African peace-making capabilities but supported and reinforced by the international community.

During the time that has passed since holding the workshop, the necessity to build African capacities to respond more effectively to the widespread conflicts on the continent has, for several reasons, become increasingly urgent. First, the turmoil in the Great Lakes region of Central Africa has continued to spread and now affects tens of millions of people over a huge area. At the time of writing, the "quiet implosion" (Williame, 1997) of the Zairian state has turned into regular warfare between a coalition of opposition forces under the banner of Laurent Kabila's Alliance of Democratic Forces for Liberation of Congo-Zaire and Zaire's long-time ruler Mobutu Sese Seko. In addition, of course, there are still a number of other severe internal conflicts on the continent; several countries are candidates for state collapse or civil war; and there are a host of other countries where present low-level ethnic and political conflict remains unresolved. The regional effects of internal conflicts are multiple, including tactical and strategic spread to neighbouring countries, growing refugee problems, arms traffic and spread of conflict through simple contagion (Stedman, 1996).

Second, in the United Nations, the United States and Europe, the debate on the role of third party intervention in African conflicts has been coloured by the traumatic experiences from the humanitarian interventions in Somalia and Rwanda. Declining resources for engagement, coupled with a fatigue borne of the apparent intractability of conflicts in Africa, has led to a situation in which it is difficult for policy makers to engage meaningfully in preventing or ending armed conflicts. This problem is particularly pronounced in the United States, where the "Mogadishu syndrome", which refers to the general lack of political will in the US for engagement in Africa following the deaths of US soldiers deployed in the United Nations' peace keeping operation in Somalia, seriously limits the ability to make credible policy commitments in dealing with actual or potential armed conflicts in Africa (Sisk, 1996). At the moment, and as clearly seen in the case of the crisis in the Great Lakes region, the international community is unable to respond quickly, constructively and sustainably to violent conflict and its tenuous aftermath.

On a more encouraging note, however, there has been an increasing African engagement in several intra-state conflict on the continent. On a more spectacular level, this has been seen in the strong and patient efforts by South Africa to bring the parties in the Zairian conflict to negotiations. Less visibly, however, but perhaps in the long run even more significantly, are the many attempts to build the capacities of civil society to play an increasing role in preventing and managing conflicts. While previous efforts have focused largely on exploring the role of OAU in managing internal and international conflicts in Africa, several concrete proposals to link civil society to the OAU Mechanism (see Chris Bakwesegha's chapter) have recently been tabled, particularly during the 1996 consultation in Cape Town between OAU and the International Peace Academy (IPA).

SOME WORDS OF CAUTION

The simple argument which runs through this chapter is based on a few basic premises, one being that social and political conflict is natural and inevitable in all societies. Further, competition and conflict are potentially positive and productive. The challenge is to manage conflict in constructive ways, to create sufficient space for legitimate struggle without causing excessive instability, violence or destruction. This is the essential, on-going business of governance. It is the responsibility of government, parliament, state institutions, the judiciary, local authorities and local communities. As Nathan argues, crises occur when these sectors lack the capacity to manage society, or when they are unwilling to accommodate diverse groups and interests (Nathan, 1996).

While this may be self-evident to most readers, certain implications follow that may be at variance with the practices of several NGOs involved in conflict resolution, conflict resolution training and preventive diplomacy. According to Voutira and Brown, the work of the NGOs is generally predicated on the notion that the ideal state of human society is "harmony", and, therefore, tends to neglect issues of power, control and justice (Voutira & Brown, 1995:6). Conflict management efforts which are based on poor understanding and analysis of ongoing conflicts may, thus, easily be in danger of trading justice with harmony, and of maintaining or exacerbating existing inequalities. At issue, therefore, is not simply finding the "right" model for managing conflict, but to engage in thorough analyses of specific conflicts and their causes before deciding on appropriate assistance or interventions.

If we do so, we will also find that some of the deep causes of conflict in African societies today are, for a variety of reasons, not on the agenda for action, mainly because they are too complex, long-term or sensitive (Nathan, 1996). They include many of the long-term permissive conditions related to such factors as distribution of resources, access to political power, basic political identities and the nature of African states and state boundaries (Stedman, 1996).

If we fail to approach African internal conflicts in such terms, interventions by the international community are likely to focus on the symptoms of conflict rather than root causes. The main challenge is to African governments, individuals, groups and organisations, and concerns policy formulation and debate around critical issues of political, social and economic justice. As Nathan observes, such issues may require the *generation* of conflict, raising complex questions for conflict resolution practitioners around the relationship between advocacy and mediation (Nathan, 1996:5). Within this perspective, a debate on conflict management which is excessively preoccupied with the experiences from the complex emergencies in places like Somalia and Rwanda is both limited and misleading.


AFRICAN INITIATIVES

Intervention fatigue and the price tag of sustaining UN-led military deployments in conflicted societies on the African continent have encouraged growing attention to the possibilities (and limits) of intervention by regional and sub-regional actors.

In the US and Europe, however, much of the public debate on the role of such actors has been coached in rather negative terms. This applies both to the OAU and to sub-regional efforts, with regard to peace enforcement as well as mediation. Thus it is commonly argued that OAU's attempts to create an organisational basis for providing early warning of impending conflicts and a capability for mediation and peace-keeping may be ineffectual, particularly because the organisation is unlikely to have the resources or the will to overcome the resistance of powerful states such as Kenya, Nigeria and Sudan, which brook no interference in their affairs (Stedman, 1996:262). The same author, in discussing the sub-regional effort by West-African countries operating under the aegis of the Economic Community of West-African states (ECOWAS) to impose a peace settlement in Liberia, argues that the intervention created the very situation it hoped to prevent. The war was transformed into a protracted struggle that continued until 1995; the adoption of enforcement action raised questions on the credibility of the military force (ECOMOG) to conduct a peace-keeping mandate while remaining an impartial arbiter; and political differences within the coalition prevented them from developing and implementing a unified and coherent strategy for ending the war.

The crucial question is whether the ECOMOG experience discredits the whole idea of sub-regional peace enforcement in Africa. Sub-regional organisations might have advantages in carrying out peace-enforcement operations in civil wars if they possess unity of purpose and common interests; if they embody regional norms of responsible conduct and good government that can be demanded of the warring parties; and if they have the capability to use force to defeat recalcitrant parties. According to Stedman, all of these things were lacking in the ECOMOG intervention in Liberia (ibid.:253).

A similar argument has been put forward regarding the role of the Inter-Governmental Authority on Development (IGAD) in peacemaking in the Sudan. IGAD has been considered a promising initiative, in that it is African led and regional, and interest and action comes from the level of the presidencies. But it could be argued that all four governments (Kenya, Uganda, Ethiopia and Eritrea) have seen their relation deteriorate enough with the Khartoum regime as a result of the latter's meddling in their internal affairs, and consequently would all like to see a change of government in Khartoum. Such a position would probably welcome in the short term a continuation of the war in order to destabilize Khartoum. On the other hand, the economic gains for neighbouring countries from peace and reconstruction are likely to be significant. An examination of the multiple and conflicting agendas of the IGAD participants demonstrates the complexity of arbitrating a civil war with regional implications, the point being that there is often a mixed agenda when it comes to external players engaging in conflict resolution (Prendergast, 1997: 65ff).

LESSONS FROM PEACE ENFORCEMENT AND HUMANITARIAN
INTERVENTIONS

While the mixed agenda of neighbouring state may hamper rather than promote a peace process, a crucial lesson to be learned from Liberia and the Sudan as well as from Somalia and Rwanda, is that once a domestic political conflict becomes militarized, the task of conflict solution whether it be done by African or non-African intervenors, is immeasurably complicated. Or put differently: the price of inaction (during earlier phases) rises dramatically once the political-military threshold is crossed and constituencies and groups with vested interests in warfare, weapon procurement, and military resource mobilization become entrenched. An important lesson, therefore, is to underscore the benefits of pre-emptive engagement in promoting negotiated alternatives to continued repression or expanding violence and upheaval (Crocker, 1996:186).

In the area of pre-emptive action, the record shows that interventions in some types of internal conflict can be successful. Without outsiders to provide much of the pressures, ideas, resources and inducements, there would have been no peace settlement in Mozambique in 1994; the Namibian transition was clearly made possible and gained from the leadership of an outstanding UN team; and, more recently, concerted action by South Africa, Botswana and Zimbabwe, acting in the name of the Southern African Development Community (SADC) defused an incipient war in Lesotho in September 1994 by quickly reversing a military coup. In Burundi, the international community still attempts, through the United Nations, the OAU, African and Western diplomats, and several NGOs, to prevent the conflict between Hutu and Tutsi from boiling over into genocidal warfare. Quite clearly, the record shows that intervention in some types of internal conflict can be effective when there are important stakes and high confidence in the possibility of shaping an acceptable outcome at a reasonable price. Thus, there is a vast range of intervention options between doing nothing and sending in the US Army (ibid.:187). Likewise, there are many potential intervenors, including African states, individuals, groups and organisations.

In both Somalia and Rwanda another important lesson has been that humanitarian action cannot substitute for political action. One of the hallmarks of a complex emergency is that the political/diplomatic (including conflict resolution), human rights, humanitarian, military/peace keeping, and development aspects get inextricably intertwined—before, during and after the peak of the crisis. The Rwanda experience is a prime example (Joint Evaluation of Emergency Assistance to Rwanda 1996).

The problem in Rwanda, as Suhrke and Anyidoho show in their contributions to this book, was that policy and strategy formulation by the international community seldom, if ever, took these elements into account in an integrated manner. There was a dramatic lack of policy coherence at and between different levels and no overall agreed understanding of the complexity of the situation, the preponderance of factors weighing against early repatriation of refugees and the resulting policy implications. In Somalia, there was a similar lack of agreed understanding, and humanitarian action was not conceived as a bridge to a political process that could provide the best basis for a successful exit. That was one of the missing ingredients that undercut the impact of US and UN intervention in Somalia (Crocker, 1996).

This is not to say that better management and coordination hold the only key to successful interventions. Rather, the point is that humanitarian assistance has only a limited, moderating influence on the political forces and the nature of violence in a target area. The same applies to humanitarian presence generally. Hence, it may be unrealistic and counter-productive to assign humanitarian assistance an ambitious agenda in terms of mitigating existing violence or preventing further conflict. Not only does this create false expectations, it may encourage political passivity towards the conflict and its underlying causes (Suhrke et al., 1997). It may also reinforce conditions creating conflict. Thus, in Somalia there is little doubt that the UN military intervention and many NGOs helped refuel and underwrite an extortionist, militarized political economy in many Somali towns. Much of the benefit was captured by General Aidid and his allied militias in Mogadishu South (Prendergast, 1997).

Among aid agencies one common response to the mounting awareness of the negative effects of humanitarian assistance in conflict situations has been to adopt the physician's motto "first do no harm" (Andersen & Woodrow, 1989).

Within this perspective, it is often conceived that the best way to ensure that relief has a mitigative aspect, rather than a negative impact, is to centre efforts on supporting local capacities for peace and development. A "no harms" position, however, may effectively abandon any claim that humanitarian assistance can be an effective tool of conflict prevention (Suhrke et al., 1997). To see humanitarian aid as a principal mechanism of conflict management in the South is clearly inadequate. Rather, the complex crises which exist in many war-torn, famine-stricken countries require much more meaningful political engagement from governments (including donors) and international organisations than they presently receive.

There seems often to be a lack of commitment on the part of the intervenors to support peace by addressing the political roots of the crises. In several cases, the efforts which have been exerted so as to find political solutions, seem to have been ill conceived. Thus, again using Somalia as an example, the strategies adopted aimed at reviving a central Somali state without, however, taking into account the structural impediments to the resuscitation of a central authority. As Prendergast has argued, centrifugal forces in Somalia—political, economic and social—clearly outweighed centralizing ones. The UN donor governments were, however, obsessed with trying to re-create a centralized authority in Mogadishu. This greatly exacerbated conflict, as competing militias positioned themselves for the potential spoils of a new aid-dependent state. In the process, the vast majority of Somalia and their local institutions were ignored and further marginalized (Prendergast, 1997).

The Somali story also shows how interventions are perceived by local actors as an imposition. In fact, people of the region and the wider international community pursued their respective agendas with little recognition that they occupied the same stage and that achieving their goals required engaging each other. The Somalis were unable to break out of the vicious spiral and violence and destruction on their own in 1992. By the same token, the international community could not rebuild political institutions or manage the humanitarian emergency without local partners. Their failure to recognize that their fates required an appreciation of common purpose made the outcome a tragedy (Lyons & Samatar, 1995).

LESSONS FOR ZAIRE?

The Somali example is instructive not just for the self-evident point that it helps to know something about a place and to understand the nature of conflict before deciding on interventions. It is also instructive in that it shows the necessity for political models for resolving conflict to be home-grown and evolutionary instead of being imported or externally imposed. The origins and contours of intra-state conflict differ substantially from country to country. Being preoccupied with crises, interventions typically focus on the symptoms of the conflict; the interventions are often perceived by local actors as an imposition; and the interventions may be ineffectual, if not counter-productive (Nathan, 1996).

During late 1996 and early 1997, a possible intervention by the international community in Zaire was debated. Zaire has, since the beginning of the 1990s, been threatened by a similar collapse of centralized authority. In contrast to the explosions in Somalia, Liberia and Rwanda, however, there was, over the years, a "quiet implosion" of the Zairian state. In fact, if not fuelled from problems related to the crisis in Rwanda, large-scale civil strife—with all that this implies for mass migration and large-scale humanitarian intervention—would not likely have occurred, at least not in the near future (Williame, 1997). One reason Zaire did not explode is that Zairians have learned over the years to live beyond the reach of the state's authority and structures, as evidenced by the development of the so-called "popular economy". Since the early 1990s the crisis in Zaire has also stimulated embryonic forms of local "good governance" in some areas. As a basis for any intervention, it would have been extremely important to understand the way Zairian society at large, as well as its economic, social and political arrangements, has held together in a somewhat bizarre and mostly paradoxical "order" preventing the explosion that one would have expected years ago. It is, e.g., still unlikely that the economic rehabilitation of Zaire will progress from the top down; nor have matters such as the rehabilitation of political legitimacy of a viable state system or of an acceptable modern economy seemed to greatly occupy political actors. Entering Kinshasa, therefore, may be the easy bit for Laurent Kabila and his forces. Changing the country's ways could be a greater problem.

If this is correct, the reconstruction of a post-war Zaire may have to start from the grassroots and the regional and local communities rather than from the top of the political pyramid. The primary objective of possible interventions should, therefore, be to utilize and build on the capacity of emergent civil and political structures and institutions, in order to reverse the erosion of civil society and communal cohesion. This calls for creativity and an understanding of local and national realities, including a recognition of the country's limited capacity to absorb aid, particularly for the economic development of the poor (Leclercq, 1997). Based on our current understanding of social and political developments in Zaire the encouragement of civil society where it is possible to build on the spontaneous action taking place in several regions of the country, as well as mediating local and regional conflicts and assisting the learning process of intergroup mediation and conflict management, will be among the most urgent issues (Williame, 1997).

## CHANGING DONOR PRIORITIES

There would seem to be two general conclusions to follow from this brief analysis; one of them being that "solutions" that are based on widespread desires for quick fixes for long-term problems are generally at odds with African realities and, therefore, mostly futile exercises (see also Stedman, 1996:263). The other, related conclusion is that the success or failure in addressing the roots of conflict or its manifestations ultimately lies in the hands of local responders (see also Prendergast, 1997:14). Recommendations and measures proposed for addressing Africa's internal wars and violent conflicts must be assessed on the basis of their ability to be consonant with such realities.

Given that, for the moment at least, the international community continues to devote limited resources to Africa, and that the track record when it comes to humanitarian interventions or peace enforcement operations does not provide much basis for optimism, there is a need for donors to put more emphasis on long-term efforts related to peace and development. In doing so, they must also work harder to Africanise the area of conflict prevention and resolution, to ensure that the analysis and proposed "solutions" are appropriate, and that all the parties involved or responsible for implementing the agreement support them.

This may seem like a rather naive statement in view of the ECOMOG and IGAD experiences referred to above. Conflict management, however, must remain the essential business of governance, and international actors can play a major role through the allocation of resources and transfer of skills to both governmental, non-governmental and community-based organisations so as to enhance the capacity to manage society. I agree with those who argue that the common donor paradigm, perhaps particularly in the area of humanitarian interventions and peace enforcement, is still very much based on the notion that African people are objects, beneficiaries, victims and receivers rather than active actors engaged in their own development and future. As Nathan writes,

> Too often we stand by helplessly as powerful external actors dash to the scene of crisis. They compete with each other to give us food and bright ideas, but they know and learn nothing about our lives, vanishing suddenly and moving on to the next crisis. (Nathan, 1996:5)

STRUCTURAL REFORM, COHERENCE AND CO-ORDINATION

This does not mean that there is no need for better overall coordination on higher levels. Today, the international community faces some key concerns:

— the need to invest in preventive and pre-emptive action and peace building, addressing a broad spectrum of measures which are necessary to avert violent conflict;

— the need to establish a sensible and workable division of labour between international actors—from the UN and regional organizations, to governments and non-governmental institutions, who become involved in conflict management;

— the need to strengthen the capacities of institutions engaged in managing conflict;

— the need to learn and apply lessons from previous and ongoing peace operations; and

— the need to build support for international action at a time when many factors tend to discourage governments from contributing to peace efforts.

Related to the second point, consultations are needed to develop a meaningful division of labour among international, regional, sub-regional organisations, governments and NGOs regarding their responsibilities for conflict management in Africa. Operative concepts to be discussed include both the "layered response" approach (international, regional and sub-regional organisations, governments and NGO's should be involved in increasingly wider concentric circles as the level of violence escalates) and the view that the United Nations and OAU should jointly serve as the central players of the response mechanism (see e.g. the contribution by Tom Vraalsen in this book). The present "architecture" of response to conflicts in Africa is diffuse, ad hoc, and often incoherent. At times, organisations seeking to ameliorate conflicts or assist the victims of conflict find themselves working at cross purposes or in competition rather than collaboration.

Since holding the Workshop, one particularly interesting initiative has been IPA's Project on Civil Society and Conflict Management in Africa which seeks to find ways and means whereby civil society efforts can contribute to the OAU's conflict management efforts and vice versa. It includes mobilizing women's networks, organizing a pool of African scholars who can serve as resources to the OAU, trying to build African capacity for humanitarian action, and developing an African conflict management database.

The following recommendations, distilled from participant discussion at the Workshop, are anchored to this fundamental notion of shared and complementary responsibilities.


BOLSTERING EXISTING ORGANISATIONS

The OAU's mechanism for conflict prevention, management, and resolution, formally approved in 1993, is now being made operational. The international community should continue to support this important diplomatic initiative and provide resources, training, and other assistance needed for the development of the OAU's early warning system.

Despite the consensus that information about emerging conflicts is widely available, there is concern that such information often exists in disparate forms and is not available to decision makers at the regional and sub-regional levels in a concise manner and at critical moments. Thus, an early warning and information management system, whose existence is well-known and whose contents are widely available to all relevant actors, should be developed within Africa. Better quality information and analyses that explore basic root causes of conflict could help develop more coherent responses.

One specific recommendation to enhance the early warning system now being developed by the OAU is to prepare briefs (comprehensive, standardised descriptions) of current or impending armed conflict situations in Africa. These briefs should be made publicly available in a central repository. The conflict briefs should be regularly updated as new information becomes available. In particular, information about deteriorating intergroup relations and regional arm flows—both vital early warning indicators according to participants—should be regularly disseminated.

African sub-regional organisations have become increasingly involved in peacemaking—and in the case of ECOWAS, peacekeeping—despite the fact that they were not initially created for such purposes. These organisations' peacemaking activities can be enhanced by efforts to professionalise their staff and increase their operational capacity. Donors play an important role in facilitating technical assistance to promote enhanced peacemaking capacities by these organisations. In view of the generally disappointing results in pursuing the primary economic aims of these bodies, any initiatives in this area should be undertaken in a spirit of caution and realism.

SPECIAL PROBLEMS OF COLLAPSED STATES

When the fundamental structures of a state collapse as a consequence of armed conflict, as in Liberia, Rwanda or Somalia, the international community faces special challenges of intervention. Restoring basic services—reliable food supplies, water and electrical supplies, sewage facilities, communication links, policing, judicial administration—as soon as possible is critical. UN peacekeeping missions in such situations can be improved (as in Haiti) through the deployment of UN police units and technical teams to complement military units. The rapid restoration of indigenous capacities in these areas should also be seen as an intrinsic component of the peace-making process.

While it may be important in a crisis to begin reconstituting the government through negotiations among political and military leaders, it is equally and sometimes even more important, as argued above, to find other "anchors of reconstruction"—organisations and individuals with close links to civil society. This approach aims to rebuild the state from the bottom up, instead of relying solely on the leaders of armed factions as the point of contact. For example, areas of Somalia where the creation of local and district councils was given priority during the UN intervention (UNOSOM II) have experienced a quicker restoration of stability.

The international community should be prepared for long-term engagement in such conflict settings. The reconstitution of a collapsed state is a difficult enterprise requiring perseverance and the investment of appropriate resources. The "staying power" of external actors has often been an issue, especially in Somalia where unreasonably short timetables were set to accomplish complex operations. Similarly, peace-keepers were withdrawn from Rwanda at a critical moment in the escalation of the crisis.

## SUSTAINABLE MEDIATION PROCESSES

Since complex emergencies require complex responses which the international system may be ill equipped to provide, one of the key lessons of the interventions in Somalia and Rwanda for other current and potential conflicts around the world is the need to invest in preventive diplomacy early on in the crisis. As early as 1990, the Addis-based Inter-Africa Group called on the UN to appoint a special envoy for the multiple conflicts in the Horn, but to no avail. Eritrea had offered to intervene in the Somali crisis long before UN and US troops landed on Mogadishu's beaches (Prendergast, 1997).

As Stedman has argued, more emphasis should be put on supporting processes of mediation, which involves modest costs and few risks; peace keeping when agreements are reached; and reconstruction to help countries recover from the ravages of war (Stedman, 1996:265).

Too often, the mediation process that leads to a negotiated settlement of a conflict is not sufficiently linked to the process of implementation. In several instances, such as in Angola and Rwanda, the peace process broke down during the implementation phase and a new round of fighting erupted. Sustained mediation can be better achieved when those responsible for implementing an agreement are involved in its formulation. For example, if the UN is expected to be involved in an implementation process with peacekeeping forces, UN personnel should participate in the negotiations that lead to an agreement. Consistency, persistent attention, and follow-through are often lacking in mediation processes in Africa, a situation that requires urgent correction.

Mediation processes should be better co-ordinated. In some instances, NGOs or other parties working to bring peace in a conflict situation are not aware of the activities of others, especially "quiet diplomacy" efforts. In each conflict situation, there should be a specified focal point or central clearing-house for co-ordination of peacemaking activities. For example, in Burundi, conflict management efforts are centrally coordinated by the UN Secretary General's Special Representative. This approach should be replicated elsewhere. It is especially important that the UN, regional, and sub-regional efforts at peacemaking be structurally integrated. Structured co-ordination can also contribute to the development of a coherent mediation framework and the implementation of a longer-term peacemaking plan.

When the international community deploys military force, diplomatic initiatives and military missions should be better coordinated. The political objectives of deployed forces must be clearly stated and should be achievable with the resources available and in keeping with the mandate of the operation. Peacemaking exercises in Liberia, Rwanda, and Somalia were hampered by the absence of commitment to provide and maintain the necessary military and political resources.


RECONCEPTUALISING SECURITY

Traditional notions of security should be reconceptualised to encompass a broader range of human needs and concerns. Traditional security issues such as military and strategic questions are still important. Increasingly, however, "security" involves the capacity to meet such basic needs as reliable food and water supplies, access to health care, freedom of movement, peaceful adjudication of land disputes, and protection of human rights.

A critical aspect of enhanced security is the curbing of the arms flow in Africa, including both legal arms transfers and the illegal arms market. A frequent underlying factor in the severity of recent conflicts in Africa is crossborder arms transfers and the use of the territory of a country as a staging point for incursions across frontiers. New and innovative approaches should be developed to limit the availability of arms and absorb the surplus of arms generated by recent wars and bloated defence budgets.

African armies and other security organisations, particularly the police, can be restructured and trained to undertake conflict management missions. Efforts should be made to inculcate democratic values in the military and police forces, and to ensure that these institutions are broadly representative of a country's population. The training of armed forces for peace operations is desirable, including preparation for the special challenges of peacekeeping and peace enforcement. Civic action skills for humanitarian relief missions and disaster response should also be cultivated. African countries should identify, train, and volunteer troops in advance of crises, a proposal being actively promoted by the OAU. Donor states can help by offering resources for training and by assisting with logistics, the development of operational guidelines, and helping draft rules of engagement. Military units designated for peacekeeping missions should also receive instruction to prepare them for the complexities and subtleties of these operations.


DEMOCRATISATION AND DEVELOPMENT

In the long run, effective conflict management in Africa requires a continued commitment to the processes of democratisation. Training in democratic and civic practices, human rights monitoring, electoral system design and administration, judicial practices, parliamentary procedures, and the responsibilities of opposition parties and the media are critical. There is no substitute for a transparent system of democratic good government as a long-term system of conflict management. In case of severe conflicts, power sharing systems can be important transitional mechanisms. It is important that the donor community not become complacent and lessen its active encouragement of democratic transitions and the strengthening of new democracies.

Africa is the world's poorest continent, and no long-term effort to address the underlying sources of conflict is complete without a dedicated commitment to economic development. Economic marginalisation in the global economy and the accumulated debt burden of African states were seen by Workshop participants as critical impediments to sustained development and economic revitalisation. They called attention to the need for programmes designed to promote economic restructuring to take account of the ways in which they may provoke inter-group tensions.

As Stedman argues, peace enforcement and humanitarian intervention, by drawing resources from African countries that have the potential to be selfsustaining, risk condemning all of Africa to collapse (Stedman, 1996:264). Those countries that are the most conflict-ridden receive more assistance than those that have achieved some measure of progress and stability. Assistance to help create and bolster democratic forms of government is often based on short-term perspectives, with little regard for the requirements for maintaining democratic stability: the development of political cultures that emphasize tolerance, inclusion, participation and accommodation. The policy implications of this should be obvious, particularly regarding the need for long-term efforts.

## CLOSING REMARKS

I would like to reinforce a general conclusion shared by Workshop participants, namely that the despair over intervention in conflicts in Africa is unwarranted. Despite severe problems in many countries, several major wars in Africa have been brought to a negotiated solution in recent years. And even short of full resolution, international intervention has helped contain conflicts that could have engulfed neighbouring states. The Workshop heard moving testimony of the difference even a small international presence can make in saving lives. As the violence in April 1994 in Rwanda was reaching its peak, a small group of twelve lightly-armed UN peace-keepers under the command of Brigadier-General Henry Anyidoho (who attended the Bergen Workshop) established a safe zone in the Amohoro Stadium in Kigali. This prompt action is credited with protecting the 20,000 internally displaced persons huddled inside. How many thousands of Rwandans would have been saved if a sizeable intervention force had been quickly dispatched by the United Nations and the major powers?

## REFERENCES

Crocker, Chester A., 1996, "The varieties of intervention: conditions for success", in Crocker, Chester A. et al., 1995, *Managing Global Chaos, Sources of and responses to international conflict*. Washington, DC: United States Institute of Peace Press.

Joint Evaluation of Emergency Assistance to Rwanda, 1996. *Synthesis Report. The international response to conflict and genocide: lessons from the Rwanda experience.*

Leclercq, Hugues, 1997, "How best to provide international economic aid in Zaire", in Williame, Jean-Claude et al., 1997, *Zaire—Predicament and Prospects*. Washington, DC: United States Institute of Peace.

Lyons, Terrence and Ahmed I. Samatar, 1995, "Somalia: State Collapse, multilateral intervention, and strategies for political reconstruction", *Brookings Occasional Papers*. Washington, DC: The Brookings Institution.

Nathan, Laurie, 1996, "Analyse, empower, accommodate. A constructive challenge to conflict resolution", in *Track Two*, Vol. 5, No. 3, September 1996, pp. 4–7. Cape Town: The Centre for Conflict Resolution.

Sisk, Timothy D., 1996, *Future U.S. engagement in Africa: opportunities and obstacles for conflict management*. Special Report. Washington, DC: United States Institute of Peace.

*Somalia*. London: Pluto Press.

Stedman, Stephen John, 1996, "Conflict and conciliation in Sub-Saharan Africa", in Brown, Michael E. (ed.), *The International Dimensions of Internal Conflict*. Cambridge: Harvard University.

Suhrke, Astri et al., 1997, *Humanitarian assistance and conflict*. Bergen: Chr. Michelsen Institute.

Voutira, Eftihia, Shaun Brown and A. Whishaw, 1995, *Conflict resolution—a cautionary tale*. Uppsala: Nordiska Afrikainstitutet.

Williame, Jean-Claude, 1997, "Understanding the unending crisis in Zaire", in Williame, Jean-Claude et al., 1997, *Zaire—Predicament and Prospects*. Washington, DC: United States Institute of Peace.

# About the Authors

*Richard Joseph* is Visiting Professor at the Massachusetts Institute of Technology (1995-1997) and Professor of Political Science at Emory University. He served as co-chairperson of the 1995 Bergen Workshop and is engaged in several writing projects on African governance, democracy and conflict resolution.

*Tom Vraalsen* is at present Norway's Ambassador to the United States. His previous assignments include: Ambassador to the UN (New York) 1982–1989, Minister of Development Cooperation 1989–1990, Ambassador to the United Kingdom 1994–1996. He is author of two books on the UN and of numerous papers and articles on African issues.

*Peter Vale* is Professor of Southern African Studies at the University of the Western Cape and a Visiting Professor of Political Science at the University of Stellenbosch. In 1995 he was Visiting Scholar at the Chr. Michelsen Institute in Bergen. His contribution for this book was written during his tenure as UNESCO Africa Chair, University of Utrecht, the Netherlands.

*Margaret Aderinsola Vogt* is currently a Senior Associate for the Africa Program at the International Peace Academy. She has been Senior Research Fellow and Head of the Strategic Studies Division at the Nigerian Institute for International Affairs, and was the first civilian Director of Studies at the Command and Staff College of Jaji. She served as a Demobilisation Officer for the United Nations Operation in Somalia (UNOSOM) in 1994. She has published extensively on peace and security topics, especially pertaining to the African continent.

*Chris J. Bakwesegha* is currently Head of the Division of Conflict Prevention, Management and Resolution of the Organization of African Unity (OAU), a post he has held since the inception of the Division in 1992. For thirteen years prior to 1992, he was the Head of the Bureau of Refugees and Internally Displaced Persons of the OAU. Dr. Bakwesegha has published numerous articles on African development issues in international journals.

*Astri Suhrke* is currently Senior Research Fellow at the Chr. Michelsen Institute. She is co-author of Study II of the Joint Evaluation of Emergency Assistance to Rwanda (1996), and is currently revising *Escape from Violence: Refugees and Conflict in the Developing World* (1989) for a French version to be published by Armand Colin in 1997 (with A. Zolberg). She is a member of the Advisory Council on Human Rights and on Disarmament and Arms Control to the Norwegian Ministry of Foreign Affairs.

*Henry Kwami Anyidoho* is currently Brigadier General and Commander of the Second Infantry Brigade Group of the Ghana Armed Forces, where he formerly served as Director General of logistics, joint operations and plans at the General Headquarters. He has participated in several UN peace-keeping missions, and was appointed as Deputy Force Commander and Chief of Staff of the UN Assistance Mission for Rwanda.

*Bethuel A. Kiplagat* is a senior consultant on peace issues to the All Africa Conference of Churches. He has served as Kenya's Ambassador to France and the United Kingdom. He is the immediate former Permanent Secretary of Kenya's Ministry of Foreign Affairs and International Cooperation. He is also Chairperson of the African Medical Research Foundation (AMREF), member of the World Bank's Council of African Advisors and Chairperson of the Kenya Rural Enterprise Programme (K-Rep).

*Josephine A. Odera* is currently a lecturer at the Institute of Diplomacy and International Studies, University of Nairobi. She has had extensive experience in Kenya's Ministry of Foreign Affairs. She is currently associated with regional and international organisations on matters of peace and conflict management, the International Resource Group for the Horn of Africa and the AACC Working Group on the Sudan. She is also a council member of the International Peace Research Association.

*Herman J. Cohen* is the Senior Advisor to the Global Coalition for Africa, an intergovernmental forum dedicated to economic and political policy reform designed to accelerate economic development in sub-Saharan Africa. He retired from the US State Department in 1993 after 38 years as a career diplomat specialising in African affairs. He was the US Assistant Secretary of State for Africa during the administration of President Bush (1989–1993).

*Timothy D. Sisk* is a Program Officer in the Grant Program at the US Institute of Peace, where he has been based since 1989, specialising in conflict management in Africa, South Asia and the Middle East. He is the author of *Power Sharing and International Mediation in Ethnic Conflicts* (1996) and *Democratization in South Africa: The Elusive Social Contract* (1995). He is currently also a professorial lecturer in the Liberal Studies Program at Georgetown University.

*Gunnar M. Sørbø* is currently Director of the Chr. Michelsen Institute, a position he has held since 1994. He is the former Director of the Centre for Development Studies at the University of Bergen (1986–1994). He has been a member of the North-South Aid Commission of the Norwegian Ministry of Foreign Affairs since 1993. He has extensive research experience from the Sudan and other African countries.